Writing Now

Writing Now

An Interactive Approach
for the Paragraph-to-Essay-Level Writer

Instructor's Edition

Janet Nay Zadina
University of New Orleans

Susan Halter
Delgado Community College

HOUGHTON MIFFLIN COMPANY   Boston   New York

Senior Sponsoring Editor: Mary Jo Southern
Development Editor: Kellie Cardone
Editorial Assistant: Peter Mooney
Senior Project Editor: Fred Burns
Manufacturing Manager: Florence Cadran
Marketing Manager: Annamarie L. Rice

Printed in the U.S.A.

Student Edition ISBN: 0-618-05099-X
Instructor's Edition ISBN: 0-618-05100-7

1 2 3 4 5 6 7 8 9—QD—06 05 04 03 02

Contents

Preface

Writing Now is a textbook for paragraph- to essay-level courses in developmental writing programs. It is a fully integrated text that includes writing instruction, reading selections, and language use.

Organization

The overall organization of *Writing Now* consists of fourteen chapters with a set of two chapters representing one unit of instruction. Each chapter pair has one overall writing assignment, as well as additional writing options. In addition to the *Start* chapter, in which the philosophy and organization of the text is presented, the book contains seven paired thematic units. The central writing assignment begins in each odd-numbered chapter and is completed in the next even-numbered chapter. This format allows students an opportunity to practice revising and editing. Writing skills are introduced in the first chapter of each pair and a draft is then written. The second chapter of a pair introduces new skills that are incorporated into that draft and allows for a revision. This revision process becomes more thorough as students progress through the book and are held accountable for more skills. Skills build on preceding skills and are reinforced throughout the book after they are introduced.

Because the first week of a semester contains certain introductory activities, such as explaining the syllabus, finalizing enrollment, and so forth, the text provides an introductory chapter entitled Start. The activities in this chapter introduce students and teachers to the organization of the book and to each other. We believe that students learn better if they are informed of the theory because knowing why an activity is important can be motivating. Therefore, the Start chapter also explains the purpose of the activities. In addition, the instructor's version contains marginal notes that provide a theoretical background to the exercises in the text.

Writing Now is organized according to the recursive writing process. Concepts in the book are introduced in a sequence approximating that of the actual writing process and then revisited in more depth in later chapters. However, instructors can use the content to suit their individual teaching style and the needs of their students. For example, an instructor who prefers to begin with "audience" can begin with Chapter 6 and then reinforce it when students focus on audience in later chapters.

The content can be addressed by using a variety of techniques and technology. Instructors can incorporate technology options into assignments, or they can occasionally use the options when visiting a computer lab. These options can also serve as enrichment activities for students who wish to use computers in their writing process. Throughout the book we provide explanations for technology use so that students can use these options independently if the instructor does not wish to cover it in class. *Help* boxes provide students with information on technology as they learn about the writing process.

Reading Selections

The text readings are high-interest and focus on real-life issues, such as communicating with the opposite sex, performing well on a job interview, and coping with technology. Each chapter pair is centered around a theme, such as music, self-image, or technology. This unifying theme builds the writer's schema on a topic, demonstrates different writing approaches to the same topic, and gives enough depth and information to help the writer get involved in the topic. The text includes readings from sources most students will encounter in their everyday lives, including magazines, textbooks, journals, newspapers, student writing, and the Internet. These readings provide fuel to fire high-interest discussions in the classroom prior to the writing assignment. We believe that writing is easier for students if the classroom is grounded in authentic discourse.

We also believe that the more students read, the better writing skills they develop. Each chapter has three to five readings, with more in the first chapter of the pair (introductory) and fewer in the second chapter of the pair (development). This provides *immersion* in a topic relevant to the student's life and/or career so that the writing is grounded in authentic communication. Instructors may use as many or as few readings as need and time permit.

You may also find more writing activities in this text than in others. Each chapter contains informal writing practice so that students practice getting their ideas on paper in a variety of ways before composing a unified essay. Each chapter pair introduces a *central assignment*. The central assignment is an essay that is started in the first chapter of the pair and is enhanced and revised in the second chapter of the pair. This unique system has several advantages. First, it builds revision into the text and the assignment process. Often instructors find it difficult to get students to revise a previous essay when the class has moved on to the next chapter. In *Writing Now*, revising an essay is built into the chapter following each assignment. In addition, the second chapter of a pair introduces language and writing skills that are practiced through the revision of the central assignment essay. We believe that it is easier for students to focus on a new skill with something that is already written. At the same time, students see how the skill and the process of revision have improved their original essay. A final advantage of the two-chapter-per-essay design is that it works with the practical needs of instructors. For instructors who wish to assign more frequent essays, additional and alternative options for writing are provided in every chapter and on the accompanying web site.

Features

The unique features of *Writing Now* reflect the recursive nature of the writing process. Each chapter is consistently organized around steps in the writing process and these steps, as well as other unique features, are indicated by "pull down menus."

▶ **Log On** Every unit begins with warm-up activity. This warm-up section provides an opportunity for reflection and metacognition regarding the ***theme*** of the two-chapter unit upon which the central assignment will be based. The warm-up stimulates recall of relevant existing knowledge, generates interest, and gets students involved in writing in a relaxed and engaging way.

▶ **File: Open** While Log On accesses existing information in a freestyle open-ended format, File: Open, the second section in every chapter, provides ***for reflection, metacognition, and critical thinking about the writing process and grammar concepts*** introduced in a more structured style. File: Open activities guide students toward making connections to existing knowledge and experiences while providing an opportunity to engage in informal writing on topics that interest them. Theorists tell us to begin with an activity in which every student can be successful before introducing more challenging work. This activity assures success and insures that every student will find that he or she has something to contribute.

▶ **File: New** As the name indicates, this section of every chapter *introduces a new step in the writing process*. In most chapters, exploration of new concepts through activities and readings occurs before explicit instruction. After the explicit instruction, additional readings on the unit's theme and attendant activities provide reinforcement of the concept. Opportunities for individual and collaborative exploration and reinforcement of the topics are given. Practical application of the concept will be provided in writing the central assignment (given in *File: Create*).

▶ **File: Create** Appearing only in the odd-numbered chapter of each pair, File: Create directs students *to begin the central writing assignment while incorporating newly learned information.* This is the student's first *draft* of a text that will be revised as he or she works through the second chapter of the pair. It also provides independent application of the concepts given in *File: New*.

▶ **Save As** This feature appears only in the odd-numbered chapters. Save: As directs students to *finish the first draft* of the central assignment. It also indicates closure of that chapter and its name reminds students that writing requires revision.

▶ **Tools** This feature appears only in even-numbered chapters (chapters dealing with further development of an essay) and contains the *language lesson* for the unit. Students are given an opportunity to explore a new language convention or writing process concept through activities and examples found in the readings. Next, explicit instruction is provided and reinforced with examples from the readings as students are given opportunities for individual, group, and/or class practice. Students apply the concept through examination and revision of their existing draft of the central assignment. Even though students are concentrating on one aspect of language per unit, each succeeding chapter holds the student responsible for all earlier lessons. In this way, each essay the student writes will illustrate a greater degree of conventional language usage.

▶ **Edit** A tool to build *revision* into the writing process, this section, appearing toward the end of the second chapter in a pair, requires students to revise their first draft. It reinforces the concepts that have been taught in the unit, as well as those that have come before.

▶ **Save** Appearing at the end of the even-numbered chapters, Save indicates that the *final revision* of the central assignment is to be completed. It contains reminders to students to incorporate all the new information learned in the two-chapter pair as well as all previously learned writing skills and language conventions into the draft, providing them with independent application of the information from *File New* and *Tools* in the chapter. It also indicates the end of a two-chapter unit.

▶ **Options: Customize** Occurring frequently throughout every chapter, *Options: Customize* enables instructors to *customize the textbook* to their own preferences and level of technological access. These optional activities may be used as alternative central assignments or as enrichment activities. Assignment options range from traditional to highly technological, addressing the needs and capabilities of the instructor, students, and technology available. It also provides opportunities for student collaboration.

▶ **Go To** Another feature that appears frequently throughout every chapter, Go To provides web sites to visit for ***additional information on a topic and web activities***. It appears after suggested classroom activities and may be useful for students who finish an assignment early or for instructors who occasionally take their class to a computer lab. It is also ideal for assigning work to be completed in a computer lab for those who teach in a traditional classroom but want to provide enrichment using technology.

▶ **C:/Prompts** Occurring at the end of each chapter, this feature gives prompts for ***alternative or additional writing assignments.*** It gives instructors another way to customize the textbook. For those who wish to assign an essay every week instead of every two weeks, this section provides additional writing activities.

▶ **Log Off** As we learn more about the importance of reflection and metacognition, we build more time into our lesson for these practices. To ***reinforce the material*** and to encourage students to take the time to see how their writing improved in each chapter, students are asked to complete a *Log Off: Review and Reflect* assignment. They answer a few questions that lead them to reflect on their progress. This can be used as a tool for student-teacher conferences, as well, or as part of the assessment process. It is the last activity in the second of the two-chapter pair, a counterpoint to the *Log On* activity that begins the first of each chapter pair.

You will find that *Writing Now* indirectly teaches other literacy skills while teaching the writing process. Highlighting key information in the readings teaches students effective reading skills and enables instructors to quickly assess whether students have effectively read the material. Questions pertaining to the readings encourage effective reading and critical thinking while paving the way for idea generation for essay writing. The use of graphic organizers, such as clustering, mapping, and outlining, is encouraged throughout the book. In sum, students learn the skills of reflection and metacognition, effective reading, outlining and other graphic organizational procedures, and critical thinking in addition to writing skills.

Theory

Writing Now is a blend of theory and practice. The approach is to model the writing process as closely as possible within the linear progression of a college course. Exercises have been designed with close attention to current composition theory and research on learning from cognitive neuroscience and cognitive psychology. Rather than focusing chapters on individual genres, these genres have been worked into real writing activities as needed to support the ideas of the writer. The genres are seen as a communication tool, rather than as an artificial modeling practice. Instructors whose curriculum calls for working with individual genres can address these by focusing on them where they are introduced in the book.

Writing Now and Faculty Diversity

Writing Now is designed to address the diverse needs within the faculty. By combining a mix of high-tech/low-tech strategies, and traditional teaching methods for reading and writing, *Writing Now* addresses the needs of today's technologically diverse faculty. As computer labs are being added to college campuses, more faculty members are enlisted to teach in them. At any given time, faculty may include instructors who have a great deal of technological expertise and experience and those who do not have the interest or perhaps the opportunity to use computers in the writing classroom. *Writing Now* is appropriate for a broad range of instructor expertise.

English faculties are diverse in other ways. Within a given faculty, instructional skills and experience vary greatly and *Writing Now* addresses this diversity. Inexperienced faculty will find a textbook that moves students smoothly through the writing process, introducing skills and reinforcing them in a seamless manner. Inexperienced instructors don't have to figure out how to approach the teaching of writing. By following the book, they are free to concentrate on the students as they work through the writing process, step-by-step, as outlined in *Writing Now*. In addition, instructor's notes in the margin explain the reasoning behind the learning activities. Quotations from a variety of theorists, such as Jerome Bruner and Nell Noddings, are provided to inform as well as to stimulate. Therefore, if desired, *Writing Now* can be a "mentoring" tool for new or adjunct instructors, either in or out of the computer classroom.

But most of all, *Writing Now* was written to engage students and instructors in meaningful and enjoyable discourse, using as many technology tools as available in an atmosphere of exploration to create successful writing experiences. *Writing Now* makes the teaching and writing process more efficient, realistic, manageable, engaging, and successful for teachers and students.

Acknowledgments

It is impossible to acknowledge the myriad influences on us that have led to the writing of this book. We have benefited from the ideas shared with us by texts we have read, the Internet, the media, colleagues, students, professors, classmates, conference presenters and attendees, and friends. As much as possible, we have attempted to cite those whose theory directly influenced us within the book and have provided a bibliography of influential texts. In addition, we would like to give special thanks to the following people:

We wish to thank our devoted Senior Sponsoring Editor, Mary Jo Southern, who developed the concept of a writing textbook designed for use in the computer classroom and worked with us on the process of creating such a book. The pleasure of her company has been one of the highlights of writing the book. Gratitude goes to Annamarie Rice, Marketing Manager, who is a powerhouse of marketing talent and organization, and to the efforts of Sophie Xie, Marketing Assistant. Kellie Cardone, in-house Development Editor, has been a joy to work with as she kept everything progressing smoothly toward completion, while serving as a role model for gracious communication skills. In addition, we have received invaluable help from our development editor, Maggie Barbieri, whose insightful questions and talent for organizing improved the text. We also wish to thank Senior Project Editor Fred Burns who kindly and patiently advised us and guided the text through the copyediting, and Peter Mooney, Editorial Assistant, for unflagging effort.

We are indebted to the Communications Division faculty and students at Delgado Community College who have taught us so much. We are proud to be among them.

We also acknowledge some of the many theorists, researchers, and practitioners who have informed this work: Carl Jung, L.S. Vygotsky, Howard Gardner, Jerome Bruner, Nell Noddings, Caine & Caine, and Maxine Green. In addition, we would like to thank the following reviewers:

Lisa Berman, Miami-Dade Community College

Jennifer E. Bradner, Virginia Commonwealth University

Mary Caldwell, El Paso Community College

Betsy Hawk-Cassriel, Oxnard College

Janet Cutshall, Sussex County Community College

Ray Foster, Scottsdale Community College

Julie Hendrickson, University of Maine at Augusta

Valerie Hennen, Gateway Technical College

Gilda Teixido Kelsey, University of Delaware

Linda G. Matthews, South Suburban College

Tim McLaughlin, Bunker Hill Community College

Christine McMahon, Montgomery College — Rockville Campus

Patricia Pallis, Naugatuck Valley Community College

Stephanie Hurst Powers, Florida Community College at Jacksonville

Daisy Price, Montgomery College — Takoma Park Campus

Jenni Runte, Metropolitan State University

Valerie Russell, Valencia Community College

Karen Standridge, Pikes Peak Community College

Dr. Tonya Strickland, Waycross College

Stacey Thompson, Austin Community College

Kendra L. Vaglienti, Brookhaven College

Dorothy Voyles, Parkland College

Jayne Williams, Texarkana College

I, Janet Nay Zadina, would like to thank those who have supported me throughout this project. I always will be indebted to my family for their continued words of encouragement. Special thanks go to my mother, Irene B. Nay, for her encouragement and support in many ways and Jeff, Kathie, Jason, Alexander, Larry, and Joelan Nay.

Thanks to the professors and doctoral students at the University of New Orleans who have contributed to this book by supporting me intellectually and emotionally. Their insight and comments about the writing process, their own writing in the field of literacy, and their modeling of exemplary practices have been a real inspiration. Thanks to John G. Barnitz, Ph.D., Linda Lonon Blanton, Ph.D., Renee Casbergue, Ph.D., Judith Kieff, Ph.D., Wilma Longstreet, Ph.D., Richard B. Speaker, Jr. Ph.D., Mary Dee Spillett, Ph.D., April Whatley, Ph.D., Deborah Darby, Rubina Khan, Rebecca Maloney, Paulette Perrin, Denise Pouliot, Julie Smith-Price, Lisa Sullivan, Lauren Tarantino, Christy Templet, Barbara Ward, and Cheryl Wheeler. I also wish to thank others who encouraged me through this process, including Chrissy Bergeron, Anne Capes, Eleanor Gordon, Patrice Haydel, Yvonne Ladegaillerie, Judy Morovich, Anita C. Prieto, Ph.D., and Alice Taylor.

Finally, I thank my husband, James E. Zadina, Ph.D., who gave me emotional and household support to write the book and never complained about anything that was neglected to meet deadlines.

I dedicate this book to him.

Biography

Janet N. Zadina, M.Ed., has twenty years of teaching experience in composition and reading and is nationally known as an expert on strategies for reaching all types of learners, especially those in developmental courses. She is currently a doctoral candidate at the University of New Orleans, specializing in the neuroscience of learning, with a doctoral minor in English. She is also a Research Associate engaged in research on the neuroanatomy of language at Tulane University School of Medicine. Ms. Zadina also conducts workshops on educational implications and teaching strategies based on current research. She can be contacted at jzadina@uno.edu.

Susan Halter is a Professor of English at Delgado Community College in New Orleans, La., and a 1998 winner of the Two-Year College English-Southwest Region's Teaching Excellence award. At numerous conferences nationally she has presented workshops on techniques for incorporating electronic communication skills into the composition classroom, as well as her design for an online composition class.

00:45

These timers are suggestions for breaking down the chapter into class time and homework. Three 45-minute timers provided in each chapter (except for this introduction) indicate suggested class activities. Optional homework activities follow the **Go To** sections. Instructors are encouraged to use any material in this book in any order that suits individual teaching styles. The only strong recommendation is that the **Connecting** activities (see page S-2) always be done before introducing new material.

This chapter is meant for those first days of class when roll isn't stabilized and all students don't yet have their books. Although the material in this section is very important, it is something that latecomers can read on their own. This chapter gives students a chance to get to know you and the class.

We are all at different times insiders or outsiders to different discourse communities. Our successful participation in those communities will have a lot to do with whether we're invited into the conversation and treated with tolerance and respect as we gradually acquire a new discourse, or whether we're kept outside of the conversations that would support that acquisition until we demonstrate a mastery that we can't achieve without participation.

E. Kutz, *Language and Literacy: Studying Discourse in Communities and Classrooms* (Portsmouth, NH: Boynton/Cook, 1997), 137.

Because of the importance of building schemas to support new learning, you will notice that many times a new concept is very simply introduced in one chapter without being fully explained. Full explanations come in a later chapter, when students are ready to build on the basic idea that has been introduced earlier. Sometimes it is helpful if a word is slightly familiar to them even if it has only been defined and not previously explained. You will also notice, along these lines, that sometimes a student is asked to work with a concept before the concept is explained or before examples are given. This design enables students to *discover* the use or value of the concept. Then the explanations that follow seem important and necessary to students. If

Start

You are already a writer. However, you may be new to the type of writing community you are now joining: the academic discourse community, or, people writing in the college setting. *Writing Now* initiates you into this new community. As with any new community you join, you will find that you will acquire certain "insider" behaviors as you become an active member.

At the same time, you are participating in another community—the community of people who use computers as a tool. If you have an e-mail account, or use a computer at work, you are already a member of this community and can look forward to acquiring additional computer skills. For those of you who are unfamiliar with computers, *Writing Now* will provide an initiation into this group as well.

It may be helpful, as you proceed into somewhat unknown territory, to remember that you have entered new communities before, whether as a new employee, a new student in a school, a new member in a social group, or a new family member through marriage. Did you feel like an outsider when you first joined a new community? You most likely did until you caught on to the behaviors and expectations of that group. Over time, you learned skills that enabled you to fit into that group. Becoming a writer of college essays is similar to your earlier experiences. You are bringing some skills to the writing task, and you will learn about new expectations and behaviors that will enable you to become a successful writer.

This may be a new way of looking at writing for you. You may have thought that there are good writers and bad writers. Instead, you will see that writing is a skill that can be learned and improved upon. You are already a writer. You are going to add to those skills and learn how to write college essays. You will see that writing is not an *event*, it is a *process*. You may recall that a process is a series of steps. You will find that none of the steps is difficult in itself. If you take writing a step at a time, you will find it manageable.

Not only is writing a process, it is a *recursive* process. This means that you will find yourself repeating some of the steps in the process as necessary—going back to earlier steps and doing them again as the writing progresses. For example, you may do the idea-generating step and later, after you are into the drafting step, find that you need to do some more idea generating.

In the same way, this textbook is recursive. You will be introduced to new skills and then find that they come up again in later chapters in more depth. In this way you can gain experience with a skill, then learn to expand upon and develop it.

Getting Acquainted

You have probably experienced what it means to be a newcomer, especially on the job. One of the first things your new employer did was introduce you to your colleagues. So it makes sense that on your first day in your new academic discourse community—your writing class—you get to know your classmates. Just as on a job, your classmates will make your day pleasanter and more interesting, and they will be able to help you when you get stuck on a task.

students don't discover the concept at that early stage, it's not problematic because the explanation soon follows. This explanation may still carry significance because students realize that there is an information gap that needs to be filled.

Jerome Bruner suggests that

the shape of a curriculum be conceived as a spiral, beginning with an intuitive depiction of a domain of knowledge, circling back to represent the domain more powerfully or formally as needed.

Jerome Bruner, *The Culture of Education* (Cambridge, MA: Harvard University Press, 1996), xii.

The following icebreaking activity teaches students about the learning process and makes for a powerful lesson. Furthermore, students find the activity exciting and memorable. Tell students that you are going to give them a quiz. (That gets their attention!) Tell them that you are going to leave the room for a fixed amount of time (allow about 15 minutes) and when you return, you expect that everyone in the class will have learned everyone else's name. *Give no further instructions and leave the room immediately.* Students devise their own learning strategies while you are gone. Return after the allotted time. Ask for volunteers to recite their classmates' names, and be sure to praise their success. Tell them that they can see how they are *natural learners.* Ask them if you had given them the list to learn overnight, would they have done as well? They should realize that they would not have studied as well as they did in that 15 minutes. Why? Ask students what they did when you were gone to learn the material so efficiently. Some of the answers given will be:

- Wrote names down
- Looked at the written names
- Said the names aloud
- Heard names said
- Used as many senses as possible to retain information
- Repeated names (key to retention)
- Made associations (key to retention)
- Felt pressure of time (brain loves some pressure—that's why game shows are popular; set time limits when studying)
- Felt positive emotion (fun, exciting = enhanced cognition)

Use the chart below to write the names, phone numbers, and e-mail addresses of three of your classmates. You've just completed the first step of getting to know your peers.

Name	Phone	E-mail address

Making Connections

In addition to meeting everyone on that first day of your new job, you had to get the "lay of the land"—find your workstation, locate the bathrooms, learn when and where you eat, and so on. If you weren't given a "grand tour" at the beginning of the day, you may have found that you felt lost your first few days on the job. You probably weren't performing at your best when you felt lost. In learning theory we call getting the "lay of the land" *acquiring schemas.* This means that you acquire some basic foundation on which to build new learning.

If someone tells you to deliver a package to your boss and you don't know where the boss's office is, then you don't have an adequate schema to carry out that task. Lack of a schema can create many difficulties with more complex tasks. For example, assume your boss asks you to write the Friday Report. You have no idea what that is and so you ask. Your boss says, "That is the report we write every Friday to give to the weekend crew. In it we tell them about everything important that happened during the week." Now you know what the Friday report is, but you have an inadequate schema. You don't know the kind of information required or how it should be presented. Without these resources, it would be difficult to write the Friday Report from scratch. However, if you were given copies of Friday Reports from the previous month and you studied those, you would have a schema on which to build new learning—the first Friday Report that you write.

Therefore, it is important for you to acquire a schema for this textbook. Before you make demands on yourself to learn the new skills required in this writing community, familiarize yourself with the important landmarks of the text.

Overall Structure

This text is unique in that its chapters are written as pairs. Both chapters in a pair are based on one *central assignment.* This means that you will start an assignment in the first of the two paired chapters and continue to work on that assignment as you proceed through both chapters.

The textbook is constructed *thematically.* This means that for every chapter pair, all of the readings and your central writing assignment will be based on a general theme or topic, such as working, technology, or music. The text has been designed this way to make writing easier by providing you with an abundance of information on the topic on which you will be writing. This information provides you with ideas for writing. That is one of the reasons that you will find so much reading in your writing textbook.

- Worked with each other
- Learned the names in logical order

Discuss these learning strategies with your students and have them write the strategies down. Ask them how they normally study, and write those methods on the board. Have them compare the two lists and discuss which is more effective and how they can incorporate these new strategies into their new study habits.

Picture yourself again beginning a new job. During your first few days, you are probably paying as much attention as possible to how other employees are performing their tasks, particularly if their tasks are similar to yours. You do this so that you can model your behavior after theirs as a way to learn to do your job effectively. *Modeling* is a basic learning tool that you have used since you were a toddler. To see modeling in action, watch how young children imitate their parents. You can also notice how teenagers model their behavior after their friends' behavior so that they can fit in.

Just as modeling has helped you learn many behaviors in the past, you can use it to improve your writing. This text contains many readings. As you read and analyze how other writers handled a topic, you will discover ways to improve your own writing.

While the readings serve these important purposes, they also help to improve your writing in subtler ways. The more you work with language, whether through discussions, writing, or reading, the better you become at all of those activities. It may be challenging for you to keep up with all the readings at first, but you will get better at it as the course goes on and you improve in all your language skills as well.

Log On ▶ Reflection

"Thinking about thinking" has to be a principal ingredient of any empowering practice of education.

Jerome Bruner, *The Culture of Education* (Cambridge, MA: Harvard University Press, 1996), 19.

Reflection is a critical aspect of all sophisticated and higher-order thinking and learning.

R. N. Caine and G. Caine, *Making Connections: Teaching and the Human Brain* (Menlo Park, CA: Addison Wesley, 1991), 158.

We value students' previous knowledge as an essential resource, one that enables the acquisition of unfamiliar terms and concepts. Given the opportunity to make connections between what they already know and what they are being asked to learn, students can take ownership of subject matter.

Vivian Zamel and Ruth Spack, eds., *Negotiating Academic Literacies: Teaching and Learning Across Languages and Cultures* (Mahweh, NJ: Lawrence Erlbaum, 1998), x.

As you drive to work on the first day of a new job, you are probably *reflecting* on what it will be like. You are imagining what kind of people you will be working with, what tasks will be involved, how your skills will support you in this job, and whether you will need to learn new skills. You are also probably thinking about what you already know about the job—what friends have told you, what you may have experienced as you interacted with that type of business as a customer, or maybe even television shows in which that kind of work has been portrayed.

As you begin a new chapter, in the **Log On: Reflection** section you will spend time reflecting on what may be coming up in the chapter. Reflecting is an activity with several purposes. First, it will begin to build schemas—that is, connect this new material to information already existing in your brain. Forging connections will make learning easier. Second, reflecting helps to "warm up" your brain by focusing your attention. It will settle your mind and help free it of distractions. In addition, this section gives you practice in writing under conditions that are comfortable and relaxing. Over time you will become more comfortable expressing your thoughts in writing and will become a better writer.

When you are reflecting, you will be writing in a style called *freewriting*. *Freewriting* is what the name implies—writing free of rules. You simply write whatever comes to mind, without worrying about whether you are writing in complete sentences or using conventional grammar. The point is to get your thoughts down quickly and easily. The more relaxed you are when you freewrite, the more easily your thoughts will flow. You will learn more about freewriting in Chapter 1.

When you use a computer, the first thing you do is *log on*. This means that you are beginning to interact with your computer. You can open files you have previously saved, add and access new information, and communicate with others. When you "log on" to a writing task, you gather materials to complete the assignment. You take time to collect your thoughts and prepare to work. In the **Log On: Reflection** section of each chapter you will be doing similar activities.

FILE ▶ Open

As you may be aware, the theories of John Dewey are once more receiving positive attention. He was ahead of his time in recognizing the importance of the schema, a concept that Nell Noddings supports:

John Dewey (1963) posited continuity as one of the criteria of educational experience. For Dewey, an educational experience had to be connected to the prior personal experience of students and also to a widening or opening of future experience.

Nell Noddings, *The Challenge to Care in Schools* (New York: Teachers College Press, 1992), 64.

The importance of this section cannot be overemphasized.

We do not come to understand a subject or master a skill by sticking bits of information to each other. Understanding a subject results from perceiving relationships. The brain is designed as a pattern detector. Our function as an educator is to provide students with the sorts of experiences that enable them to perceive [patterns]. All knowledge is embedded in other knowledge. The ability to perceive this interpenetration and both understand it and teach it constitutes one of the cornerstones of brain-based learning.

R. N. Caine and G. Caine, *Making Connections: Teaching and the Human Brain* (Menlo Park, CA: Addison Wesley, 1991), 39.

Using the **File: Open** section as a starting point for class or small-group discussion is highly recommended because

if . . . the purpose . . . is to encourage exploration, risk-taking, and discovery, while creating a supportive learning community and providing a scaffold that connects everyone's prior discourse experience to the new demands of a community where not everyone shares the same prior knowledge, then the conversational strategies for creating involvement

This section of the book might be compared to the lunchtime at work. It's the easiest, pleasantest time of the day on your job, and it is also very important! If you don't have a good foundation of energy and nutrition, then it is hard to put in a good day's work. The **File: Open** section is easy, pleasant, and foundational in enabling you to do a good job in the chapter. This section activates the schemas in your mind so that the new information you learn can connect to what you already know. You already bring knowledge to the task in every chapter. Some of this knowledge may be something you haven't thought about in a while or something you may not have *connected* with the new learning. This section enables you to make connections, thus bringing more brain power to the task.

The importance of making these connections cannot be overemphasized. Learning and thinking consist of your brain's making connections between neurons. Certain parts of your brain are activated when you perform specific tasks—when you are learning and thinking. When you learn something new, you build connections between existing neurons. The more you can connect neurons, the more brain power you can bring to a task. If you already have many connections, many pathways, then additional learning becomes easier.

This is one reason it is difficult to learn something entirely new. If you want to learn in-line skating but have never done any type of skating before, your brain will have to create new connections to perform these motor skills. That means you will not perform well at first and your progress might be slow. However, someone who has previously ice skated would have formed connections in these motor skill areas of the brain and could make use of them in performing the new task. Because that person is connecting the new skills to a web of previously existing strong connections, he or she will immediately perform better and will learn the skill more quickly. This may explain why sometimes you see another student catch on more quickly than you do. You immediately assume that student is smarter than you, but now you see that it could be because that student had already formed a web of connections of earlier learning that made the new material easier.

In completing the **File: Open** section of each chapter, you may be writing by yourself or you may be talking as a class or in small groups. *Speaking* about reading and writing is an important part of the writing process. By speaking about the writing process, you are thinking about the ideas that you will write about and you gain experience in expressing those ideas.

Therefore, as you can see, you will want to activate any existing connections before you try to incorporate new material. The **File: Open** section of the text is like opening a file on a computer where you have already saved information; you simply have to build on that information rather than start completely from scratch.

FILE ▶ New

and negotiating newly shared meanings need to have a more prominent role.

E. Kutz, *Language and Literacy: Studying Discourse in Communities and Classrooms* (Portsmouth, NH: Boynton/Cook, 1997), 184.

This book is based on themes that are relevant to the lives of students, thus providing them with meaningful activities.

Because people learn to be literate when they are able to/asked to engage in meaningful literate acts, the foundation is formed by giving learners, adult and children alike, occasions for genuine literate action. Instruction then builds on that foundation by helping students to enter into a discourse practice.

L. Flower, *The Construction of Negotiated Meaning: A Social Cognitive Theory of Writing.* (Carbondale and Edwardsville: Southern Illinois University Press, 1994), 25.

Another challenge of your first day on the job is learning new information and skills. Most new activities can seem overwhelming at first, but you realize that you will learn them in time. Remember the first time you were shown how to operate an unfamiliar piece of equipment? You may have felt uncertain at first, but later you became experienced and comfortable with the task.

File: New is the section of each chapter that introduces new material. You may already be familiar with some of this "new" material. For example, when you learn to operate a state-of-the-art copy machine, you have some knowledge of older models, and so you have some experience on which to draw. Some of the new material in this text may seem totally unfamiliar at first. However, since you have already made connections in the **File: Open** section, you have some experience on which to draw and you are ready to integrate this new material.

As you are introduced to the new material, you will be given examples and explanations of the material. As you experiment with integrating the new information into your writing, you won't be expected to be perfect the first time. Since writing is a recursive process, you will have continued opportunities to become better at the tasks presented in this new material.

Think of the **File: New** section of the text as opening a new file on the computer and beginning to work from scratch.

FILE ▶ Create

Because some students are not familiar with computers, each section's explanations begin with a workplace metaphor and end with a computer metaphor. This frame gives students some computer schemas as well.

Since most instructors assign one formal piece of writing every two weeks, this text is based on starting a writing assignment one week and finishing it the next. Each chapter is designed to contain one week's work. Most instructors using this text work with one chapter per week, devoting two weeks (two chapters) to one central writing assignment, with students revising the beginning draft throughout both chapters. If instructors want to make one formal writing assignment per week, there are additional options. (See **Options: Customize** and **C:\Prompt.**)

This section begins the central writing assignment that carries through the paired chapters. If you don't want to use the suggested central assignment, you will find alternative topics under **C:\Prompts for Writing** at the end of the chapter.

Once again, picture yourself in a new job. You have familiarized yourself with your surroundings. You have brought some information and skills to the new job, and as you were introduced to its tasks, you made connections in your mind between what you already knew and how you would apply that information to the new situation. Then you were told about tasks that would be new and unfamiliar to you but that you knew would connect in some way to your existing skills (or you would not have been hired in the first place!). This section of the book can be compared to your first task in your new job.

When you get to the **File: Create** section, you are ready to write your first *draft* of the central assignment. The purpose of this draft is to get as much content into your paper as you can. Your writing at this stage may be roughly organized and almost certainly will contain spelling, punctuation, and other mechanical inconsistencies. Do not interrupt your train of thought at this stage to focus on such details.

Since this is your first attempt with new material, keep in mind that it will not be your best version. That is why you will continue to work with this text throughout two chapters, rewriting and making your draft better.

Documents and Files

The **File: Create** section of the text is similar to working on a computer. When you create a new document after you open a new file you create that document in a new file.

OPTIONS ▶ Customize

This section allows you to individualize the course according to the resources you have available and the technological skills you bring to it.

If you have held more than one job in your field, you may have noticed that each company has its own way of doing things. Although you may have performed a task one way for a given company and had successful results, another company wants you to get the same results using a different method. Or you may notice that individual employees in one company have different ways of accomplishing the same job tasks.

The same is true for learning. Some people learn best by listening while others learn best by seeing or reading. Others learn best by doing things with their hands or on a computer. Therefore, this text offers periodic suggestions for alternative ways of handling a lesson. Your instructor may elect to use one or more of these alternatives, or you may want to try one if you think it suits your learning style. Another reason the **Options: Customize** section is included is that available technology varies from school to school. If your school doesn't offer frequent access to a computer lab, your instructor may choose an alternative lesson. Because some schools have specialized equipment and software, those options are also included. In other words, the text aims to work with the resources you have on a variety of levels and enable you to use many kinds of learning styles.

Customize

Later in the course you may learn that you can *customize* your text on the computer by changing its appearance to suit your own purpose and taste. In fact, one of the advantages of using a computer is that it allows you to customize, or *format*, text, not only by determining the appearance of the text itself but by adding pictures, text boxes, and other options you may become familiar with later in the course.

Go To ▶ You will come across the **Go To** section periodically throughout the text. Its purpose is to refer you to places that you can *go to* on the computer for additional help with the new material or for more information on the topic.

<developmentalenglish.college.hmco.com/students>

This section is designed to be as much help to the instructor as it is to the student. If you are teaching in a computer classroom, it is ideal for students who finish their in-class assignment early or for spare time once you have finished a lesson. If you use a computer lab infrequently, this feature provides worthwhile activities for students as they learn to use the computer when you do have lab access. You may want to use this section for extra credit or for alternative assignments. In addition to specific sites given in **Go To,** you will find more help on the Houghton Mifflin Company web site: <http://college.hmco.com>

C:\Prompts for Writing ▶

This section includes alternative topics for writing. These topics could be used instead of, or in addition to, the central assignment. If you have time at the end of the course, you may want to return to a topic your students particularly enjoyed and give another writing assignment on it. Students can see how much progress they have made in handling the topic.

Most jobs include regular assigned tasks. In addition, you may occasionally be asked to perform alternative or further tasks to help out where needed. In the same way, additional opportunities for writing are provided in this section of the text. Your instructor may use the **C:\Prompts for Writing** section instead of or in addition to the central writing assignment.

TOOLS ▶ **Language**

For our students, standard English and the standard forms of academic discourse are a new style, a new dialect, in a sense, a new language. They will not learn that new language effectively from the application of rules of grammar or from the application of discourse models, just as children will not attend to language features that seem to conflict with the meaning they intend. All of these language learners will, however, learn out of communicative need, in real contexts in which language is pushed by meaning.

E. Kutz, "Between Students' Language and Academic Discourse: Interlanguage as Middle Ground," in *Negotiating Academic Literacies: Teaching and Learning Across Languages and Cultures,* ed. Vivian Zamel and Ruth Spack (Mahweh, NJ: Lawrence Erlbaum Associates, 1998), 41.

Most jobs have specialized "tools of the trade" that enable the user to create the best possible finished product. A carpenter may use an electric tool that drives nails quickly and an electronic level to ensure proper alignment. A waiter may use a *crumber*—a tool used to sweep crumbs off a table—and a corkscrew to open wine. A writer works with the tool of written language to express thoughts effectively. A writer in an academic discourse community uses *conventional language*—that is, language appropriate to the college community.

You may have noticed that most groups you belong to have their own language conventions. The language style you use with your friends is different from the language style you use at home with your family. You may use another language style for school. Academic writing (and most on-the-job writing) has its own language, often called *Standard English.* Throughout the text in the **Tools: Language** section you will learn the appropriate language conventions for your new group—the college community.

Toolbar

If you look at the top of a computer screen, you will see a *toolbar.* This is a series of pictures—*icons*—that indicate word processing features, or *tools.* In addition, there is a pull-down menu bar with the word "Tools" on it. This feature provides you with the tools to check spelling, mechanics, and word count, among other features of your writing.

EDIT ▶

This section consists of revising the central assignment. Revision is seen in this text as a major, and recursive, part of the writing process.

Once in a while you may not get something right on a job the first time you do it. Therefore, you will have to go back and correct it. This is especially true if you are doing word processing. You may find errors in what you have keyed and will have to make changes. In writing, finding errors and correcting them is always part of the writing process. Even professional writers do not get their text into good final form on their first draft; they always have to *edit.* Editing is

Throughout the text we separate the creative work of making meaning from the detail work of editing.

We know . . . that attending to both meaning and form simultaneously may be impossible at some moments for writers working in a secondary discourse, and we can anticipate that, as she gains fluency as a writer and as a speaker of the standard variety of English, she'll both acquire more of these forms and find it easier to monitor for those she has learned but has not fully acquired.

E. Kutz, *Language and Literacy: Studying Discourse in Communities and Classrooms* (Portsmouth, NH: Boynton/Cook, 1997), 135.

the process of going back, looking critically at what you wrote, and finding ways to improve it. It is a step that you will take with every essay you write. In fact, you will probably have to take this step several times when writing your essay.

You may notice in the sequence of tasks in this text you are asked to write an essay before you edit, that is, before you are concerned with the specifics of the language you use. That order is provided for a purpose. When you are writing down your ideas, you want to use the creative part of your brain. You want to focus on *what* you are saying, not on *how* you are saying it. Then, when you come to the **Edit** section of the chapter, it is appropriate to focus on the *how*— the language conventions. It is time to let the linear left side of the brain take over and carefully examine the writing in its *details,* rather than taking the *holistic* (big picture) approach that you use in the first of each pair of chapters.

Editing

Because editing is such a fundamental part of writing, a word processor has a pull-down menu for editing, too. It allows you to cut and paste so you can move sentences and paragraphs around to organize your paper effectively. It also includes a Find-and-Replace function for making consistent changes throughout your paper.

FILE ▶ Save As/Save

File: Save as refers to a completed *draft* of your essay. The name "Save as" helps you remember that your essay isn't finished. You will continue to work with your draft until the end of the second chapter in a pair. Once you get to the second chapter in a pair, you will find a section called "Save." "Save" tells you that it is time to turn in a final version of your essay.

File: Save is the final stage of the writing process. You have completed all the stages of the writing process (some of them more than once), and you are ready for the result—a polished piece of writing. Now you perform a final check, making sure that you have taken advantage of everything you have learned up to this point. When you are sure that the piece of writing has been through all the steps, you are ready to "save" it, in computer language—to turn it in for a grade.

Save

If you are using a computer to write your essay, you will literally save the text to a disk so that it is available to you in the future. You will print a hard copy for your instructor or, in some classes, post it to a software application that allows your instructor to grade it online.

Log Off: Review and Reflect ▶

We've taken special pains with two aspects of the language lessons. First, since research shows that students are likely to remember examples at random from a text, we are careful to use only examples that we would want students to mimic. For this reason, we don't show students what *not* to do. You will notice occasional nonacademic usage in some of the readings that come from newspapers or student writing. You may want to point out examples of different usages and discuss language *codes*. Language codes are appropriate language for different situations or different audiences. Our second area of concern is that exercises be as close to real writing as possible rather than a series of isolated sentences given out of context. Therefore, we have included language lesson activities in which students are asked to *rewrite* a given text. This is *not* busy work, though it appears deceptively easy. The student is required to look at the language usage in the *context* of an entire sentence or paragraph and then make whatever changes are necessary throughout the sentence or paragraph—changing, say, a noun from singular to plural when rewriting. These exercises are designed to resemble a real editing experience as much as possible without providing incorrect examples.

Achieving skill and accumulating knowledge are not enough. The learner can be helped to achieve full mastery by reflecting as well upon how she is going about her job, and how her approach can be improved.

Jerome Bruner, *The Culture of Education* (Cambridge, MA: Harvard University Press, 1996), 64.

As you finish a project, whether at work, home, or school, you might take time to look it over one last time, remember the work that you put into it, and evaluate the final result. You might think about what you liked best about the project, how completing it made you feel, and what you learned that might help you if you do a similar project.

Similarly, when you have finished the long, hard work of writing your central assignment, it is time for you to take a moment to wrap things up. You pause and reflect on what you have learned in the chapter. The ability to think about your thinking is called *metacognition*, a skill that enhances learning. As you spend a few moments writing about what you learned in the paired chapters, you are consolidating and storing this information in an effective way. Furthermore, sometimes you don't even realize what you have actually learned until you stop and think about it. Realizing the improvements you have made in your writing as a result of the work in those chapters helps to ensure that these improvements become more solidly fixed in your mind. The **Log Off** section of the even-numbered chapters is crucial to the long-range consolidation of your new skills and should never be omitted.

Logging Off

Logging off the computer means you are shutting the machine down, but it doesn't mean that you are putting what's in it away, never to see or use again. On the contrary, when you log on the next time, you should find everything stored on your computer just as you left it, and you may access and build on it to continue creating, organizing, and storing more information.

Besides all these helpful sites in your chapter, you can find additional help on the web site for this text:

<developmentalenglish.college.hmco.com/students>

Now that you are familiar with the structure of your textbook, you are ready to begin using it. If at any time you forget what you are supposed to be doing in each section, refer back to these pages to reorient yourself.

You have gotten acquainted with your fellow students and with the layout of the book. Perhaps it would be a good idea for your instructor to get acquainted with you.

Warm-Up Exercise

Now you are going to write a letter about yourself. However—pay careful attention because this is definitely an unusual task—you are going to write a letter *to* yourself *from* your instructor about who you are and your anticipated performance in class. You will be writing the letter from the *point of view* (you will learn more about this term later) of your instructor. For now, it just means to pretend that you are the instructor and as the instructor you write yourself a letter. Assume the instructor knows you and is writing you about how you will do in the class, discussing your strengths, weaknesses, attitude, lifestyle, or anything else that might affect your performance. Just keep in mind that you are writing from the instructor's point of view, addressed to yourself.

You may find it helpful to use the following format to get started. Be sure to talk about your attitudes, homework, class participation, contributions to the class as a whole, strengths, weaknesses, and fears and hopes about the class. Write at least ten sentences.

Dear _____
(your name)

I can tell that you are someone who . . .

You may want to begin the homework assignment with the letter to you, or, if you have time, have students write it in class. If you ask for volunteers to read their letters, you will find that some students enjoy reading their assignments out loud to the class. However, unless you warn students beforehand, it is probably best not to require all students to read their letters to the class. This can be quite an eye-opening experience. Students may surprise themselves as well as you with their insight into their strengths and weaknesses. This assignment will also give you a rough idea of students' writing skills while still providing them with a nonthreatening and enjoyable initial writing experience.

This page is formatted so that you can have students tear it out and turn it in if you like.

Additional Notes to Teachers

We realize that instructors want to base their instruction on sound teaching and learning principles. In addition, instructors like to know the *why* of what they are doing. This may especially be the case in this text, since some of the material is based on the most recent findings in the neuroscience of learning. Therefore, we are providing here some of the theory and principles on which this book is based, which will be familiar to seasoned instructors. A brief bibliography is also provided. Of course, the book is primarily grounded in our years of study and of instructional practice.

One of the most valuable tools we have come across is Linda Lonon Blanton's concept of a holistic design for each unit of coursework.[1] Although Blanton provided this model in an article on teaching ESL students, it is based on what we currently know to be effective, brain-friendly teaching strategies for all students. We have modified the model for this text as indicated by the information in brackets.

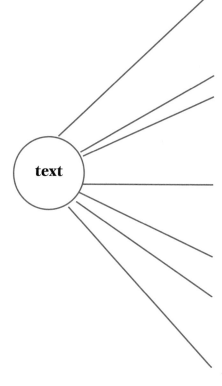

- **Listening Activities**   For example: The teacher talks about the topic of the text, giving background information. [Since this text is not written for ESL students specifically, we use the schema work in **File: Open,** suggesting that you use a combination of writing and discussion techniques with that section.]

- **Reading**   For example: Students read text, in class or at home.

- **Talking**   For example: Students role-play, compose a different title, verbally "design" illustrations to the text. [Our activities vary, but with the same purpose—to get students to interact with the text using a variety of learning styles. This is why you will see notations suggesting small-group work throughout the text.]

- **Writing**   For example: Students write in journals in response to questions related to the text, such as "What do you consider significant about the text?" [We have students do this writing in the text as they analyze the readings.]

- **Talking**   For example: In small groups of two or three, students react to the text by talking about any related experience.

- **Writing**   For example: Students write about a related experience. [This is comparable to our central assignment, which takes place after students have had time to explore the topic in discussion and writing, as above.]

- **Reading**   For example: Students read each other's papers, which constitute new texts. [We encourage group work in the composing and revising process.]

---

1. Linda Lonon Blanton, "A Holistic Approach to College ESL: Integrating Language and Content," in *Teaching of Writing to U.S.-Educated Learners of ESL*, Linda Harkiau, Kay M. Losey, Meryl Siegal. Mahwah, NJ: Lawrence Erlbaum, 1999, 285–293.

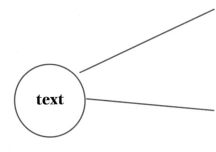

- **Reading**   For example: Students return to the original text to check for new insights. [We occasionally refer students back to earlier writing and earlier readings, but this activity is most comparable to our stage of having students continue to explore additional readings on the topic as they continue to process and modify the ideas in their text.]

- **Talking and Listening**   For example: Students discuss any features of the text worthy of note. [Talking and listening are built into some of the activities in the final **File: Create** stage. We end our work with a metacognitive activity in **Log Off.** We encourage you to have students share these reflections in a talking and listening process, as in a class or in small groups.]

Blanton discusses the flexibility of this holistic design:

> The model is flexible and can be easily changed to accommodate more of any kind of activity—more reading, writing, listening, and speaking. Neither is the order sacred, although common sense dictates that students talk about a text or the topic related to it and listen to others do the same before being asked to write about it. It is also a good practice to go back to the text and have students read it again after they have had the experience of talking more about the topic and writing about it. It is wonderful to observe their deeper reading and fuller comprehension the second time around. In asking students to respond to the text, reading must not be reduced to the simple transmission of information. Comprehension questions often do little more than ask readers to remember what the author of the text said, and should be avoided.[2]

Caine and Caine offer a similar view: "The learner needs to be engaged in talking, listening, reading, viewing, acting, and valuing. Brain research supports this."[3]

Another heuristic is the following contrast between assigning writing and teaching the writing process. We have attempted to base the instruction in this text on the principles of *teaching the writing process* and believe that Haugen, Kean, and Mohan have provided valuable guidelines:

Assigning Writing

1. The teacher asks the student to write on one topic from a list.
2. The topic is general and unstructured.
3. There is no specific audience.
4. The topic allows for general thinking.
5. The purpose is vague.
6. The student writes for a grade.
7. The student is asked to write spontaneously. [Note: We believe this means without brainstorming.]

---

2. Blanton, "A Holistic Approach," 285–293.
3. R. N. Caine and G. Caine, *Making Connections: Teaching and the Human Brain* (Menlo Park, CA: Addison Wesley, 1991), 6. This and other excerpts from *Making Connections: Teaching and the Human Brain* © 1994 by Geoffrey Caine and Renate Nummela Caine. Published by Dale Seymour Publications. Used by permission of Pearson Education, Inc.

8. Time and/or work limit is imposed.

9. A first draft is required for a grade.

10. There are negative comments.

11. Corrections are usually for mechanical errors.

12. All errors are corrected by the teacher.

13. Teacher's time is spent correcting papers.

14. Student is unsure of how grade evolved.

15. Student is unsure of significant changes.

16. Student and teacher are bored by the student's writing.

Teaching the Writing Process

1. The teacher encourages the student to write precisely and effectively.

2. The topic is specific and structured.

3. There is a clear audience.

4. The topic allows for precise thought and supporting details.

5. The purpose is specific.

6. The student writes to improve ability to express ideas.

7. The student is encouraged to think about the topic.

8. The student evaluates purpose, then perceives the amount of work needed to fulfill it.

9. Student is encouraged to review and rewrite the first draft.

10. Comments are positive and constructive.

11. Recommendations include suggestions for improvement.

12. Only specific errors are corrected by the teacher.
[Note: We suggest you focus on errors taught in the current lesson and in preceding chapters, not on errors not yet covered.]

13. Teacher's time is spent in class, teaching.

14. Student earns and understands the grade.

15. Student sees changes.

16. Student and teacher are excited by student's writing.[4]

A third schema that has provided theoretical underpinning to this text comes from Caine and Caine, who assert that the following conditions "increase the brain's capacity to function in complex ways and create new connections":

1. Outcomes should be relatively open ended.

2. Personal meaning should be maximized.

3. Emphasis should be on intrinsic motivation.

---

4. N. Haugen, J. M. Kean, and M. B. Mohan, eds., *A Guide to the Teacher's Role in the Writing Program* (Madison: University of Wisconsin, Wisconsin Writing Project, 1981). Copyright 1981 by Wisconsin Writing Project. Reprinted by permission.

4. Tasks should have relatively open-ended time lines.

5. Tasks should be manageable and supported.[5]

You may notice that this text has not been structured around rhetorical modes. Rhetorical modes, called *patterns of development* in this text, are discussed as *tools* for the reader in expressing thoughts or in organizing material within a paragraph as opposed to assigning a cause and effect essay, for example. We agree with Blanton:

> Infused with an antiquated perception of English discourse as "fitting" rhetorical modes (Bain, 1866), like muffins in a tin, remedial writing lessons model, say, expository essay structure or cause-effect arrangements. With little concern for reading, except for analyzing texts as models of rhetorical modes, traditional pedagogy gets students operating in conceptual frames that, true, can manifest themselves in English discourse (whether academic or not), but—herein lies the fundamental instructional problem—with form externally imposed on writerly efforts, effectively stifling a writer's possibility to generate thoughtful prose.[6]

Instead, students are encouraged to respond to readings and to present their responses through speaking and writing. Students are given meaningful topics and readings primarily from the type of material they are likely to encounter in real life, such as newspaper and magazine articles or texts by bestselling authors who are being discussed in the media. Students read on the topic, then thoughtfully develop their own opinions and present them in an essay. This activity also allows students to practice critical thinking and to express views in the arena of public discourse. Blanton finds that this experience can empower students:

> Empowerment as a critical reader, then, comes about through the practice of interacting with texts, and through developing individualized responses to them (Bartholomae & Petrosky, 1986). Reader-writers who develop individualized responses to texts—who can "talk" to them and about them, who can agree or disagree with them, who can relate their own response to texts and write about them—are empowered to practice literacy as academics do (Heath & Mangiola, 1991).[7]

We strongly believe that the classroom atmosphere is of utmost importance, more important than the pedagogical methods or the content of a lesson. Wherever possible, we have incorporated activities that will enable students to relax and enjoy themselves as they learn. We encourage a puzzle-solving attitude that encourages guessing, risk taking, and exploration. Group activities are encouraged throughout the text so that students can make attempts without fear that they will be embarrassed, give the "wrong answers," or receive a lowered grade. We do this because we believe that no matter how excellent a lesson is, a student cannot learn well in a negative emotional state. On the contrary, evidence suggests that positive emotion enhances learning.

---

5. Caine and Caine, *Making Connections*, 85.
6. Linda Lonon Blanton, "Instruction and Language Minority Students," in *Generation 1.5 Meets College Composition: Issues in the Teaching of Writing to U.S.-Educated Learners of ESL,* ed. Linda Harkiau, Kay M. Losey, and Meryl Siegal (Mahweh, NJ: Lawrence Erlbaum, 1999), 127.
7. Blanton, "Instruction and Language Minority Students," 135.

All three layers of the brain interact. It means that none of the ingredients that we deal with in education, such as concepts and emotions and behaviors, is separate. They influence and shape each other. . . . The interconnectedness of concepts and emotions, however, should be expected, given the fact that the limbic system mediates both emotion and memory. . . . The practical consequence is that the enthusiastic involvement of students is essential to most learning. There is more, however. . . . Concepts are actually shaped by emotions. . . . Content that is emotionally sterile is made more difficult to understand. . . . To teach someone any subject adequately, the subject must be embedded in all the elements that give it meaning. People must have a way to relate to the subject in terms of what is personally important and this means acknowledging both the emotional impact and their deeply held needs and drives. Our emotions are integral to learning. When we ignore the emotional components of any subject we teach, we deprive students of meaningfulness.[8]

Our hope is that students can have fun with many of the activities in *Writing Now* and that you, as the instructor, have fun with the material as well.

For further information regarding some of the philosophical and theoretical foundations of this textbook, we have included a brief bibliography.

Suggested Readings

Bruner, J. *Acts of Meaning.* Cambridge, MA: Harvard University Press, 1990.

————. *The Culture of Education.* Cambridge, MA: Harvard University Press, 1996.

Caine, R. N., and G. Caine. *Making Connections: Teaching and the Human Brain.* Menlo Park, CA: Addison Wesley, 1991.

Cross, K. P. Learning Is About Making Connections. *The Cross Papers* 3 (June 1999).

Dewey, J. *Moral Principles in Education.* Carbondale: Southern Illinois University Press, 1909.

Flower, L., ed. *The Construction of Negotiated Meaning: A Social Cognitive Theory of Writing.* Carbondale: Southern Illinois University Press, 1994.

Gardner, H. *Multiple Intelligences: The Theory in Practice.* New York: Basic Books, 1993.

Greene, M. *Releasing the Imagination.* San Francisco: Jossey-Bass, 1995.

Harkiau, L., K. M. Losey, and M. Siegal, eds. *Generation 1.5 Meets College Composition: Issues in the Teaching of Writing to U.S.-Educated Learners of ESL.* Mahweh, NJ: Lawrence Erlbaum, 1995.

Jackendoff, R. *Languages of the Mind: Essays on Mental Representation.* Cambridge, MA: MIT Press, 1996.

Klauser, H. A. *Writing on Both Sides of the Brain.* New York: Harper & Row, 1987.

Kutz, E. *Language and Literacy: Studying Discourse in Communities and Classrooms.* Portsmouth, NH: Boynton/Cook, 1997.

---

8. Caine and Caine, *Making Connections,* 63–64.

Mehan, H., I. Villanueva, L. Hubbard, and A. Lintz. *Constructing School Success.* Cambridge, UK: Cambridge University Press, 1996.

Noddings, N. *The Challenge to Care in Schools.* New York: Teachers College Press, 1992.

Rico, G. L. *Writing the Natural Way.* New York: Jeremy P. Tarcher/Putnam, 1983.

————, and M. F. Claggett. *Balancing the Hemispheres: Brain Research and the Teaching of Writing.* Berkeley: University of California and Bay Area Writing Project, 1980.

Vygotsky, L. S. *Mind in Society: The Development of Higher Psychological Processes.* Cambridge, MA: Harvard University Press, 1978.

Zamel, V., and R. Spack, eds. *Teaching Academic Literacies: Teaching and Learning Across Languages and Cultures.* Mahweh, NJ: Lawrence Erlbaum, 1998.

The authors welcome feedback from you about which activities have or have not been helpful for your students, as well as any suggestions regarding improvements to future editions. Please e-mail us at the address appearing on our web site.

Chapter 1
We Are All Writers

I must write it all out, at any cost. Writing is thinking. It is more than living, for it is being conscious of living.

—Anne Morrow Lindbergh

Chapter Contents

1

Log On ▶ **Reflection**

Write whatever comes to mind upon reading the chapter title and opening quotation. (If you forget how to do this, go to **Start,** page S-3, for a reminder.)

_____

_____

_____

_____

_____

_____

_____

_____

_____

_____

_____

_____

_____

_____

_____

_____

_____

_____

_____

_____

_____

_____

FILE ▶ Open

Remember, making connections is a critical first step in the writing process. It enables students to start making connections in a relaxed situation. It taps into the creative part of the brain, putting students where they need to be at this point—the creative, idea-generating stage. Keeping this in mind, this writing exercise probably should not be collected or evaluated.

00:45

Reminder: This freewriting activity has several important purposes. First, you want students to write early and often. Second, you want students' early writing attempts to feel successful and nonthreatening in order to build their confidence. However, one of the most important functional purposes of freewriting is to generate connections to familiar material. Students *absorb* new material more easily when they can *connect* it to something they already know. To make these important connections, students must activate known material before encountering new material. Therefore, it is best if students write out the answers to these questions as much as time allows. You may ask them to keep a composition notebook, a kind of journal, just for this purpose.

For this first class session, allow 5–15 minutes for the Connecting exercises (while you take roll and perform other classroom management activities).

Remember, in the File: Open section of each chapter you are warming up for the work that follows. Like stretching exercises before a workout, these thinking exercises warm up the brain, making the learning that follows easier. Always devote as much time as possible to the activities in this section. They will help your brain make the connections it needs to make learning and writing easier!

Connecting with Experience

▶ What is your definition of a writer?

▶ Are you a writer? Explain what it means to be a writer.

▶ Compile a list of things you have written. Remember to include papers for school, e-mails to friends, a journal, or letters.

▶ Will you ever have to write anything on your job (job descriptions, memos, e-mails . . .)? Think of your long-range job status.

▶ Has your definition of a writer changed as a result of your answers to the above questions?

▶ How do you feel about writing in general? Explain.

▶ How do you feel about *your* writing? Why?

Connecting with Writing

▶ When you are writing for your own purposes, how do you get started?

▶ Specifically, when you are assigned to write an essay for school, how do you start the assignment?

▶ Do you use a general process or list of steps when you tackle a writing task? Explain the process or steps that you use when you tackle a writing task.

▶ How would it help if you could be aware of some small steps writers take when they begin a piece of writing?

Connecting with the Topic

▶ What do you think are the most important things you will learn about being a writer?

▶ How do you expect your writing ability to affect your life? Your education? Your career?

▶ What do you want to learn about writing?

Connecting with New Material

◗ Have you ever heard the term *brainstorming* used before? If so, under what conditions? What did you assume it meant? If the term is not familiar, attempt a definition and see how close you get to the meaning.

◗ Why do people make lists? What purpose do they serve? Under what conditions do you find making a list helpful?

◗ What is a *process*?

FILE ▶ New

Generating Ideas for Writing

A common writing misconception is that the first step in writing an essay is to sit down with a piece of paper and start trying to write something. This is not the case. In almost every instance of writing anything (directions to your house, a recipe, a list, an e-mail, or even a report for school), the first step is *prewriting.* Even a task as simple as making a grocery list has a prewriting stage of thinking about the purpose of the list, what items are needed, and how much information needs to be written down; sometimes it even involves organizing the information mentally into groups. Then, in actually writing the list, you engage in the rest of the *writing process.* In making a list you generate as much information as possible, perhaps organizing the items into logical categories (such as dairy, meat, and produce), and revising the list (perhaps deciding to omit one item and add others later). As a student in a writing course, you will also follow the natural steps of a writing process.

One of the most difficult tasks for student writers is generating ideas to include in their writing. And yet, as you know from experience, when friends get together to talk, there is no shortage of things to say. In fact, have you ever experienced the frustration of waiting to use a phone while someone else in the house talks endlessly?

So why does the mind go blank when it comes time to write? One reason for this mental freezing is the anxiety associated with writing. When anxiety sets in, it can shut down our creative thinking process.

To get their creative juices flowing, therefore, writers start with the first phase of the writing process: prewriting. This is an important step during which you explore a topic and generate ideas. When you are generating ideas, it is important to keep the process simple and relaxed.

A few techniques are especially helpful in keeping the prewriting step simple and relaxed. The first two are *brainstorming* and *freewriting.* It doesn't matter which you do first. As a matter of fact, you may find that one technique works better for you than the other or that doing a specific one first and then going to the other suits your writing style best.

Brainstorming

Brainstorming is a powerful technique, not only for generating ideas for writing, but also for problem solving or for any situation in which you want to explore options creatively. The purpose of brainstorming is to generate as many ideas as possible as quickly as possible, using the creative part of your brain. It should be a stress-free, exploratory activity. Brainstorming is simple to do. First, set aside a specified amount of time, perhaps 5 minutes. (Some people find it useful to use a timer.) During that time, fire off as many ideas as you can, writing each one down without regard for whether you think it is a good idea or not. Typically, you do not write these ideas in complete sentences but simply in words and phrases. They can be written anywhere—on a sheet of paper or typed in a word processor.

Once all of your ideas are on paper and time is up, you can evaluate your ideas. If you are still generating ideas when your time is up, by all means continue until you can think of no more ideas. The purpose of the set amount of time is so that you won't give up too easily. People often find that their best ideas come after a period of struggle, when all of their superficial thoughts have been written down and they are delving deep into their minds to come up with the really worthwhile ideas. That is why you don't want to give up until you have stared at that paper or computer screen for a period of time, letting ideas slowly connect and surface.

The reason you shouldn't judge your ideas is that judging shuts down the creative side of your mind, creates anxiety, and inhibits the idea-generating process.

It can also be helpful to brainstorm in groups. Many corporations use a brainstorming session when they need to generate ideas to solve a problem. It works like this: The group is given a set amount of time, perhaps 15–60 minutes or even longer, depending upon the complexity of the problem. One person is assigned to record the ideas. Then members contribute *any ideas that come to mind,* without regard to whether they are "good" or "bad." In fact, at no time in the brainstorming process are ideas judged. Any and every idea is written down.

Experiment with Brainstorming

1. Your instructor will give you a topic on which to brainstorm and a specified amount of time to complete the activity. During that time, write down as many ideas on the given subject as you can think of. Do not judge or eliminate any ideas. Write down every idea that comes to mind.

2. When the time is up, look over your ideas. Do not eliminate any ideas at this time.

3. Now break into small groups. Again, your instructor will give you a specified amount of time to complete the activity. Before you begin brainstorming as a group, select someone to record all of the ideas. Now brainstorm by saying your ideas aloud as you think of them. Remember, do not judge anyone's idea as bad, or even good. Even positive judgments can block creativity. Write down everything.

4. When that process is finished, discuss as a class whether you found group brainstorming or individual brainstorming more helpful. What did you notice about the group brainstorming?

5. Your instructor will select one group to write all of the ideas on the board. After the first group notes all of its ideas, the other groups can add anything to their lists that is not already written on the board. Continue until you have a master list.

6. Once again, this time as an entire class, brainstorm for a few more minutes on the same topic. Sometimes seeing one idea leads you to think of other ideas. As a class, were you able to come up with even more ideas?

About 10–15 minutes is sufficient for this activity. Students need time to make a master list of what they came up with individually and more time to generate new ideas. You may find it better not to say how much time you are giving, and then monitor students' progress and determine the time accordingly.

Provide a rather broad topic with which to begin.

Some topics are:
- writing
- first year of college
- things you might do in this course
- computers
- e-mail

7. It is finally time to let the left part of your brain, the "editor," take over—at least temporarily. The part of your brain that wants to judge and evaluate or express thoughts in a linear, organized fashion is valuable for this activity. You just didn't want it interfering with the previous creative, idea-generating activity. How does the editor take charge? It takes over automatically when you begin evaluating and organizing. Individually (not in groups), write down the ideas you would want to include if you were writing a paragraph on this topic.

Freewriting

Another effective prewriting technique is *freewriting.* It is also a relaxing exploratory method for tapping into your creativity. As its name implies, this is very free writing—free of rules and *shoulds.* Just let whatever comes to mind flow onto the page. And, as in brainstorming, sometimes the best ideas come after a minute or two of blankness, while deeper connections and explorations are taking place in your head. Freewriting is the technique you use when you are completing the **Log On** section of each chapter, except that you are freewriting for a different purpose there. In **Log On** you are writing to tap into deeper sources of knowledge in order to make connections in your brain from that knowledge to the new material you will be learning. Freewriting is a prewriting technique that taps into your creativity to generate connections and ideas for writing.

In brainstorming, you generated ideas in the form of words or phrases. In freewriting, you typically write in sentences, though without regard for standard sentence construction or spelling conventions. As in brainstorming, you simply write anything that comes to mind when you freewrite. A few aspects of freewriting are challenging, but they are the reason you will be able to tap into deeper levels of thinking. First, you must *keep writing* for the entire specified amount of time. In fact, you should not even lift your pen off the paper. Keep your pen moving at all times. You may have to write something like "I don't know what else to say," but keep writing.

The second feature of freewriting is the same as for brainstorming: Do not judge what you have written. Simply write anything and everything that comes to mind without regard for "correctness" of any type.

Explore Freewriting

1. Take out a composition notebook or some paper (or sit in front of a blank screen at a computer). Put yourself in a state of relaxed alertness.

2. The instructor will give you a topic. When the instructor says to begin, write without pausing or lifting the pen from the paper (or your hands from the keyboard) until the instructor says to stop. Don't think too much about what you are writing.

3. When the time is up, read what you wrote. On the lines below, describe what surprises you about this process and your writing.

_____

_____

_____

Since this freewriting activity is probably done at the end of the period, you have flexibility in the amount of time you allow for it. However, too much time can frustrate students, especially at the beginning of the term. You might find 5 minutes appropriate for your class. Suggested topics:

1. Ideas from the brainstorming session
2. Concerns about this course
3. Strengths students are bringing to the course

_____

_____

_____

_____

_____

 Go To ▶

1. Go to the online course pack for Northwestern University's Engineering Design and Communication course, to see how engineers use brainstorming to find and organize ideas: **<http://www.edc.northwestern.edu/cp/2002/4.1_brainstorming.html>**.

2. The _Writing Now_ web site, for links to other web sites that discuss or demonstrate a writing process: **<developmentalenglish.college.hmco.com/students>**.

Help Screen

Finding a Web Site

URLs are web addresses. In this book, whenever you see something in angle brackets, < >, you are looking at a URL.

The Web—or the World Wide Web—is a part of the Internet. The Web allows you to see pictures and other graphics, video clips, and audio files. By using a mouse you can click on links to other sites.

To access the Web, you need to open a Web browser, such as Internet Explorer or Netscape, on a computer that has an Internet connection. You open the browser just as you would open any other computer program.

Once the browser is open, you are ready to get information from the Web. To access one of the sites mentioned in this book, or any other URL you want to find, click in the white bar, titled "Address" or "Netsite," for instance, that runs across the top of the screen. Key in the URL. Copy everything between the angle brackets, < >, exactly as you see it. Then hit the Enter key, and you are there!

When you do key in a URL and hit the Enter key, remember that you are sending a command to a computer. You must be exact when typing in a URL—one letter or even one dot off, and the browser won't take you where you want to go.

Once you arrive at the desired web site, move the cursor (mouse pointer) over the page. When the pointer turns into a hand with the index finger pointing upward, you are on a link to another web page; to get to the other web pages, just click your mouse on the link. Most links show up in blue and are underlined, but a link can be hidden under anything—plain text, a graphic image, even a section of a photograph.

OPTIONS ▶ Customize

1. List what you already know about the writing process.

2. In small groups, share what you know about the writing process and generate a master list to put on the board or on an overhead projector.

3. Circle all of the items that show up on more than one group's list. Underline the items that show up on one list only. Discuss and make another master list, including the items on which everyone agrees.

Journaling

Journaling is similar to freewriting but is done for other purposes—personal purposes—such as to understand yourself better, to relieve stress, or to record memories. Some studies have even found that journaling can improve health. While freewriting is done to generate ideas, many writers keep journals on an ongoing basis to generate and record ideas as well as for sheer enjoyment. Journaling helps writers improve their writing because through journaling they practice expressing themselves frequently. An important reason that you may want to start journaling now is that it will not only help you relieve some of the stress of school but also help you improve your writing in the classroom. The more you do of anything, even if it is for personal, enjoyable reasons, the better at it you will become.

Read the following articles about journaling and decide if you think keeping a journal would serve you well. While you read the following articles, consider how each author sees the "rules" for journaling differently. Prepare to discuss which rules you would follow and which you would reject if you were to start a journal. Those of you who are experienced journal writers can discuss which of the rules you follow and whether you would consider adding any of the rules or enhancements the authors suggest.

How-To Sources Aid Aspiring *Journal*-ists

Janis Fontaine

1 "Keeping a journal will absolutely change your life in ways you never imagined," Oprah proclaims on her Web site, Oprah.com.

2 Whether you call it a diary, a journal or the silly-sounding jouniary, in the search to discover your "authentic self," the best place to look may be between the pages of a 99-cent notebook.

3 Journaling—yes, it's become a verb—is hotter than ever, mainly because of Oprah Winfrey's pitch for women to nurture their selves and simplify their lives.

4 In 1995, Sarah Ban Breathnach (pronounced "Bon Brannock") wrote a little inspirational book called *Simple Abundance: A Daybook of Comfort*

and Joy. It revisited the idea of building a positive outlook by counting your blessings.

5 When Oprah called the book "life-changing" and named it among her favorite books in 1996, *Simple Abundance* blessed Ban Breathnach by becoming a bestseller, with more than 4 million copies sold in the United States alone. A year later she published *The Simple Abundance Journal of Gratitude* and dedicated it to Oprah. In April, Ban Breathnach released *The Simple Abundance Companion.*

6 By recording five things each day that you feel grateful for, Ban Breathnach said, the gratitude journal will help you discover and re-member what's truly important in your life.

7 Don't feel like feeling grateful today? Try a fitness journal. Or a pri-vate journal on Oprah.com. Or a journal of your family history. Frank McCourt's family journal became a bestseller: *Angela's Ashes.*

8 Still need help delving into your deepest feelings?

9 There are lots of books, Web sites like www.thriveonline.com, and even a magazine to guide you on your journey of self-discovery. *Per-sonal Journaling, Writing about Your Life,* a bimonthly magazine, hit shelves in 1999. The magazine ($4.95 a copy) boasts a circulation of 70,000 scribbling subscribers.

10 And consider this: Two castaways on CBS's *Survivor* show chose journals as their one luxury item. Both Jenna and Ramona preferred paper to, well, just about everything.

Ten Rules for Successful Journal Writing

Dennis J. Cleary

1. Date each entry and note the time and place.

2. Find the right type of pen tip and style for your journal work.

3. Buy a quality journal book that meets your specific standards for use.

4. Always write your journal in a special atmosphere or place for best results.

5. Use visual items to decorate your journal and bring it new ideas.

6. Use the journal as a storehouse for items about your life.

7. Do not worry about length; rather, just write.

8. Guard your journal from loss and incursions by others.

9. Discipline yourself to make the Joys of Journaling a daily routine.

10. Capture the beauty and conflict of your life day by day and year by year.

Source: "Ten Rules for Successful Journal Writing" from *Joys of Journaling* by Dennis J. Cleary. Copyright © 2000 by Dennis J. Cleary. All Rights Reserved. Reprinted by permission of the author.

Ten Joys of Journaling

Dennis J. Cleary

1. Use the journal as a way to alleviate or dispel depression and anxiety.
2. Write when you are alone to really focus on your life.
3. Take your journal writing to a favorite coffee shop.
4. Review your journal entries weekly and monthly.
5. If you are feeling physical or emotional pain, write about it.
6. Add favorite jokes, visuals, photos, and quotes to add joy to your life.
7. Keep ideas, projects, and brainstorms noted and documented in your journal.
8. Seek out only the best in paper and writing utensils for your journal entries.
9. Create a small chapbook of journal entries for making gifts to your friends.
10. Keep up the habit of journal writing on a daily and weekly basis.

Source: "Ten Joys of Journaling" from *Joys of Journaling* by Dennis J. Cleary. Copyright © 2000 by Dennis J. Cleary. All Rights Reserved. Reprinted by permission of the author.

Jessica on Journaling

Fareeda Philip
senior
Simley High School
Inver Grove Heights

Jessica Wilber is 15. Like most girls her age, she likes hanging out with her friends and going to movies. But unlike most 15-year-olds, Jessica is the author of a book, *Totally Private and Personal: Journaling Ideas for Girls and Young Women.* The Racine, Wis., teen says it's the kind of book she wishes had been available when she began her own journal writing. "My goal in writing this book is to communicate to other girls how much journaling helped me and how much it could be able to help them too."

The book . . . focuses on everything from what you can do to decorate a journal to the rules of journaling. Jessica says, "I have two rules when it comes to journaling. My first rule is to date every entry, and my second rule is to not make any more rules." The book also focuses on stronger issues such as sexual harassment, puberty and sexually transmitted diseases. It targets girls, from 11 to 16, and emphasizes that they can feel good about themselves in a world that constantly gives them reason not to.

"A journal is there to help teens express their feelings (self-therapy). Writing in my journal helped me because there's not a lot of people that you can talk to, but I can talk to my journal and put things in it and it won't tell or make fun of me."

Source: Fareeda Philip, "Jessica on Journaling/Classroom Assignment Becomes Published Book," Minneapolis *Star Tribune*, May 22, 1997, p. 2E. Reprinted by permission of the author.

Journaling for Speaking to Your Heart

Pennie Boyett

1 These days, bookstores have shelves filled with elegant journals.

2 Covers are fabric or leather, artsy or plain. Pages may have lines to write on, photos and artwork for inspiration and quotations from famous people to set the tone, or they may be blank to allow you to sketch or paint.

3 My first journal had a pink vinyl cover embossed with the words, "Dear Diary," and a picture of a teenager with a ponytail.

4 It locked with a tiny key.

5 My younger brother, had he been old enough to read, could probably have gotten past that lock in a matter of seconds.

6 But he was only 4, and no one else paid attention. So I could write and write like no one would ever read it.

7 Filling up the pages.

8 Thoughts on paper.

9 After I filled the pink diary, a page a day, with all the joys and woes of surviving fifth and sixth grade, I started another one, a plainer book, again filling a page a day.

10 In adolescence, one page a day wasn't near enough for all the euphoria and the despair that fueled my life. I advanced to filling spiral notebooks with teenage angst and bad poetry.

11 I have recorded thoughts, ideas, dreams, story ideas, rough drafts, political rants, to do lists, menus, party plans, remodeling schemes, travel experiences, cute stories about our children, complaints about same, births of kittens and puppies, deaths of friends and relatives, good moods and bad days in spiral notebooks—nothing so formal as a journal—intermittently ever since.

12 Some people keep their journals on computer, but I would not consider doing this.

13 Most of us spend far too much time in front of a computer as it is, plus I find that my writing style is different when I make words on a keyboard to appear (and disappear) on a screen.

14 The intimate contact between paper and pen leads to more personal thoughts perhaps, or maybe it's because the pace is slower so a writer can wait for ideas to come.

15 Journaling, after all, tends to be introspective, even when the subjects written about are mundane.

16 Notebooks going back to the early 1980s are stacked on a closet shelf upstairs. I rarely look at them although I'm frequently surprised by all I discover when I do.

17 It is not reading, but the act of writing that makes them valuable.

18 Plain will do when words beckon.

19 It is sitting in a quiet place actually writing . . . conversing on paper when the listener never criticizes, working out plans and dreams only half-formed in thought, keeping a favorite moment alive . . . that makes journaling worthwhile.

20 Friends have given me pretty books with blank pages for gifts, but I tend to stay with my college-rule spiral notebooks. They are less intimidating.

Source: Pennie Boyett, "Journaling for Speaking to Your Heart." *Arlington Morning News,* July 16, 2000, p. 1B. Reprinted by permission of the *Arlington Morning News.*

21

If you've always wanted to start a journal, I think this is the way to go. It's the perfect time to buy them, too, as colorful assortments of notebooks and fat ballpoint pens lure shoppers to back-to-school sales.

22

When you're writing in a 79-cent spiral, you can just scribble to your heart's content. You don't mind crossing out words, even tearing out a page, if things aren't going the way you like.

23

You can write and write, like no one will ever read it.

24

It's almost as good as that pink vinyl diary. All it needs is a lock with a tiny key.

Analyze the Reading

If groups are responding to one reading only, then discuss whether the reading convinced them to keep a journal, and why or why not.

1. Which reading was most convincing about the advantages of keeping a journal? In your opinion, why was that reading convincing?

_____

_____

_____

2. Based on what you just read (or discussed in class), if you were going to keep a journal, which style would you prefer, and why? What rules for maintaining a journal in that style were given in the reading?

_____

_____

_____

3. What would your journal cover look like? What type of information would it contain? Did any of the readings describe the type of journal you write (or would write)?

_____

_____

_____

_____

4. In your opinion, what rules should journal writing follow?

_____

_____

_____

5. In your opinion, what rules should journal writing *not* follow?

_____

_____

_____

Clustering (or Mapping)

The words *clustering* and *mapping* or *mind mapping* are often used interchangeably. Although mapping is more complex than clustering, in many ways the two techniques are similar. Both involve getting ideas down on paper in a prewriting session, but in a slightly more organized manner than you may have done in your brainstorming session earlier. Mapping is more organized and linear than clustering, and you will learn more about mapping in Chapter 2.

When you brainstorm, you get the ideas down in any order, usually in the form of a list. A *cluster* is more organized. *Clustering* is based on the concept that ideas relate to each other in some fashion. In other words, certain ideas tend to cluster together in a brainstorming session. As you think of the ideas, you group them in clusters, usually in the form of offshoots from a central circle containing the main idea. For example, if you were brainstorming earlier in this chapter about ways to succeed in school, you probably wrote your ideas in a list. However, within that list, certain ideas could cluster together. Some of your ideas may have related to what you do in the classroom and others may have related to what you do for homework. Some ideas may have related to mental attitudes. These ideas could form three clusters off a central circle containing the main idea, "ways to succeed in school." You can give each cluster a main idea, such as "school," "home," or "attitudes."

Often you don't see these relationships until after you have brainstormed for a while and have several ideas on paper. Then you begin to see relationships between the ideas. Therefore, after brainstorming, you will want to organize the ideas in your list into a *clustering diagram* or *mind map*. Some writers cluster as their first step because they recognize that an idea belongs in a new category as they think of it and they cluster as they write down their ideas. You can experiment and find out whether brainstorming or clustering works better as a first step for you.

After you have clustered a few categories on your topic, you will find that you can focus on one category at a time and come up with even more ideas. Sometimes you will find that a cluster will generate many more ideas and eventually you can break it into two or more offshoot clusters. You can continue clustering until you run out of ideas in every offshoot. Then you can decide which clusters to include in your writing. Clustering is an excellent tool for generating ideas. On page 14 you see a cluster diagram of the steps in the writing process. The following activity will help you analyze this cluster so that you will know how to create a more detailed cluster diagram yourself.

Sample Cluster

The following assignment will help you become familiar with using clusters when writing.

1. On page 14 there is a clustering map of the writing process. Turn to that page and analyze the cluster carefully. Be sure to read every item.

2. Using your green highlighter, highlight the topic of the cluster, the central circle in the cluster. In the remainder of this book, you will highlight in green the *thesis*, or the overall main idea, of each reading selection.

3. Using your blue highlighter, highlight the circles that are attached directly to the main circle. These are the *main supporting ideas* (they support

This is a good place to end the homework assignment.

00:45

You may want to begin class with a discussion of the journaling articles on pages 8–12. You could allow approximately half of the class period for that discussion and half to discuss the analysis of the clustering diagram. Clustering is a key concept, so sufficient time must be allowed for its discussion. If you are short on time, the key learning from the journaling assignment is the perception that the authors handled the same topic very differently. You may want to either encourage or assign students to begin journaling. Of course, we believe it is critical that journaling, if assigned, should not be read by the teacher. If you want to grade the journal assignment, one alternative is to have students turn the book upside down so that they can see that you are not actually reading their entries. You can flip through it and note the *quantity* of writing. The *quality* of journal writing should not be evaluated, and actually should not be read by an instructor in our opinion.

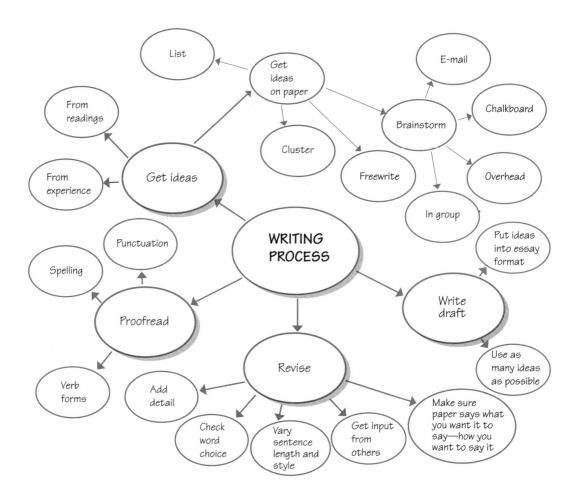

the thesis). In the readings that you analyze in the remainder of this book, you will highlight main supporting ideas in blue. Notice how the main supporting ideas—in this case, the steps in the writing process—form one layer or a group of central clusters.

4. Now turn to the next level. This is the level of *supporting details*. As you will learn later, supporting details can be examples (we will use yellow for these) or facts (pink). In this case, we will use both yellow and pink interchangeably to represent supporting details. First, look at the circle *Proofread*. It should be colored blue because it is a main supporting idea. Note that three lines come off the circle *Proofread*, leading to three other circles: *Punctuation, Spelling, Verb forms*. The three circles represent ideas that relate to the blue idea—three aspects of the idea. These are support-ing details for the main idea of *Proofread*. Highlight the three circles in yellow.

5. Examine another major cluster—*Write draft*. The *Write draft* circle should be blue because it extends from the central circle, *Writing process*. Notice that two ideas are related to *Write draft*: *Put ideas into essay format* and *Use as many ideas as possible*. Highlight these two circles in yellow. They are supporting details. They support the blue main idea *Write draft*, which in turn supports the topic or green central idea *Writing process*.

6. How many supporting details are given for *Revise*? _____ Color these supporting details pink. We are using pink so that the supporting details for *Revise* will not be confused with the yellow groups next to them. Remember, both pink and yellow represent supporting details.

7. What do you notice that is different about the cluster *Get ideas*?

_____

_____

_____

Notice that three lines come off the *Get ideas* cluster—three aspects or supporting ideas: *Get ideas on paper, From readings, From experience.* Color these three attached circles pink. They support the concept of *Get ideas.* However, note that one of the supporting details, *Get ideas on paper,* has four lines coming off it: *List, Brainstorm, Freewrite, Cluster.* These are four details that support the supporting idea. Color these supporting details yellow. There is yet another difference in this cluster. *Brainstorm,* a supporting idea for *Get ideas on paper,* has four lines or supporting ideas coming off it: *E-mail, Chalkboard, Overhead, In group* (Confused yet? That's why the colors help!). Color these circles pink.

8. Now examine the map again. Do you see how ideas cluster? We will look at this organizational pattern in more detail in Chapter 2.

This may be a good place to begin the second homework assignment. Assign students to read pp. 16–20, and answer questions 1–5.

The reason that clustering is effective is that it works in a manner similar to the way your brain works. Your brain doesn't categorize items. In other words, it doesn't think of all the ideas in one category and then all the ideas in the next (that is, in outline form). Rather, ideas pour out and fall all over the place. When you were brainstorming about the writing process, you may have generated one idea about revision and then one about brainstorming and then one about revision again, and then one about *proofreading.* Clustering allows you to add ideas to the appropriate location when you think of them. In other words, you are roughly organizing your thoughts as you go. The form of an outline or list makes it harder to add ideas that relate to each other—in the order in which they relate.

However, bear in mind that to keep your creativity flowing, do not spend too much time on linear, left-brain activities such as organizing, judging, deciding relevance, and the like. You can always draw the connections after brainstorming. That is one of the advantages of clustering. The main point of clustering is to get the ideas down, on paper or on screen. If you *see* how ideas relate, then put them where they belong on the cluster diagram. If you aren't sure, just get the ideas down and look at them later.

You can also use clustering as a tool for understanding what you read and for taking study notes. Clustering is a more effective study tool than taking linear notes because it is more visual. Visualizing the groups makes it easier to remember the supporting details. Furthermore, it helps you see and understand relationships.

If you really want to learn something well and make a map that will help you to do so, make a map that is entirely pictures. First, make a cluster map of the concepts. Then turn every concept into a picture that represents the concept. This is the step that creates real learning. In order to create a visual image of an idea or process, you have to understand it and think about it. Then you have to figure out how to draw it. By the time you draw it, you will find the visual image is very easy to remember.

The following article contains some helpful points about how to be successful in college. In addition to reading for those points, read with the intention of clustering the information when you are finished reading. That means you will look for main ideas and supporting details, noticing the relationship between them.

How to Make It in College, Now That You're Here

Brian O'Keeney

1   Today is your first day on campus. You were a high school senior three months ago. Or maybe you've been at home with your children for the last ten years. Or maybe you work full time and you're coming to school to start the process that leads to a better job. Whatever your background is, you're probably not too concerned today with staying in college. After all, you just got over the hurdle (and the paperwork) of applying to this place and organizing your life so that you could attend. And today, you're confused and tired. Everything is a hassle, from finding the classrooms to standing in line at the bookstore. But read my advice anyway. And if you don't read it today, clip and save this article. You might want to look at it a little further down the road.

2   By the way, if this isn't your very first day, don't skip this article. Maybe you haven't been doing as well in your studies as you'd hoped. Or perhaps you've had problems juggling your work schedule, your class schedule, and your social life. If so, read on. You're about to get the inside story on making it in college. On the basis of my own experience as a final-year student, and on dozens of interviews with successful students, I've worked out a no-fail system for coping with college. These are the inside tips every student needs to do well in school. I've put myself in your place, and I'm going to answer the questions that will cross (or have already crossed) your mind during your stay here.

What's the Secret of Getting Good Grades?

3   It all comes down to getting those grades, doesn't it? After all, you came here for some reason, and you're going to need passing grades to get the credits or degree you want. Many of us never did much studying in high school; most of the learning we did took place in the classroom. College, however, is a lot different. You're really on your own when it comes to passing courses. In fact, sometimes you'll feel as if nobody cares if you make it or not. Therefore, you've got to figure out a study system that gets results. Sooner or later, you'll be alone with those books. After that, you'll be sitting in a classroom with an exam sheet on

Source: Brian O'Keeney, "How to Make It in College, Now That You're Here" from J. Langhan's *College Writing Skills with Readings*, 4/e. New York: McGraw-Hill, 1997, pp. 632–643. Reprinted by permission of Townsend Press.

your desk. Whether you stare at that exam with a queasy stomach or whip through it fairly confidently depends on your study techniques. Most of the successful students I talked to agreed that the following eight study tips deliver solid results.

1. ***Set Up a Study Place.*** Those students you see "studying" in the cafeteria or game room aren't learning much. You just can't learn when you're distracted by people and noise. Even the library can be a bad place to study if you constantly find yourself watching the clouds outside or the students walking through the stacks. It takes guts to sit, alone, in a quiet place in order to study. But you have to do it. Find a room at home or a spot in the library that's relatively quiet—and boring. When you sit there, you won't have much to do except study.

2. ***Get into a Study Frame of Mind.*** When you sit down, do it with the attitude that you're going to get this studying done. You're not going to doodle in your notebook or make a list for the supermarket. Decide that you're going to study and learn *now,* so that you can move on to more interesting things as soon as possible.

3. ***Give Yourself Rewards.*** If you sweat out a block of study time, and do a good job on it, treat yourself. You deserve it. You can "psych" yourself up for studying by promising to reward yourself afterward. A present for yourself can be anything from a favorite TV show to a relaxing bath to a dish of double chocolate ice cream.

4. ***Skim the Textbook First.*** Lots of students sit down with an assignment like "read chapter five, pages 125–150" and do just that. They turn to page 125 and start to read. After a while, they find that they have no idea what they just read. For the last ten minutes, they've been thinking about their five-year-old or what they're going to eat for dinner. Eventually, they plod through all the pages but don't remember much afterward.

   In order to prevent this problem, skim the textbook chapter first. This means: look at the title, the subtitles, the headings, the pictures, the first and last paragraphs. Try to find out what the person who wrote the book had in mind when he or she organized the chapter. What was important enough to set off as a title or in bold type? After skimming, you should be able to explain to yourself what the main points of the chapter are. Unless you're the kind of person who would step into an empty elevator shaft without looking first, you'll soon discover the value of skimming.

5. ***Take Notes on What You're Studying.*** This sounds like a hassle, but it works. Go back over the material after you've read it, and jot down key words and phrases in the margins. When you review the chapter for a test, you'll have handy little things like "definition of rationalization" or "example of assimilation" in the margins. If the material is especially tough, organize a separate sheet of notes. Write down definitions, examples, lists, and main ideas. The idea is to have a single sheet that boils the entire chapter down to a digestible lump.

6. ***Review After You've Read and Taken Notes.*** Some people swear that talking to yourself works. Tell yourself about the most important points in the chapter. Once you've said them out loud, they seem to stick better in your mind. If you can't talk to yourself about the material after reading it, that's a sure sign you don't really know it.

7. ***Give Up.*** This may sound contradictory, but give up when you've had enough. You should try to make it through at least an hour, though. Ten minutes here and there are useless. When your head starts to pound and your eyes develop spidery red lines, quit. You won't do much learning when you're exhausted.

8. ***Take a College Skills Course If You Need It.*** Don't hesitate or feel embarrassed about enrolling in a study skills course. Many students say they wouldn't have made it without one.

How Can I Keep Up with All My Responsibilities Without Going Crazy?

You've got a class schedule. You're supposed to study. You've got a family. You've got a husband, wife, boyfriend, girlfriend, child. You've got a job. How are you possibly going to cover all the bases in your life and maintain your sanity? This is one of the toughest problems students face. Even if they start the semester with the best of intentions, they eventually find themselves tearing their hair out trying to do everything they're supposed to do. Believe it or not, though, it is possible to meet all your responsibilities. And you don't have to turn into a hermit or give up your loved ones to do it.

The secret here is to organize your time. But don't just sit around half the semester planning to get everything together soon. Before you know it, you'll be confronted with midterms, papers, family, and work all at once. Don't let yourself reach that breaking point. Instead, try these three tactics.

1. ***Monthly Calendar.*** Get one of those calendars with big blocks around the dates. Give yourself an overview of the whole term by marking down the due dates for papers and projects. Circle test and exam days. This way those days don't sneak up on you unexpectedly.

2. ***Study Schedule.*** Sit down during the first few days of this semester and make up a sheet listing the days and hours of the week. Fill in your work and class hours first. Then try to block out some study hours. It's better to study a little every day than to create a huge once-or-twice-a-week marathon session. Schedule study hours for your hardest classes for the times when you feel most energetic. For example, I battled my tax law textbook in the mornings; when I looked at it after 7:00 P.M., I might as well have been reading Chinese. The usual proportion, by the way, is one hour of study time for every class hour.

    In case you're one of those people who get carried away, remember to leave blocks of free time, too. You won't be any good to yourself or anyone else if you don't relax and pack in the studying once in a while.

3. ***"To-Do" List.*** This is the secret that single-handedly got me through college. Once a week (or every day if you want to), write a list of what you have to do. Write down everything from "write English paper" to "buy cold cuts for lunches." The best thing about a "to-do" list is that it seems to tame all those stray "I have to" thoughts that nag at your mind. Just making the list seems to make the tasks "doable." After you finish something on the list, cross it off. Don't be compulsive about finishing everything; you're not Superman or Wonder Woman. Get the important things done first. The secondary things you don't finish can simply be moved to your next "to-do" list.

What Can I Do If Personal Problems Get in the Way of My Studies?

6   One student, Roger, told me this story:

> Everything was going OK for me until the middle of the spring semester. I went through a terrible time when I broke up with my girlfriend and started seeing her best friend. I was trying to deal with my ex-girlfriend's hurt and anger, my new girlfriend's guilt, and my own worries and anxieties at the same time. In addition to this, my mother was sick and on a medication that made her really irritable. I hated to go home because the atmosphere was so uncomfortable. Soon, I started missing classes because I couldn't deal with the academic pressures as well as my own personal problems. It seemed easier to hang around my girl-friend's apartment than to face all my problems at home and at school.

7   Another student, Marian, told me:

> I'd been married for eight years and the relationship wasn't going too well. I saw the handwriting on the wall, and I decided to prepare for the future. I enrolled in college, because I knew I'd need a decent job to support myself. Well, my husband had a fit because I was going to school. We were arguing a lot anyway, and he made it almost impossible for me to study at home. I think he was angry and almost jealous because I was drawing away from him. It got so bad that I thought about quitting college for a while. I wasn't getting any support at home and it was just too hard to go on.

8   Personal troubles like these are overwhelming when you're going through them. School seems like the least important thing in your life. The two students above are perfect examples of this. But if you think about it, quitting or failing school would be the worst thing for these two students. Roger's problems, at least with his girlfriends, would simmer down eventually, and then he'd regret having left school. Marian had to finish college if she wanted to be able to live independently. Sometimes you've just got to hang tough.

9   But what do you do while you're trying to live through a lousy time? First of all, do something difficult. Ask yourself, honestly, if you're exaggerating small problems as an excuse to avoid classes and studying. It takes strength to admit this, but there's no sense in kidding yourself. If your problems are serious, and real, try to make some human contacts at school. Lots of students hide inside a miserable shell made of their own troubles and feel isolated and lonely. Believe me, there are plenty of students with problems. Not everyone is getting A's and having a fabulous social and home life at the same time. As you go through the term, you'll pick up some vibrations about the students in your classes. Perhaps someone strikes you as a compatible person. Why not speak to that person after class? Share a cup of coffee in the cafeteria or walk to the parking lot together. You're not looking for a best friend or the love of your life. You just want to build a little network of support for yourself. Sharing your difficulties, questions, and complaints with a friendly person on campus can make a world of difference in how you feel.

10   Finally, if your problems are overwhelming, get some professional help. Why do you think colleges spend countless dollars on counseling departments and campus psychiatric services? More than ever, students all over the country are taking advantage of the help offered by support groups and therapy sessions. There's no shame attached to asking for help, either; in fact, almost 40 percent of college students (according to one survey) will use counseling services during their time in school. Just walk into a student center or counseling office and ask for an appointment. You wouldn't think twice about asking a dentist to help you get rid of your toothache. Counselors are paid—and want—to help you with your problems.

Why Do Some People Make It and Some Drop Out?

11 Anyone who spends at least one semester in college notices that some students give up on their classes. The person who sits behind you in accounting, for example, begins to miss a lot of class meetings and eventually vanishes. Or another student comes to class without the assignment, doodles in a notebook during the lecture, and leaves during the break. What's the difference between students like this and the ones who succeed in school? My survey may be nonscientific, but everyone I asked said the same thing: attitude. A positive attitude is the key to everything else—good study habits, smart time scheduling, and coping with personal difficulties.

12 What does "a positive attitude" mean? Well, for one thing, it means avoiding the zombie syndrome. It means not only showing up for your classes, but also doing something while you're there. Really listen. Take notes. Ask a question if you want to. Don't just walk into a class, put your mind in neutral, and drift away to never-never land.

13 Having a positive attitude goes deeper than this, though. It means being mature about college as an institution. Too many students approach college classes like six-year-olds who expect first grade to be as much fun as *Sesame Street.* First grade, as we all know, isn't as much fun as *Sesame Street.* And college classes can sometimes be downright dull and boring. If you let a boring class discourage you so much that you want to leave school, you'll lose in the long run. Look at your priorities. You want a degree, or a certificate, or a career. If you have to, you can make it through a less-than-interesting class in order to achieve what you want. Get whatever you can out of every class. But if you simply can't stand a certain class, be determined to fulfill its requirements and be done with it once and for all.

14 After the initial high of starting school, you have to settle in for the long haul. If you follow the advice here, you'll be prepared to face the academic crunch. You'll also live through the semester without giving up your family, your job, or *Monday Night Football*. Finally, going to college can be an exciting time. You do learn. And when you learn things, the world becomes a more interesting place.

Analyze the Reading

1. Refer to the section "What's the Secret of Getting Good Grades?" (pp. 16–17). Highlight in green the part of the title that contains the thesis or the overall central idea of the section.

2. In the same section "What's the Secret of Getting Good Grades?" highlight the main supporting ideas in blue. *Help:* Look closely at the numbered list.

3. Now highlight in yellow the key details that support the main supporting (blue) ideas. For your purposes here, you do not need to highlight entire examples, as you will usually do in the future for other reading selections.

Although it's enjoyable, this activity is not the activities in the "Analyze the Reading" portion of the text that are "just for fun." Color coding helps students to see relationships. Because color is a powerful trigger in the brain, it can help students remember associations more easily. Students will continue working with these color-coding concepts throughout the book.

Activities 1–6 are effective, not only for bringing home the concept of clustering, but also for enabling students to see the impact of visual representation on their long-range learning. When you ask students to recall this activity in a week or two, they will be amazed at how much they remember. If approached with a playful attitude, this is an exciting, brain-friendly way to begin the semester with very good results. To set the right tone, it is helpful to discuss this homework assignment before assigning it. Remember, the more physical activity, visualization, color, and emotion you can build into an activity, the better the learning will be.

00:45

If possible, stop the homework with #5. Ask students to bring the finished product to class. Then, if at all possible, bring to class large sheets of paper, from the copy machine room or elsewhere. (If you have to, use standard-sized plain paper.) Also bring a large set or sets of colored pencils or marking pens, or assign students to bring in whatever they can. Then have students do #6 in class. If students seem insecure (they will all moan that they can't draw), you could let them do this in small groups. We have always found this activity to be highly successful, no matter what age students are. Remember, students cannot write any words on the entire page! Allow time at the end of number 6 for volunteers to hold up their drawings and explain to everyone "The Secret of Getting Good Grades" by looking only at the drawings and not at any notes. This activity demonstrates that students can remember everything they've learned (without studying!) by using pictures to jog their memories.

4. Cluster the main supporting ideas on a sheet of plain white paper.

5. Repeat steps 1–4 with the section entitled "How Can I Keep Up with All My Responsibilities Without Going Crazy?" *Help:* The overall central idea is in the second paragraph.

6. Now for the fun part. Best of all, although this activity should be stress-free and enjoyable, it is where the real learning takes place. On a sheet of paper re-create the clustering for "How Can I Keep Up with All My Responsibilities Without Going Crazy?" but this time *you cannot use words.* Yes, you read that right. Each main idea (blue) must be represented in a drawing. Okay, so you can't draw. That's great—you will learn even more. All that thinking you will put into representing the concept in a simple image will let you remember that concept for a long, long time. Feel free to use stick figures and primitive drawings. It is the process of figuring out *how* that creates the learning, not the drawing itself. In fact, even if no one in the class but you can figure out what your symbol is or even why you chose it, *you* will remember it very well. Use as many colors as you can. Just enjoy your drawing without thinking judgmentally about it.

7. Create a cluster map of "What's the Secret of Getting Good Grades?" without using any words, not even for the central idea in the center circle. Use a large sheet of paper or posterboard and use as many colors as you like. Make it fun. As long as you don't break the only rule—*no words!*—you cannot do this assignment incorrectly.

 Go To ▶

1. Go to the *Writing Now* web site and read the articles on how to keep a family journal on the Web.

2. Go to the sites listed below for additional information about clustering. You may find a style of clustering you like better than the style presented in the text, or you may find out how to use this technique more effectively.

   ▶ Help on clustering is available from the University of Richmond at **<http://writing.richmond.edu:16080/writing/wweb/cluster.html>**.

   ▶ Another source for generating cluster maps can be found at **<www.powa.org/orgnfrms.htm>**.

3. Go to the *Writing Now* web site, for updated information on "Blogs." *Blogs,* short for "weblogs," are online journals. The *Writing Now* web site will point you to sites where you can read other people's Blogs, where you can post one of your own, and where you can find downloads that allow you to add a Blog to your web site, if you have one.

FILE ▶ Create

00:45

Have students list the eight techniques for getting good grades outlined in O'Keeney's article. See how many techniques students remember without studying in their usual manner. Of course, the quiz is illustrative and doesn't count toward a grade since students haven't been told to memorize those items. No reading homework is given here.

You might want to let students brainstorm individually at first and then in groups, using the same process for the clustering step. At this point, your goal is to ensure success with students' first formal writing attempt.

Reminder: This is the central assignment that will be continued throughout this chapter and the next. You may wish to substitute an alternative topic, either from ideas in this chapter or from your own sources.

Clustering for Writing

It is time to put all the prewriting pieces that you've learned so far in place. In the next chapter you will turn the material that you generate here into a text.

1. The first step in generating new material is to generate ideas. Start with a freewriting exercise. Freewrite for 5 minutes on the topic "How to Be Successful in This Writing Course" (or an alternative topic suggested by your instructor). Write anything that comes to mind, but do not stop writing until your instructor says to stop. You might find it helpful to begin with the phrase "I can be successful by. . . ." Do not let your pen lift off the page. Write nonsense if you must.

2. With any luck, this freewriting exercise generated some connections and attuned your mind to the subject. Now explore the brainstorming technique. For 5 minutes, list in any format everything you can think of that relates to succeeding in composition class (or the alternative topic suggested by your instructor). Do not evaluate any of your ideas, no matter how silly they might seem once you start writing them on paper. As you create the brainstorming list, write down just words and phrases, not complete sentences.

3. Now try clustering for generating ideas (rather than for organizing ideas). Draw a circle in the center of a sheet of paper and write in the circle "How to Be Successful in This Writing Course" (or the alternative topic suggested by your instructor). For 5 minutes, or the amount of time given by your instructor, cluster the main ideas off the circle.

At this point you should have some ideas to work with. Review the brainstorming list and the cluster you have created. Look for relationships between the ideas. Some ideas might be "main" ideas and others might be "supporting" ideas or offshoots of the main idea. On a new sheet of paper, combine your brainstorming list and your cluster map, cluster those ideas again (you may use the cluster you have already created, if you think it is organized enough), drawing lines between ideas that are related. Write "How to Be Successful in This Writing Course" (or the alternative topic suggested by your instructor) in a circle in the center of the page. Cluster the main supporting ideas off the central circle and cluster any supporting details off the main supporting ideas.

Help Screen

Saving Documents

Virtually all of us who have used a word processor have a catastrophic story about the one and only time we forgot to save a document. A good way to avoid adding yourself to this unfortunate group is to save early and save often.

When you create a new document, save it before you begin typing. Go to **File: Save As** on the pull-down menu bar at the top of your screen. You will be prompted to fill in or select information in several boxes.

File name: Name your file whatever you wish. Note that each new file needs a unique name.

File type: If you will be working on a document on one computer only, or if you will be using a number of computers that have the same word processing program (for instance, Microsoft Word) don't change the automatic (default) file type. If there is a chance that you will be using different word processing software, save the document as a *rich text format* (.rtf) file. Formatting should not change, and most word processors can open .rtf files.

Location: You must specify a drive and possibly a location on that drive where your file will be stored. The C drive (C:\) is usually the computer's hard drive, and if you save your file to the hard drive, you must work on the same computer to be able to open the file at a later time. If you're working on more than one computer and need to bring files with you, many formats for movable storage exist. Movable storage formats include 3.5-inch floppy disks (A:), Zip disks, CD-W or CD-R (writable or rewritable compact discs), and many others. You can bring these files with you. As long as the computer you move to has the same storage media, you should be able to open your documents. Make yourself familiar with the storage options available on all computers you expect to use while working on your document, and choose the format most convenient for you.

Most people use either Macintosh® (Mac) or personal computers (PCs). Mac computers will usually open a PC disk, but PCs won't open Mac disks without special programs, and these programs don't work well consistently. Plan ahead: If you are working on both Macs and PCs, make sure you can move your documents back and forth.

Just a reminder, it never hurts to press the Save button every few minutes. If your program crashes, you will lose only the work that you have added since your last save.

FILE ▶ Save As

You may want to assign students to write just one paragraph from the cluster since Chapters 3 and 4 discuss how to turn a paragraph into a longer essay. You may want to leave the assignment open ended to see what students do on their own. This assignment is a *discovery process*, so you don't want to give students too much direction. In the next chapter students will learn to organize and outline the ideas they clustered in this chapter. Then students will revise this paragraph and see how much better it is. In this way, students will learn the value of organization through a before-and-after experience.

Basic Cluster for Writing

It is hard to get a cluster lined up exactly the way you want it on a first draft. At this point, it is a good idea to make a final copy of the cluster, with all the ideas laid out and clearly grouped and connected. Draw your final version of your cluster on a separate piece of paper and save it to work with in Chapter 2.

Then, using the ideas in your cluster, write a draft of an essay on your topic. As you may have noticed in the cluster diagram of the writing process, the purpose of a draft is to get as many ideas as you can on paper, in essay format. Remember, you aren't concerned with proofreading, or even revising much, at the draft stage.

OPTIONS ▸ Customize

Clustering

1. If you have mapping software, such as Inspiration, this is a good opportunity to learn to use it. Re-create your final cluster in the software and print out a neat version from which to work. Select "Outline Version" from the menu and print it also as a tool for guiding your writing.

2. You can use the drawing toolbar in Microsoft Word to create clusters. Check out the *Writing Now* web site for detailed instructions.

 Go To ▸ These Go to activities offer more help with the prewriting process.

1. The Purdue University Online Writing Lab at **<http://owl.english.purdue .edu/handouts/general/gl_plan3.html>**, for Thought Starters, which is a list of questions that will help you develop your topic. This may be a system that works well for you.

2. Go to the Purdue University Online Writing Lab at **<http://owl.english .purdue.edu/handouts/general/gl_plan1.html>** for Invention, which provides information on a variety of writing techniques. In the previously mentioned URL, substitute "plan 2" for "plan 1" in that address and find "Planning (Invention): When you start to write," which provides additional writing techniques.

3. Go to Donna M. Avery's site at Arizona State University, for additional help with prewriting: **<http://www.public.asu.edu/~donam/invntion .htm>**.

4. Go to Lisa R. Cohen's site, for help with overcoming writer's block at: **<http://www.sff.net/people/LisaRC/>**.

C:\Prompts for Writing ▸

1. Freewrite, brainstorm, and cluster on the advantages of journaling. Be sure to refer back to the ideas you generated from the articles you read in this chapter.

2. Freewrite, brainstorm, and cluster on how your ideas about writing have changed as a result of the work you have done in this chapter.

3. Freewrite, brainstorm, and cluster on the prewriting process, using information you have learned in this chapter.

4. Freewrite, brainstorm, and cluster on a writing experience of which you have strong memories, using information you have learned in this chapter. For example, can you recall a writing experience that produced a

piece of writing that you were proud of? Or think of a time when a writing instructor responded very positively to your writing. Perhaps you have had an enjoyable journal writing experience or a pen pal with whom you like to communicate. You could freewrite, brainstorm, and cluster on any of the previously mentioned examples or come up with one of your own.

Chapter 2
Learning Is Seeing with Fresh Eyes

It is impossible for anyone to begin to learn what he thinks that he already knows.
Epictetus

Chapter Contents

00:45

Log On ▶ Reflection

Write whatever comes to mind when you read the chapter title and opening quotation on the previous page.

_____

_____

_____

_____

_____

_____

_____

_____

_____

_____

_____

_____

_____

_____

_____

_____

_____

_____

_____

_____

_____

_____

FILE ▶ Open

This section is designed to activate schemas—to allow students to make connections between what they know and new material they will learn. You can use this section for freewriting while you take roll or for class or small-group discussion. This section is not as extensive in the second of the paired chapters as it is in the first, where the overall topic and lesson are introduced.

In Chapter 1 you worked with several techniques for generating ideas. In this chapter you will take the *next step* in writing—organizing those ideas into an appropriate order. If you approach this step as if it were simply a puzzle, you may find it stress-free and even interesting. You will also begin to learn about *revision*—a method all writers use to improve their writing.

Connecting with Writing

▶ What is an outline?

▶ What is the purpose of an outline? Why would someone write an outline?

▶ What is a map?

Connecting with Experience

▶ What is the purpose of a map?

▶ What is your best guess of what a *mind map* is?

▶ If you had a map to follow, would it be easier for you to write an essay? Explain your answer.

▶ What are some of the things to keep in mind when you are deciding in what order to put things?

▶ If you were organizing your closet, what are some of the ways you could decide to order the items?

▶ Have you ever noticed that a text you read is organized in a particular order? Describe any of those orders.

Connecting with the Topic

▶ What does it mean to collaborate?

▶ Why do people form committees? What is the advantage of a committee over an individual?

▶ Why do people form study groups?

▶ How could it help you in school if you were allowed to work with other students when doing an assignment?

▶ If you saw a highway sign that said EIXT instead of EXIT, what thoughts would come to your mind?

▶ Everyone has trouble spelling certain words. What are your "trouble words"?

▶ What does it mean to *revise* something?

▶ How many times do you think a writer rewrites a text to get it to the point where he or she is pleased with it? Support your estimate.

▶ Under what conditions would you repeat a task in order to improve the result?

FILE ▶ New

Organizing Your Information

In Chapter 1 you were concerned mostly with getting as many ideas as possible down on paper. You roughly organized your ideas when you clustered, especially when you drew lines between ideas that were related or when you clustered supporting details around a main idea. In this chapter, you will focus less on generating ideas and more on organizing them. You will let the linear, structured part of your brain take over to create an effective organization of your ideas, again using some of the tools that you used in Chapter 1.

Mind Mapping

Look back at some of the prewriting exercises you did in Chapter 1. When you were brainstorming, you wrote ideas anywhere on the page, possibly forming some relationships. Later you wrote a cluster, grouping similar ideas. This kind of a cluster, like the one shown on page 14, is also called a *map* or *mind map*. Just like a road map, where everything is placed according to how it relates to other locations, a mind map places ideas according to related ideas. In other words, an organized cluster can be called a mind map. A mind map takes what is in your mind and arranges it.

In Chapter 1 you learned that you could use organized clusters to help review and study material. These organized clusters are maps of the important ideas and relationships in material. Mind maps help you organize material and see relationships.

Experiment with Mapping

In this activity you will experiment with how mapping helps you understand relationships and organize information.

1. Map the following information.

whipped cream	toothpaste	tomato sauce
hair spray	paper towels	hamburger buns
frozen peas	hamburger	frozen corn
pork chops	milk	cucumbers
cereal	orange juice	soup
canned beans	tomatoes	plums
cheddar cheese	dish soap	chicken
bread	napkins	milk
oranges	green peppers	canned beets
yogurt	shampoo	crackers
spaghetti	cinnamon rolls	root beer
laundry soap	lettuce	Swiss cheese

Students can do this activity individually or in small groups. This activity is also effective when done as boardwork involving the entire class.

Help: Look for relationships, and draw a cluster that shows the relationships. Your map will have three levels. The overall topic goes in the center of the cluster. First determine the topic—a word or phrase broad enough to include everything in the list. Then determine the categories into which you can divide the overall topic and use to group the items. These categories will form the second level of supporting information. Now place the items in the categories by clustering off from this second level. The items in the above list cluster off from the second level to make up the third level.

2. After you create the map, add two more details to every category.

3. How did you order these items? Why did you put them in the categories that you did?

_____

_____

_____

4. How did that order help? Why would the order be helpful when you are shopping?

_____

_____

_____

Now work with a map with five levels. Turn to page 14 and examine the Writing Process cluster. There are five levels of information in that cluster.

1. Level 1 is the center cluster from which everything evolves. We refer to this center circle as the topic or title of the cluster. Write the main idea from the center cluster here:

_____

2. Four circles contain supporting ideas or information for that main idea. They form Level 2. Write the four ideas in Level 2 here:

_____

_____

_____

3. The supporting ideas that fall under the Level 2 circles form Level 3. Each Level 2 circle has its own Level 3 circles. Examine the Level 2 cluster *Get Ideas.* Write the Level 3 supporting ideas here. *Help:* Look for the three lines coming off the Level 2 cluster *Get Ideas.*

_____

_____

_____

4. Notice that one of those supporting ideas, *Get ideas on paper,* has four of its own supporting ideas. These ideas form Level 4. They are three steps down from the central idea. Write those ideas here.

_____

_____

_____

_____

5. There also is a Level 5. Notice that one of the Level 4 ideas, *Brainstorm,* has four supporting ideas. Write those ideas here.

_____

_____

_____

_____

You may have found this activity confusing. If you found the levels difficult to spot, there is a method for organizing your information that may be easier for you to work with.

Outlining

You may have worked with outlines in school before. You may even have found them difficult because it is difficult to start with an outline. As mentioned before, the creative part of our brain doesn't always work in the linear method suited to outlining. Working with an outline when you are trying to be creative and generate ideas, therefore, can be defeating.

Sometimes, however, we do want to make use of the linear part of our brain. That is when we are ready to make a final organization of our ideas. Make an outline when you know what you are going to write about and when you want to get the ideas down in the best order for your topic.

Experiment with Outlining

Before you start your outline, look at the cluster on page 14 in Chapter 1 again and complete Questions 1–4.

1. Write the four ideas off the central cluster, the Level 2 ideas, here.

_____

_____

_____

_____

The ideas must be listed in the order they are done in the writing process because it is a *process, a how-to.* Other ways of ordering information will be discussed later in this chapter. You may wish to discuss this with the students.

2. Read over the ideas you listed in number 1. There is one order best suited to this topic. Write down the ideas again in the order in which you think it would be best to present them.

_____

_____

_____

_____

3. Why did you choose that order?

_____

_____

_____

_____

4. Why would another order be more difficult to follow?

_____

_____

_____

_____

You have just completed two steps in organizing your material: (1) mapping out your ideas and their relationships, and (2) putting your ideas into the best order. That wasn't so hard. Once you know what direction you want your ideas to take, it is much easier to get them down on paper, in a way that makes sense for you and for the reader.

Using the information in the cluster on page 14 in Chapter 1, fill in the following outline. Before you begin your outline, look at the overall structure of the outline below. Notice that

title or topic   Level 1 ideas are indicated by _____.

Roman numerals   Level 2 ideas are indicated by _____.

capital letters   Level 3 ideas are indicated by _____.

Arabic numerals   Level 4 ideas are indicated by _____.

lowercase letters   Level 5 ideas are indicated by _____.

If you had a Level 6, it would be indicated by a number, Level 7 would be a letter and the levels would continue in that fashion, alternating numbers and small letters.

Now fill in the outline below, using the information given in the cluster on page 14 in Chapter 1. The letters and numbers along the side will give you clues.

Topic: Writing process   Topic:
I. Get ideas   I.
   A. from experience
   B. from readings   A.
   C. get ideas on paper   B.
      1. list
      2. cluster   C.
      3. freewrite
      4. brainstorm   1.
         (a) e-mail   2.
         (b) chalkboard
         (c) overhead   3.
         (d) in group
II. Write draft   4.
   A. use as many ideas as possible
   B. put ideas into essay format   (a)
III. Revise
   A. add detail   (b)
   B. check word choice
   C. vary sentence length and   (c)
      style
   D. get input from others   (d)
   E. make sure paper says what
      you want it to say—how you   II.
      want it to say it
IV. Proofread   A.
   A. punctuation
   B. spelling   B.
   C. verb forms

III.

    A.

    B.

    C.

    D.

    E.

IV.

    A.

    B.

    C.

You do not always need to make a detailed outline that includes every supporting detail at Levels 3, 4, and so on, as you may prefer other brainstorming or prewriting strategies. But one little saying will help you remember that you always need to know your supporting ideas and the best order in which to present them: *Be sure you know your ABCs.* In other words, before you begin writing, you will determine through your prewriting activities the supporting ideas that will best back up your main idea. These supporting ideas are your ABCs. For example, if you were going to write one paragraph about the main idea *Get ideas* (see cluster on page 14 in Chapter 1), then the supporting information about how to get ideas would be your ABCs.

There are three basic ways to get ideas:

    A. From experience

    B. From readings

    C. From generating on paper

If you have five ideas, they would actually be A, B, C, D, and E, but the shortcut reminder is "Know your ABCs."

Outlining doesn't work for every writing situation. There are two important things to keep in mind:

1. Different kinds of writing may call for different techniques. For example, if you are doing creative writing, telling a story, or describing something that happened to you, you don't always need an outline. Sometimes writers just follow "where the writing leads them." However, doing that to answer an essay question, for example, would not be the most effective technique.

2. The writing process has different phases, as we have shown in this chapter. Most of the time when you want to see where the writing leads you, you should be doing freewriting (or perhaps clustering or brainstorming). When you let the writing lead you, you let the creative side take over.

However, when you are finished with that phase (although you may come back to it if the writing presents you with additional ideas or if you get stuck), let the linear, organizing side take over and decide how best to present the material. Remember when you need to organize your ideas, mapping and outlining are helpful tools.

Sometimes students work with both methods, using mind mapping as a first step and then getting the information down in a more linear form such as outlining right before writing. Experiment and see what works best for you. Many instructors require an outline, so you may find it easier to do the mind map first and then turn it into an outline for your instructor. You will be making brief outlines before writing throughout this textbook.

 Go To ▶ 1. Go to the Purdue University OWL (Online Writing Lab) to see a sample outline handout:
<http://owl.english.purdue.edu/handouts/general/gl_outlinS .html>.

OPTIONS ▶ **Customize**

Mapping

1. Find a short nonfiction article in a magazine. Make an idea map based on your reading of the article. Ask your instructor to give you an overhead transparency on which you can draw the map. Once you've completed your map, show it to the class.

2. Find a short story in a book or magazine. Map the story using pictures and words. Draw pictures or cut them out of magazines. Transfer your map to poster board and display your map to the class.

3. Make an idea map to help you prepare for a test in another class–using the subject matter that will be on the test. If the map helps you do well, tell your classmates about it.

4. Turn the topic and brainstorming from Chapter 1, File: Save As, into an outline and bring it to class.

Help Screen

Color Printer

If you have access to a color printer and know how to search the Web, find pictures on the Web related to your idea map. Print the pictures you find and use them on your map.

Turn the topic and brainstorming from Chapter 1, **File: Save As,** into an outline and bring it to class.

Sometimes, if you find it difficult to make an outline or decide how to order your ideas, it is helpful to work with your classmates. Each person has a unique set of skills. You may be good at mapping; someone else may be better at outlining. If you work together, you can each learn to be better at both activities. During this course, therefore, you will be engaging in *collaborative learning.* This popular learning technique is effective in helping you master new skills.

Read the following article to understand what collaborative learning is and to see why you will be working in groups.

Collaboration

Toni Haring-Smith

We work together, whether together or apart.

Robert Frost

1   When you think of writing, what do you visualize? Do you see a solitary individual like Emily Dickinson sitting alone in an attic room? Do you imagine F. Scott Fitzgerald lying drunk in his lonely study? Or, do you see people working together—the early leaders of this country huddled in candlelight, talking, writing, and revising the Declaration of Independence? Do you see a famous novelist like Hemingway leaning over the typescript of a new book with his editor? . . .

2   Although most of our familiar images of writers and students present them as solitary, in fact most writers and thinkers work together to share ideas with one another. Our historical and cultural mythology encourages us to think of great ideas, discoveries, and events as the product of individual effort when they usually result from group effort. We remember Alexander Graham Bell and his telephone, Marie Curie and radium, Aristotle and the definition of tragedy, or Martin Luther King and the civil rights movement. But none of these people worked alone. Bell developed his invention with his associate, Thomas Watson; Curie performed most of her experiments with her husband or her daughter; Aristotle spent twenty years discussing ideas with thinkers in Plato's Academy and later with his friend Theophrastus; and Martin Luther King had a small army of supporters surrounding him as he marched out of Selma. There are, of course, hermits and solitary geniuses in our society, but they are the exceptions—so exceptional, in fact, that we frequently brand them peculiar or even insane.

3   It is not surprising, then, that recent research in education, psychology, and business management shows us that people can accomplish more if they work together. Dozens of studies have revealed that people working as a group to solve mazes or number puzzles can outperform individuals working alone at the same task. And perhaps the most

Source: Excerpts from pp. 3–10 from *Writing Together* by Tori Haring-Smith. Copyright © 1994 by HarperCollins College Publishers. Reprinted by permission of Addison-Wesley Educational Publishers, Inc.

interesting research demonstrates that groups even solve puzzles more accurately than the brightest individual in them could alone. . . .

4   The classroom in which collaborative learning is used looks quite different from a more traditional lecture or class discussion. You will work in pairs or small groups, you may move about the room rather than sit still, and you will find out answers for yourselves rather than wait for the teacher to give you the answer. In fact, in most of these exercises, there is no "right answer," so you and your groups will be developing and defending your own ideas, not just trying to figure out "what the teacher wants."

5   Have you been asked to work in groups before and thought, "What a waste of time. Why doesn't the teacher just lecture?" Have you ever waited patiently through a class discussion in order to find out what the teacher really thinks? If you have been asked to read and comment on another student's paper, have you wondered what you could possibly have to say? Have you assumed that your classmates wouldn't be able to help you write, and have you wished that the teacher would read your essay drafts? Or maybe most of your teachers have spent class time presenting material to you, while you took notes or worked on homework.

6   If any of these experiences sounds familiar, you will find collaborative learning a new approach. Of course, it is not a new kind of learning—in fact, reading, talking, and learning together was the practice in most schools until the twentieth century. But collaborative learning is not very common in American schools now. The first rules that most students learn in school are

- Be quiet.

- Don't talk to other students.

- Do your own work.

Our school systems have become so concerned with testing individual comprehension of material that they have stopped students from learning together. This has had a very serious effect on how well students learn and it has warped our assumptions about teachers' and students' roles in the classroom. Let's look at how collaborative learning challenges the kind of schooling most Americans now receive.

7   In order to work together with your classmates, you will have to recognize the knowledge and experience that you and your classmates have. Why work with others if you don't think that they have anything worthwhile to share? Why ask someone to respond to your writing if you think that only the teacher can do that? Most students have gradually come to distrust the knowledge they and their classmates have. The American educational system teaches most students that they should listen to the teacher, memorize what she and the textbooks say, and then regurgitate that information on exams and in papers. In many cases, students find it easier to forget or ignore what they think and just concentrate on what the teacher thinks.

8   I know that when I was a student, I was often afraid to speak in class. It seemed safer to be quiet than to be wrong. I remember sitting in English class and thinking, "Where did the teacher get that interpretation of this text? I thought that the poem was about a flower and she says that it is about existentialism." I learned to keep quiet rather than reveal my ignorance. I think many students share my fear of being wrong. Consequently, it is not surprising that American educators today bemoan the fact that their students are passive. . . .

9   In most colleges and universities, teachers and students alike assume that students are empty vessels, waiting to be filled with the knowledge of calculus, Chinese history, modern American architecture, or whatever. The basic definition of a teacher is one who knows a subject, while a student is assumed to be ignorant of the subject. Now to some extent, this is true. You take a class in organic chemistry because you want to learn organic chemistry. If you already knew the subject, you would probably try to "test out" of the course and take a different one. Of course, you might take a diagnostic test at the beginning of a course to see how much American history or calculus you remember, but these random questions can't really tell teachers what you know about a subject. If you know that Washington was president before Lincoln, does this mean that you also understand the different cultural or political climates in which these two men worked? . . .

10   Most of the time, you do know something about the subject of the courses you take. Your courses up to this point have prepared you for organic chemistry. You have learned methods for balancing chemical equations, and you understand the basic structure of chemical compounds. Similarly, although you may never have taken a course in Chinese history, you probably know something about it—that it involves many dynasties, that China was a great silk producer, that Chinese women used to bind their feet, that the Chinese built the Great Wall, that the Communist party has been crushing political dissent, and so on. Some of the things you "know" about a subject may not be "true." For example, based on popular media, you might assume that the Chinese were especially ruthless warriors. You might also have memorized incorrect valences for certain chemical elements. In any case, your mind is not a blank slate.

11   Not only do you come into a course with knowledge and experience that is relevant to it, but, as you go along in the course, you gradually come to understand its content. You will be learning about the subject from the teacher, the texts, and the other students in the class. What you learn will shape the way you hear the teacher, argue with your classmates, or read the texts.

12   If we teachers treat you as if you knew nothing about the subject, and if you are afraid to speak for fear of being wrong, then you will become passive. You will wait for us to tell you what you think, and then you will write it down, and tell it back to us in papers and on exams. In this kind of system, there is little reward for thinking on your own. There is also little reward for listening to other, apparently equally ignorant students. This is why students often complain about group work of any kind. They want to know why the teacher does not just give them the answer.

13   Collaborative learning asks that you

- Have the courage to recognize and speak your own ideas.

- Respect the ideas and knowledge that other students bring to the class.

- Trust the teacher to listen to you with respect and to care about your ideas.

Collaborative learning redefines your relationship to your teacher and to the other students in the class. Rather than assume that your mind is a blank slate, waiting to be written on by the teacher, collaborative learning focuses on the knowledge and experience that you bring to a classroom. It works by finding out what you know and then allowing the teacher to respond and give you exercises that will let you learn. The teacher does not digest all the knowledge and feed it to you like the predigested food fed to baby birds. The teacher does not report her learning. You learn for yourself, and the teacher is there as a kind of coach to guide your learning, to point you to important ideas and books, to give you exercises that will help you sharpen your skills. . . .

Analyze the Reading

1. Reflect on what you read. Where do you agree and disagree with the points the author made?

_____

_____

_____

_____

_____

_____

_____

_____

_____

_____

_____

_____

_____

_____

Be sure that students bring their first essay so that they will have something to work with when they learn to use peer revision in the next class.

Be sure to bring the essay you wrote in Chapter 1, **File: Save As,** to class. Bring a neat copy, because you will collaborate with your classmates to improve the essay.

TOOLS ▶ Language

00:45

You will probably want to spend a few minutes going over the outlines students completed for homework. Alternatively, you could save the outlines for group work.

Spelling

When we meet people in person, they sometimes judge us not only by what we say and do, but also by our appearance—by the clothes we wear or our personal grooming. When people read your writing, they form opinions of you not only from what you say, but also from the appearance of your text (neat-

Most instructors find it helpful to let students read from their reflections rather than simply have an open discussion. First, it encourages students to do their homework. Second, it elicits more thoughtful responses. Third, it serves to make the time used more productive because the class does not get sidetracked.

To keep students active, alert, and involved, you may want to spend a few minutes having students list on the board all of the e-mail language conventions they know. Inexperienced students can guess what the conventions mean.

ness and format) and from *how* you say things—spelling, grammar, and sentence structure. Just as the appropriateness of certain language can depend upon where you are (school, work, parties), there is a style of language appropriate to certain *types of writing.* We call this *conventional language use* or *appropriate language conventions.* You will want to follow these conventions in your essay writing for school, although you do not need to in other forms of writing such as brainstorming, freewriting, journal writing, and e-mails. As you may realize, e-mails have their own language conventions, such as LOL for *laughing out loud,* U for *you,* and R for *are.* "R U LOL?" might be an appropriate sentence in an informal e-mail, such as a message to a friend. However, this usage would not be effective in academic or professional writing, and that also includes academic or professional e-mail.

One of the conventions you must abide by in academic writing is correct spelling. Fortunately, if you have access to a computer, this is somewhat easier now, thanks to a tool called the spell checker.

> **Help Screen**
>
> ### Spell Checker
>
> The spell checker is a wonderful tool, but like all tools it must be used with some care.
>
> Most word processing programs now have a feature that automatically shows if there is a problem with a word. It might indicate a word that is misspelled or a word that is spelled correctly but is not in the program's dictionary.
>
> To check the spelling of a word, select the word by double-clicking on it, then go to the toolbar at the top of your screen and select "Tools" from the toolbar to access the spell checker. Newer word processing programs will automatically show you spelling options if you right-click on a word.
>
> To check the entire document, click on the spell checker and it will guide you through the document. If you are working on your own computer and know that a word is spelled correctly, although the spell checker indicates it is wrong (a proper name, for example), you can click on the "Add" feature so that the word does not show up as incorrect again. Do not add words to school computers unless your teacher says to do so.
>
> If a word shows up as misspelled and it is not a word that you know is correct, then you can choose one of the computer's suggestions to change the word, or you can type in a correction yourself.
>
> Using a spell checker is a good way to correct spelling mistakes, but it does not substitute for a good, close proofreading that you do yourself.

As you can see by the following poem, the spell checker is not without its dangers. All of the words in this poem are spelled correctly. Many of them, however, are not correct as they are used here. That is, if you use the wrong word, such as *there* for *their,* the spell checker will not catch it.

As you read the poem, notice the words that would actually be considered misspelled as they are used here.

Spell Chequer

by Carl Heitzman

>Eye halve a spelling chequer
>It came with my pea sea
>It plainly marques four my revue
>Miss steaks eye kin knot sea
>Eye strike a key and type a word
>And weight four it two say
>Weather eye am wrong oar write
>It shows me strait a weigh
>As soon as a mist ache is maid
>It nose bee fore two long
>And eye can put the error rite
>Its rare lea ever wrong.
>Eye have run this poem threw it
>I am shore your pleased two no
>Its letter perfect awl the weigh
>My chequer tolled me sew.

Source: "Spell Chequer" by Roger Herman from *News-Sun*, April 19, 2000. Reprinted by permission of the author.

Analyze the Reading

1. Highlight all of the words in the poem for which the spell checker inserted words that sound like the words the writer meant to use but that are incorrect.

2. On a separate sheet of paper, rewrite the poem using the word spelling the writer intended.

This poem contains some of the most troublesome words for students. Words that sound alike but mean different things and are spelled differently can be difficult to catch. When you read the word, you hear in your head the word you intended to write. Therefore, it is very important that, in addition to using the spell checker, you carefully proofread your essay for spelling errors. Several techniques are helpful in this process. You will probably want to use more than one of them for a careful proofreading.

First, using the draft you're currently working on, read your paper starting with the last sentence first.* This way you are somewhat less likely to hear what you think you wrote and more likely to actually see what you did write.

Second, make a proofreading frame. Use it to frame each word as you read your paper, one word at a time. Look closely at what is in the frame. Too

You can have students do this activity individually or in groups. One effective technique is for students to highlight the incorrect words individually and then get into groups and compare their work. Doing this enables students to learn early in the semester the value of group work, as they see that others caught words that they missed. Finally students can try to rewrite the poem as a group.

---

*To make a proofreading frame, take a 3"×5" index card and in the center of the card cut out an opening approximately 2" wide by 1/4" high. This opening will "frame" a group of words enabling you to focus on one phrase at a time when proofreading. By framing a few words at a time, you can catch errors more easily.

often, we see what we wanted to write rather than what we actually put on the page.

Third, it is always helpful to have another person review your paper and look for these errors. When you work together in a classroom (or other setting) with your peers, it is called *peer editing*.

When you finish revising your paper, you should use the abovementioned techniques before doing a final rewrite of your paper. Then, after you've completed your final copy, check one more time for copying errors that may have crept into your paper.

Of course, it is always better if you do not write a word incorrectly in the first place. You will find it helpful to keep a page in your notebook to list commonly misspelled words. You can review these words before and after writing. When you notice words that give you trouble as you or someone else proofreads your paper, add the words to your list. Eventually the words will no longer give you trouble.

Start right now to make your list. Brainstorm for a few minutes on the words that you know you have trouble with. At this point, do not worry about how you are spelling the words as you try to brainstorm and get them all down. After the creative brainstorming session is over, you can look the words up and record them correctly in a list. Put the list on the inside cover of your notebook or on a sheet of paper close to the front of your notebook. This is your reminder of your trouble words that you need to watch out for.

Some words tend to give more trouble than others. Try to memorize the following helpful hints about commonly misused words.

there/their *Help:* For the word *there*, think that you are either here or there. See the word *here* in the word *there* and remember that it is a place. If you are talking about people, use *their.*

accept/except *Help:* I **a**ccept = I **a**gree. Both words, accept and agree, begin with *a* and have similar meanings. But everyone gets to go *except* you because you are the *exception.*

to, too, two *Help: Too* has too many *o*s, as in "too much, too little, too late"; the *w* in *two* stands on two feet, so it means the number 2. Otherwise, use *to.*

breathe, breath *Help: Breathe* is longer, so the first *e* is long, pronounced *EE* as in *free.*

cloths, clothes *Help: Clothes* is longer, so the first *o* is long, pronounced as in *owe.*

an, and *Help: And* has one letter added to *an*; *and* means plus or added to, whereas *an* is a tiny word meaning just one.

Students will learn more about peer editing in later chapters.

It is a good idea to give students a few minutes to generate this list and to start their master list of trouble words. You may want students to write these words on the board after the brainstorming as a reminder to other students of words they have trouble with. Students must, however, write the words on the board correctly. (Research shows that when students see a word written incorrectly, they are just as likely to remember the incorrect as the correct version. That is why you won't see words written incorrectly in this textbook. The "incorrect" spellings in the poem are actually correctly spelled words; they are just used incorrectly.)

Go To ▶

1. Go to the *About.com* site for help with spelling and other writing problems: **<http://teenwriting.about.com/teens/teenwriting/msubject24.htm>**.

2. Go to California State University Northridge's *Spell Checker Doesn't Always Work* site, for a list of links to sites that discuss spell-checker problems: **<http://www.csun.edu/~vcecn006/spell.html>**.

3. Go to Judy Vorfeld's Webgrammar page, which includes a list of many more confusing words: **<http://www.webgrammar.com/grammar.html>**.

OPTIONS ▶ Customize

Spell Checking

1. Make a list of words you often confuse. Create a crossword puzzle to help you remember the words.

2. Organize an old-fashioned spelling bee that uses confusing words in sentences; then spell those words. Split into teams to make up the sentences. Then challenge the other teams to write the sentences on the board using the appropriate spelling. To test another team's ability to sort out confusing words, for example, you might create the following sentence: "She *peeked* through the window at the mountain *peak* that *piqued* her curiosity."

FILE ▶ Edit

This is a good place to begin the homework assignment. Remind students that they must have a written draft in order to participate in the next session's class activities.

Revision for Organization

As you may recall from the Start chapter, revision is one of the most important parts of the writing process. This means that after you have *finished writing*, you are ready to *begin revising*. Basically, *revision* is a process of rewriting your paper in order to improve *how* you said everything instead of what you have been doing so far: concentrating on *what* you said. During revision you let your linear left brain take over. When you review your paper looking for ways to improve it and questioning what you have done, you are using the part of your brain that can be critical and judgmental. You don't want to use that part too early in the writing process or you will become discouraged. But as with most steps in the process, there is a time and place for everything. This is the time to read your paper and look for weaknesses.

Because you are learning more about writing, this textbook is designed to allow you to learn gradually and to concentrate on one skill at a time rather than to try to learn everything at once. In every chapter, you will learn new ways to improve your writing. After you learn one skill, you can add another skill to it and revise your writing with both skills. Later, you can revise using additional skills until eventually you will be able to look for many ways to improve your writing when you revise. For now, concentrate on what you have learned in this chapter: how to revise for organization.

So far in this chapter you have worked with organizing your information. You used mapping or outlining to put your information in groups or clusters. Then you had to decide in what order you wanted the groups to appear in your final written text.

When you worked with the grocery list, you found that it was best to organize that information by categories or types. You put all of the canned goods together and all of the frozen foods together, for example.

When you worked with the cluster step of the writing process, you found that you had to put the writing activities in the order in which they are performed—in steps. That is because you were organizing a process.

Students will learn other patterns of organization in later chapters.

Other methods of organization are available to you. How many ways can you think of to order information? Brainstorm on this topic.

Did you come up with *order of importance* as one of the ways to order information? An effective method of organizing ideas is either to start with the most important idea and work through to the least important or to do the opposite—start with the least important idea and work through to the most important. This may be the method you want to use for your essay in this chapter.

Read the following article on how to make a smooth transition to college. As you read, decide whether the author is moving from the least to the most important points or from the most to the least important points.

Making the Transition to College

Lexington Herald Leader

1   "The biggest problem I see students have is they have not had to study in their senior years, and then they get into college and they're expected to do so much more and they're not prepared for it."

2   For that reason, Sawyer* said she strongly recommends that all high school students take a fourth year of math, no matter what course of study they intend to follow in college.

3   Once you do get to college, most experts recommend that you live in the dorms for at least your freshman year, and there's something to be said for that advice. The dorms are usually competitive with, if not cheaper than, off-campus housing, plus they're set up with students' needs in mind.

4   For one thing, someone else keeps the lights on and the bathroom clean (in dorms with communal bathrooms, at least), and meals are available already cooked, so you can concentrate on studying and not paying bills on time or shopping for groceries.

5   And living with hundreds of other students is a great way to meet people and feel like you belong. Studies show that students who live in the dorms their freshman year are less likely to drop out of school.

6   Plus, most dorms have special amenities just for students: computer labs, study rooms and exercise facilities, for instance. They're generally within walking or biking distance of classrooms and the library, which eliminates the need and hassle of having a car on campus. (Show me a campus, and I'll show you a parking problem.)

7   Some other advice for making the adjustment to college life:

- Participate in all orientation programs offered, which range from a few hours at some schools to an entire semester at others. Western Kentucky University offers a week-long orientation program for incoming students held the week before classes start. "On the first day of classes I can stand outside my office and pick out the students

---

*Jenny Sawyer, executive director of admissions at the University of Louisville, Louisville, Kentucky.

Source: *Lexington Herald Leader*, "Making the Transition to College," from *College Guide 1996.* Reprinted with permission Knight Ridder Productions, Lexington, KY, USA.

who didn't participate in that program because they look lost," said Debi Jordan, associate director of admissions at Western Kentucky University.

"And the students who did participate feel like they own the school."

- Take advantage of academic support services when you need them. That might mean visiting the writing center, taking a course in study skills or talking to an academic adviser if you are uncertain about your major.

  "Stay in contact with your academic adviser," says Jordan. "And don't wait until you're failing the class before you go talk to a teacher about it. The academic side of it is important—you have to take responsibility for that."

- Get involved in extracurricular activities, whether you live on campus or off. Jordan recommends one activity related to your major and another that's just for fun—the campus chapter of the Society of Professional Journalists and intramural soccer, perhaps. You'll make new friends and feel more connected to your new school.

- Organize or join a small study group. Many dorms have sign-up sheets for study groups. You might find that helping someone else learn material is a great way to learn it yourself.

- Be patient. It will take a while to feel comfortable with all aspects of college life.

- Manage your time. Students should be careful not to overschedule themselves, said Ed Ford, public relations director at Berea College. "Look at things from the perspective of why you are really there—you're at any college to get an education. So you should look at that academic program first and say, 'All right, here's what I need to do to be successful.'"

- Stay in touch with your family and friends back home. If you have limited money for long-distance calls, write letters, send e-mail or exchange audiocassettes.

- And the final, perhaps most important, bit of advice: Never, never be afraid to ask questions.

8   Remember, everyone on that campus was a freshman once.

Analyze the Reading

1. Did the author go from the least to the most important point or from the most to the least important point?

2. How could you tell?

You may have noticed that many of the items would be hard to rank as more or less important, and, of course, opinions would vary from person to person, as well. It is not necessary for the items to fall in a strict order when you use this pattern of organization. If you are going from the least to the most important points, then you might decide which are the least important points and list those first, then which are the most important points and list those last, and finally list the remaining points in the middle. Don't get bogged down in ranking each and every item.

You will learn more about the other ways of organizing your material when you are further along in the text. Since writing is a recursive process—meaning that you often repeat steps in the process at various times—as you go through the writing process in this book, you will find that you keep coming back to some of the same ideas. Each time you return to the same ideas, you will become more experienced and more skilled.

Revise

You are now ready to begin your first revision. Reread the draft you wrote in Chapter 1 to see if you were consciously using an effective order in the information you presented. Try to determine whether there might be a more effective order in which to present the information. Revise your essay—rewrite it, rearranging any supporting details that you think need to be rearranged. Remember, at this point you are dealing primarily with *content*, with *what* you are saying. Read your essay aloud to see if it will be clear to the reader. When you are finished with this process, write or print a clean copy of your essay for class. Whenever possible, you want to recruit some classmates to review your draft. Ask what they like about your essay, what they don't like, and, especially, what they find confusing. Make any further revisions to improve your essay, based on the feedback you received from your classmates.

You can help yourself as well as your classmates by reading and offering ideas to improve their papers. It is easier to see problems in someone else's work than in your own, and critical reading of others' papers can help you learn to read your writing with a more critical eye. Remember that everyone probably feels insecure about showing their work, so be kind and helpful with your comments. If you read a classmate's paper, look for just two things at this point: the pattern of organization (appropriate order of supporting details) and spelling. Read the paper once for pattern and once again for spelling. Remember, it is hard to think about *what* you are saying and *how* you are saying it at the same time. That applies to reading, too.

Proofread

Once you've finished revising your essay, it's time to put it into final form.

As you write, you are tweaking your essay to make the meaning clear. You probably make corrections—in spelling, word choice, word endings—as you go. You add a comma here and there. Maybe you rewrite a sentence until it sounds right, or move it, or take it out. Finally, the essay reads the way you want it to read, and you've almost reached the deadline for turning it in. The last step before submitting an essay is proofreading. Your meaning is clear, but you need to go over what you've written very carefully, word by word, to make sure what you think you've written is what actually appears on the page. You will be checking for mistakes you have made in spelling, punctuation, and

You may want to end the homework assignment here so that students can work collaboratively and experience peer revision. The concept of peer revision is addressed in more detail later, but this is an introduction to it. Students can use revision forms and engage in more intense revision later. For now, you may want to keep the activity informal and nonthreatening.

00:45

usage, things that you meant to write one way and accidentally wrote another, or usages you weren't sure of as you wrote your essay.

Most students think they can "read over" their essays once or twice and consider their essays proofread. Students are horrified when they get essays back covered with markings of mistakes that they could have corrected if they had noticed them. Your task in proofreading, then, becomes one of forcing your mind to stop reading for meaning and to begin seeing the actual words that appear on the page.

The first step in proofreading is to read word by word, pronouncing each word in your mind or, if you are alone, out loud. Sound out longer words by syllables. If you have used a spell checker, make sure it didn't accidentally change a word you meant into something that has nothing to do with what you wrote. If you hear yourself pronouncing an *s* or an *ed,* make sure it appears at the end of the word.

One way to help yourself see individual words is to use a proofreading frame that you created earlier on in this chapter. Lay it on your essay, with the first word showing through the frame. Push the frame along, word by word, focusing on what is actually written on your page, not what you meant to write. You can even use it on a computer screen, although for the final proofreading it is probably better to print a copy of your essay.

The second step is to read your essay backward, sentence by sentence. You will be listening to yourself read each sentence in this step, looking for punctuation problems. You should refer to your handbook or the *Writing Now* web site for help with punctuation when you have a question about it, but thinking of punctuation as traffic indicators will provide a rough gauge of what to do in this final step.

Punctuation marks are signals the writer gives to help the reader match the cadence of the writing that the writer intends. Just as a Yield sign warns a driver to pause or slow down, the comma signals the reader to do the same. Occasionally, a writer might use a dash, a colon, or even a semicolon to slow the reader down, but the comma is generally preferred. A Stop sign requires the driver to come to a complete stop, as do the end punctuation marks: the period, the question mark, the exclamation point, and the semicolon (when used to separate two closely linked sentences). A red light obliges the driver to stop and wait until the light turns green. A new paragraph does the same for the reader, indicating that a new idea is starting.

Some students find it helpful to use their index fingers to help identify word groups they have written as sentences. Put both of your index fingers on the very last period on the last page of your essay, then slide your left finger back until you run into an end punctuation mark (Stop sign). Read the sentence forward, listening for pauses and stops. Did you end with a pause instead of a stop? Then it is likely you have written a sentence fragment. Check it out and fix it if you did. Did you stop more than once in this word group? Unless you stopped at a semicolon, you may have a comma splice or a run-on sentence. Refer to a handbook to see how your sentence would conventionally have been punctuated. When you are satisfied that you have a well-punctuated sentence, slide your right finger back to meet the left, then slide your left finger back to the next end punctuation mark it runs into, and repeat what you just did. This may appear to be a great deal of work, but many students have found that it helps.

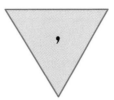

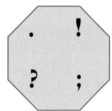

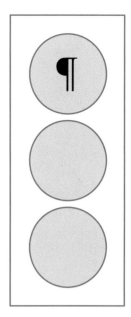

A third proofreading step is to go through your essay looking for problems you know you commonly make. If you have discovered that you tend to shift verb tenses unnecessarily or leave off *-ed* endings, read through your essay one more time looking for that specific problem and make changes where necessary.

Go To ▶

1. Go to the *Writing Now* web site for information on Online Writing Labs (OWLs), sites that can answer your questions about usage and mechanics: **<http://owl.english/purdue.edu/handouts/general/gl_outlinS .html>**.

2. Go to Dolphinville, on the Houghton Mifflin web site, and stop at the gym to "tone and strengthen your grammar skills": **<developmentalenglish.college.hmco.com/students>**. Scroll down the page and on the right-hand side of your screen, click on Dolphinville: A Place to Write. A Log In/Registration screen will appear. Once you register, you'll be ready to go.

Word Processing Quick Tips

These are tips that students have found helpful as they begin using word processors.

Find out how to Undo right away! Look at the menu at the top of your screen. Select "Edit." A drop-down menu will appear. Click on "Undo typing," which will undo your last command. If you make a mistake, such as accidentally deleting a paragraph you have written, use the Undo command in your word processor to restore your work. Most word processors allow multiple (one hundred or more) Undo commands.

Use the Enter key only to start a new paragraph. Word processors have a feature called "word wrap" that starts a new line automatically when you reach the end of a line. Using the Enter key to start a new line will cause all sorts of problems if you change the formatting of the document.

To double-space, select the double-space command. In Microsoft Word, it's under Format, Paragraph, Line Spacing: Double. Do not press the Enter key twice to double-space manually, because you are likely to find that each new line will begin with a capital letter. In WordPerfect, click on Format, then Paragraph, then Format again and you will see the options for line spacing. In other word processing programs, go to Format where you will find similar options.

Generally, for your text, you should choose a proportional font, such as Arial (sans serif) or Times New Roman (serif), in a point size of 11 or 12. Save the fancy fonts for nonacademic writing or for documents using many graphics.

FILE ▶ Save

Basic Cluster for Writing

You are now ready for a final revision. This checklist will help you to make sure you have performed all of the necessary revision and proofreading steps. The checklist will keep getting longer as you progress through the book and learn more writing, revision, and proofreading skills.

Name: _____   Date: _____

Revision Checklist

❑ I have arranged my ideas in an order appropriate to the topic.

❑ I have had someone read and annotate my essay.

Proofreading Checklist

❑ I proofread my paper for spelling.

❑ I have read each sentence aloud, starting with the last sentence first and working backward, to make sure that each sentence is clear and uses appropriate language conventions.

You are now ready to "save" your file—that is, to prepare the final version of your paper. Some students like to call this step *publishing* the paper.

Take your final revision and prepare the final text that you will submit to your instructor, either by rewriting the paper by hand or by saving the final version of it on your computer and then printing a copy of it.

C:\Prompts for Writing ▶

1. Write about the advantages of working in groups over working alone. Be sure to decide how you want to order the advantages.

2. Write a letter of advice to a friend or relative who is still in high school. Explain, from your own experience, what changes that person should expect to make when he or she starts college.

3. Write about a writing experience you have had that you remember well. Have you written a poem or letter that influenced someone special to you? Did you write a paper for school that turned out better or worse than you thought it would? Discuss the entire experience.

4. Have you kept a diary or journal? Write about what prompted you to begin writing it, how long you kept the diary or journal, what sorts of things you wrote about, and whether you found keeping the diary or journal helpful or fun.

5. Begin keeping a journal. Review what the writers in Chapter 1 have to say about journaling, and decide whether there is a place in your life for a journal.

Log Off: ▶ Review and Reflect

Take some time to reflect on what you have learned about writing so far in this course. Write about what you have learned and how your writing has changed as a result of the discussion, readings, and activities in this chapter.

_____

_____

_____

_____

_____

_____

_____

_____

_____

_____

_____

_____

_____

How is the final version of your paper different from what you wrote at the end of Chapter 1 in **File: Save As**? Reread both entries and discuss the differences between them.

_____

_____

_____

_____

_____

_____

CHAPTER 3
He Said, She Said

Men are from Mars; women are from Venus.

John Gray

Chapter Contents

Log On ▶ **Reflection**

Write whatever comes to mind as you read the chapter title and opening quotation.

_____

_____

_____

_____

_____

_____

_____

_____

_____

_____

_____

_____

_____

_____

_____

_____

_____

_____

_____

_____

_____

_____

FILE ▶ Open

`00:45`

Connecting with Experience

▶ What does it mean to *narrow* something?

▶ If you were to ask someone to go to the grocery store to buy some fruit, a vegetable, a cleaning product, and a beverage, there is no telling what that person might come back with. You may have hoped for peaches and got grapes instead. Narrow each of these words to as specific an item as you can think of. For example, instead of *fruit*, name a specific fruit.

▶ What does it mean to *respond* to something?

▶ Describe the extent, if any, of your experience with e-mail.

▶ What does it mean to reply or respond to e-mail?

Connecting with Writing

▶ What do you think it means to "narrow your topic before writing"?

▶ What is the *subject line* in e-mail? What is its purpose?

▶ What would an essay be like that responds to another essay?

Connecting with the Topic

▶ Do men and women communicate differently? Explain.

▶ List some instances in which poor communication, or miscommunication, could have serious or tragic consequences.

Connecting to New Material

▶ Cluster the term *narrow* in your notebook or on a separate sheet of paper. Then cluster the term *response*.

▶ What difficulties have you had in the past with the topics on which you have written?

▶ Think about a paper that you have written well or enjoyed writing. What can you remember about the topic that made it easier to write the paper?

▶ What would you like to know that could help you select a topic for a paper?

FILE ▶ **New**

Narrowing the Topic

The most important idea to keep in mind when you sit down to write is that writing is simply *communication.* We communicate in many ways. Body language, such as a raised fist, can express anger. Facial expressions, such as a smile, can express friendliness. Sometimes our tone of voice can communicate the exact opposite of what our words mean—for example, we might say, "Go ahead and do it," but what we really mean is, "If you do that, I am going to be very angry." In this instance, our tone of voice would communicate sarcasm or threat. We most commonly communicate, however, through speech. It is important to remember that when we do so, our listeners have the advantage of any combination of body language, facial expressions, and/or tone of voice to help them interpret what we are saying. In addition, there are *context clues.* If we are in a mall shopping with a friend and we say, "I would really like to have that," the listener can use the context to determine what we mean—see where we are looking or what we are holding or where we are pointing. In contrast, if we use the word *that* in writing, for example, it must be clear what *that* is.

What makes writing different from spoken communication is that the reader does not have all the clues available to a listener. The reader is relying solely on our words to determine the exact meaning. Beginning writers often don't think about this difference and start their paragraphs with vague statements or use words that are not very descriptive. As a result, the reader either does not understand the text or is not interested in it. It is, therefore, your concern as a writer to make sure that the *topic* is stated clearly and that when you move from one aspect of the topic to another you give the reader a hint that you are changing direction. You can do this either by starting a new paragraph or by using transition words such as *however, on the other hand,* or *another reason.* You also have to be sure that the words you use convey the information that is normally expressed in body language, facial expressions, or tone of voice. You will learn more about how to do this later in this chapter.

The first step in communicating well is to have a clear and defined topic. If the topic isn't specific, then you may not be able to write something interesting, and the reader may be either confused or bored. One of the first skills a beginning writer must learn is to control the topic. If you have ever experienced an overwhelming feeling of not knowing where to begin with your topic, then you may have been working with a topic that was too broad—too general. If you have a topic that is very general or that covers many aspects of a topic, then there is simply too much to say to do a good job. If entire books have been written on that topic, then how much can you say that is interesting and important in a few paragraphs?

On the other hand, if you have ever experienced not being able to think of enough to say about your topic, it may be that you have chosen a topic that is too specific—too narrow. Sometimes a beginning writer will select a fact or minor detail to write about and then find that there isn't much to say on this topic. The writer may resort to saying the same things over in different ways, but this is not a good solution to the problem.

Students will learn more about transitions later. This is introductory material.

The skill lies in choosing a topic you can narrow appropriately to one aspect about which you have something meaningful and interesting to say. Most topics can be made both broader and narrower. The appropriateness of a topic is determined by the assignment, the purpose of the writing, the length of the essay, and the intended audience.

Activities
Working with Topics

1. For the following topics, determine two broader topics and two narrower topics. The first one is done for you.

Broader	Broader	Topic	Narrower	Narrower
Communication	Communication in the business world	E-mail	E-mail privacy	E-mail privacy for teenagers
		Parent interactions with child		
		Male/female relationship skills		
		Impressions people create		
		Safety procedures		
		Behavior guidelines		
		Management styles		
		Education		
		Work ethic		
		Retirement planning		

2. The broad topic of this chapter is *communication.* Use this topic to experiment with narrowing.

   a. On a separate sheet of paper, cluster the topic of communication into as many smaller topics as you can.

   b. On the same sheet of paper, using the smaller topics as the center of another cluster, break the smaller topics into even narrower topics or subtopics.

   c. Highlight five of the topics or subtopics you would find it easiest to write about. Then write a one- or two-sentence statement explaining why these topics would be easier for you to write about than other topics.

_____

_____

_____

_____

d. Continue clustering. Break each new cluster into smaller clusters.

e. Where in the clustering did most of the highlighted topics occur (center, second level, third level, fourth level)? Why do you suppose this is the case?

_____

_____

_____

The more experienced you become at broadening and narrowing a topic, the easier it will be for you to write. An appropriately defined topic is much easier to write about than a topic that is too broad or too narrow.

Go To ▶

Students will learn to perform a limited Internet search in Chapter 11. Some students in your class, though, are likely to know how to search the Internet already. As an alternative activity, you could show students how to perform an Internet search by doing one on your computer and projecting your computer screen onto the board. This would be faster, and you could do several of the activities in the **Options:Customize** section of this chapter.

Go to the following URL: **<http://www.northernlight.com>**. This search engine is not only a valuable tool for searching the web, but when you are writing a paper, it can also be used to help you narrow a search or maybe even a topic. Key in a topic to search—in this case, *communication*. When the Northern Light search engine provides the results, look at the left side of the screen. Northern Light narrows the topic for you in *custom search folders* so that you can refine your web search, making it more specific and more relevant to your needs. What subtopics did Northern Light provide for *communication*?

_____

_____

_____

_____

_____

Now perform a search on the subtopic *communication between the sexes*. Notice the difference in the results provided by Northern Light. Which topic, the broader (*communication*) or the narrower one (*communication between the sexes*), helped you locate the best subtopics? Using one of your topics from the clustering activity on p. 55, try narrowing your topic further and see what subtopics Northern Light provides.

All of the following reading selections are about communication between men and women. As you read each selection, determine on which specific aspect or subtopic of male–female communication the selection focuses. Notice how many different approaches to the topic of male–female communication are possible.

Doing Business by Gender

Caryn Eve Murray

He's a male executive whose business persona radiates with the highest power, a man whose every decision is a muscle that ripples across the nation.

But from the start, his high-profile style of relating in business seemed decidedly, uh, unmacho.

"He would go and ask for consensus on things, seek out people's advice," displaying much of the consideration and thoughtfulness generally accorded women, says Elizabeth Miu-Lau Young, a consultant specializing on gender and communications in business.

And so, given this quality, the White House press concluded that President Bill Clinton was simply weak, indecisive, and unsure.

"Do men and women do business differently?" Young asks. "Yes. Women generally take more time to build a relationship or get to know a person, whereas men usually want to take three or four minutes to break the ice and then get down to business. That's generally, of course—not everyone."

From Caryn Eve Murray, "The Art of Deal," *Newsday*, February 27, 1994, p. 3.

Analyze the Reading

What is the narrowed topic? (Hint: Remember, it must relate to communication between the sexes but be more specific.)

_____

_____

Communication: Bridging the Gender Gap

Cultural differences and the communication problems they create are not limited to nationality or ethnic background. The same difficulties often arise during conversations between men and women. Certain techniques can improve the way men and women talk to each other.

"When men and women adapt to each other's different communication styles in the same way they adapt to the language of another country, this will help alleviate communication barriers between the two sexes," said Judith Tingley, Ph.D., a Phoenix-based psychologist and business communication consultant. Tingley has coined a term for this process—genderflex—which refers to temporarily using communication behaviors typical of the other gender to increase potential for influence.

In her book, *Genderflex: Ending the Workplace War Between the Sexes* (Performance Improvement Pros, 1993), Tingley identifies gender-specific communication barriers and presents ways to break down these barriers that hinder communication.

Source: From "Communication: Bridging the Gender Gap," from Vol. 71, HR Focus, April 1, 1994, p. 22. Reprinted by permission. © IOMA's HRFocus (212) 244-0360 http://www.ioma.com/.

Different Styles

4 Why do some men and women get frustrated when they talk to someone of the opposite sex?

5 Following are gender-specific communication differences identified in Tingley's research:

Content: Men and women prefer to talk about different things. Men favor sports, money and business. Women prefer to talk about people, feelings and relationships. There are, however, exceptions.

Style: Men want to resolve a problem; they view conversation as a competition. Women seek understanding; they want to support a conversation and use it to connect with another individual.

Structure: Men tend to get to the point without using descriptive details. Women often are detailed, apologetic and vague.

(See the *Writing Now* web site for the rest of the article and find out how you can adapt to these differences.)

Analyze the Reading

1. What is the narrowed topic?

_____

_____

Don't Ask

Deborah Tannen

1 Talking about troubles is just one of many conversational tasks that women and men view differently, and that consequently cause trouble in talk between them. Another is asking for information. And this difference too is traceable to the asymmetries of status and connection.

2 A man and a woman were standing beside the information booth at the Washington Folk Life Festival, a sprawling complex of booths and displays. "You ask," the man was saying to the woman. "I don't ask."

3 Sitting in the front seat of the car beside Harold, Sybil is fuming. They have been driving around for half an hour looking for a street he is sure is close by. Sybil is angry not because Harold does not know the way, but because he insists on trying to find it himself rather than stopping and asking someone. Her anger stems from viewing his behavior through the lens of her own: If she were driving, she would have asked directions as soon as she realized she didn't know which way to go, and they'd now be comfortably ensconced in their friends' living room instead of driving in circles, as the hour gets later and later. Since asking directions does not make Sybil uncomfortable, refusing to ask makes no sense to her. But in Harold's world, driving around until he finds his way is the reasonable thing to do, since asking for help makes

Source: Deborah Tannen, "Don't Ask," pp. 420–422 from *You Just Don't Understand* by Deborah Tannen. Copyright © 1990 by Deborah Tannen. Reprinted by permission HarperCollins Publishers, Inc. William Morrow.

him uncomfortable. He's avoiding that discomfort and trying to maintain his sense of himself as a self-sufficient person.

4   Why do many men resist asking for directions and other kinds of information? And, it is just as reasonable to ask, why is it that many women don't? By the paradox of independence and intimacy, there are two simultaneous and different metamessages implied in asking for and giving information. Many men tend to focus on one, many women on the other.

5   When you offer information, the information itself is the message. But the fact that you have the information, and the person you are speaking to doesn't, also sends a metamessage of superiority. If relations are inherently hierarchical, then the one who has more information is framed as higher up on the ladder, by virtue of being more knowledgeable and competent. From this perspective, finding one's own way is an essential part of the independence that men perceive to be a prerequisite for self-respect. If self-respect is bought at the cost of a few extra minutes of travel time, it is well worth the price.

6   Because they are implicit, metamessages are hard to talk about. When Sybil begs to know why Harold won't just ask someone for directions, he answers in terms of the message, the information: He says there's no point in asking, because anyone he asks may not know and may give him wrong directions. This is theoretically reasonable. There are many countries, such as, for example, Mexico, where it is standard procedure for people to make up directions rather than refuse to give requested information. But this explanation frustrates Sybil, because it doesn't make sense to her. Although she realizes that someone might give faulty directions, she believes this is relatively unlikely, and surely it cannot happen every time. Even if it did happen, they would be in no worse shape than they are in now anyway.

7   Part of the reason for their different approaches is that Sybil believes that a person who doesn't know the answer will say so, because it is easy to say, "I don't know." But Harold believes that saying "I don't know" is humiliating, so people might well take a wild guess. Because of their different assumptions, and the invisibility of framing, Harold and Sybil can never get to the bottom of this difference; they can only get more frustrated with each other. Keeping talk on the message level is common, because it is the level we are most clearly aware of. But it is unlikely to resolve confusion since our true motivations lie elsewhere.

8   To the extent that giving information, directions, or help is of use to another, it reinforces bonds between people. But to the extent that it is asymmetrical, it creates hierarchy: Insofar as giving information frames one as the expert, superior in knowledge, and the other as uninformed, inferior in knowledge, it is a move in the negotiation of status.

9   It is easy to see that there are many situations where those who give information are higher in status. For example, parents explain things to children and answer their questions, just as teachers give information to students. An awareness of this dynamic underlies one requirement for proper behavior at Japanese dinner entertainment, according to anthropologist Harumi Befu. In order to help the highest-status member of the party to dominate the conversation, others at the dinner are expected to ask him questions that they know he can answer with authority.

10   Because of this potential for asymmetry, some men resist receiving information from others, especially women, and some women are cautious about stating information that they know, especially to men. For example, a man with whom I discussed these dynamics later told me that my perspective clarified a comment made by his wife. They had gotten into their car and were about to go to a destination that she

knew well but he did not know at all. Consciously resisting an impulse to just drive off and find his own way, he began by asking his wife if she had any advice about the best way to get there. She told him the way, then added, "But I don't know. That's how I would go, but there might be a better way." Her comment was a move to redress the imbalance of power created by her knowing something he didn't know. She was also saving face in advance, in case he decided not to take her advice. Furthermore, she was reframing her directions as "just a suggestion" rather than "giving instructions."

Analyze the Reading

1. What is the narrowed topic?

_____

_____

You may already realize that *subject* and *topic* are often used to mean the same thing. If you have used e-mail, you have noticed that. The "Subject:" line alerts users to the field of the e-mail, giving them a chance to gather their thoughts on that subject and/or decide whether or not to read the e-mail. So the subject field acts as a screening and comprehension device, much as a title does. When you use e-mail, be sure to put a subject in the "Subject:" line. If you don't have an e-mail account or know how to use e-mail, this is a good time to learn.

This is a good place to end the homework assignment. Most instructors with access to a computer lab require students to establish an e-mail account early in the semester. If you have not already done so, this is an ideal time. If you have, you may use the information here as a follow-up. If you are not able to require students to establish an e-mail account, then you will want to skip the next class activity (pages 62–64) and substitute activities of your own or just proceed to the next section, where the homework assignment begins. The first tandem writing activity in **Options: Customize:** is a great alternative to the e-mail activity.

00:45

You may want to begin this class session by reviewing the homework. However, if your students are unfamiliar with e-mail, you may want to spend the entire class on the following activities and postpone discussion of the homework deadline until the next class.

Help Screen

E-Mail Guidelines

▶ Always sign your e-mail. E-mail addresses don't always identify you clearly to your reader, so at the end of your message, key in your name. Some programs allow automatic signature files to be added. To set up an automatic signature file, follow the directions on your e-mail site.

▶ In the "To:" line, make sure you type the complete e-mail address of the person to whom you are sending a message.

▶ Fill in the "Subject:" line with a clear phrase that indicates the topic of your e-mail.

▶ Your e-mail address has three components: (1) a *userid* (followed by @), (2) the name of your Internet service provider, or ISP (followed by .), and (3) an abbreviation that indicates the type of institution your ISP is. You might think of these as being like the address on a letter sent by snail-mail, which has (1) name, (2) street address, and (3) city and state. For example, Professor John Smith at Very Best University might have this e-mail address: *jsmith@vbu.edu. jsmith* is the userid; *vbu* is the ISP; *edu* indicates that the ISP is a school.

If .edu indicates an educational organization, what do you think the following indicate about the nature of the Internet service provider?

_____ .com

_____ .org

Commercial (for-profit business)

Organization (nonprofit organization)

Government

Network (similar to .com)

_____ .gov

_____ .net

▶ When you write e-mails, use the same capitalization as you would in an essay. Writing e-mail in ALL CAPS means you are YELLING; all lowercase means you are whispering. Both are difficult for your reader to read.

▶ Proofread your e-mail before you send it.

▶ Don't send or forward *spam*, which is junk e-mail sent to large groups of people. Commonly you will see advertisements, virus warnings (often hoaxes), and chain letters sent out as spam. It is not considered professional, or even friendly, to spam anyone.

▶ Always sign your e-mail. Unsigned e-mails, especially ones sent by class members to a teacher, for a class, are almost as annoying as spam.

Activities
Experimenting with E-mail and Subject Lines

1. Establish an e-mail account. Your instructor can let you know if your school has assigned an e-mail account to you. If your school does not have accounts available, you can obtain a free e-mail account that you can open on any computer that is connected to the Web. The *Writing Now* site has information on how to obtain free e-mail accounts.

2. Once everyone has established an e-mail account, put your e-mail address on the classroom chalkboard. Your classmates will do the same. Copy their addresses. Alternatively, your instructor can pass around a sheet of paper, asking each student to write his or her name and e-mail address on it. The instructor can photocopy the list and distribute it during the next class session.

3. E-mail the classmate whose name follows yours on the list. Use one of the following topics as a "Subject:" line and write four to five sentences on that topic.

The purpose of asking students to e-mail the classmate whose name follows theirs on the list is so that every student receives an e-mail message. You may, however, wish to use another method.

Hard Day (or Frustrating, Discouraging, etc.)

Good Day (or Special, Exciting, Memorable, etc.)

Homework Question

Grades

Schedule

After School

Exciting Movie

New CD

An Exciting Web Page

4. When you receive an e-mail, respond specifically to what your classmate wrote. The "Subject:" line of your response can and should stay the same, since a response means that you are addressing the same subject. The response for this assignment should be a paragraph of at least five sentences.

5. After you respond to your classmate's original e-mail, write and send a new e-mail to another classmate. Choose one of the other topics listed on page 63. Continue in this manner as time allows, sending and receiving e-mails. You will be both initiating new e-mails and responding to e-mails you receive.

Analyze new learning

1. Comment in writing, or in class discussion, about the effectiveness of the e-mail messages you received on a topic. In each e-mail, did your classmates stick to the topic listed in the "Subject:" line?

2. Comment in writing, or in class discussion, about the responses you received. Did they relate specifically to the issues you brought up?

 Go To ▶

1. Go to the *Writing Now* web site for a list of chat rooms that allow you to talk with your friends and classmates online. Keep in mind that there are many more chat rooms available, but we can't list them all here. If you have a favorite chat room, e-mail your classmates to let them know about it and when you will likely be online. Chat rooms make it easy for you and your classmates to meet via the Web to discuss questions you may have about your class, to get help on assignments when you have missed a class, or just to get to know one another better. Some chat rooms are more supportive of this sort of activity than others. Look for ones that let you go to a private room if you want to discuss something serious.

2. Go to the *Writing Now* web site to find the rest of the article "Communication: Bridging the Gender Gap." It will provide you with hints about how to communicate better with the opposite sex.

OPTIONS ▶ **Customize**

This activity could be added to the homework assignment that follows.

1. E-mail a selected classmate. In four or five sentences, give your opinion about the ideas stated in one of the articles you read on pages 59–62. *Be sure to use an appropriate "Subject:" line.*

2. Check out the Address Book function in your e-mail program. Each e-mail program is different, so you will need to go into yours to look for the address book and to find the directions for using it. Add your instructor's and some of your classmates' e-mail addresses to your address book. If your address book allows it, group the list of all of your classmates' e-mail addresses under one name or heading such as "writing class." Then you write one message and send it to your entire class.

3. As a class project, create a class list using special list software. Your school's computer system may support lists, or you can go to the *Writing Now* site to find places on the Web that offer free lists to groups.

You may wish to begin the second homework assignment here. The central assignment is based on this homework.

Here is an article about communication. The author, however, has narrowed the topic to a discussion of issues in teenage communication, particularly e-mail, which she then narrows again into one specific aspect that she addresses in depth. As you read this selection, determine the author's specific topic within the broader topic of e-mail. Your central assignment may be related to this essay, so read carefully and mark important ideas.

Researchers Worrying as Teens Grow Up Online

Patricia Wen

1 Teens don't understand the big fuss. As the first generation to grow up in a wired world, they hardly know a time when computers weren't around, and they leap at the chance to spend hours online, chatting with friends. So what?

2 But researchers nationwide are increasingly concerned that, as cyberspace replaces the pizza parlor as the local hangout, adolescents are becoming more isolated, less adept at interpersonal relationships, and perhaps numb to the small—and big—deceptions that are so much a part of the e-mail world.

3 From Massachusetts Institute of Technology to the Internet Addiction Center at McLean Hospital in Belmont, researchers are asking just how the futures of teenagers are changed when so many of them are spending an hour or two on the Internet each day, replacing face-to-face contact with virtual reality.

4 "We're not only looking at what the computer can do for us, but what are they doing to us," said Sherry Turkle, an MIT sociologist who has secured start-up funding for a Center for Technology and Identity. "It's on so many people's minds."

5 Turkle's center will study, among other things, how today's teens are affected by growing up with interactive computer technology. She wants to know how a teen's sense of self and values may be altered in a world where personal connections and the creation of new identities can be limitless.

6 Carnegie Mellon University in Pittsburgh is beginning a study on the long-term effect on teenagers when the computer becomes a central part of their social lives. Social psychologist Robert Kraut said he's concerned about the "opportunity costs" of so much online time for youths.

7 Kraut found that teens who used computers, even just a few hours a week, showed increased signs of loneliness and social isolation. In his 1998 study of 100 Pittsburgh families that use the Internet, Kraut said these teens reported having fewer friends to hang around with, possibly because their computer time replaced hours they would have spent with others.

Source: Republished with permission of *The Boston Globe* from Patricia Wen, "Researchers Worrying as Teens Grow Up Online," *Boston Globe,* April 21, 2000. © 2000. Permission conveyed through Copyright Clearance Center, Inc.

8   "Chatting online may be better than watching television, but it's worse than hanging out with real friends," he said.

9   The interest in cyber-chatting teens goes beyond academia. Next month, a White House conference on teenagers is sponsoring a session on teens and online behavior, including warnings about cyber-stalkers and other predators.

10   But today's teens don't see anything strange in the fact that the computer screen occupies a central place in their social lives. Just as their parents' generation quickly adjusted to microwave ovens and touch-tone phones, so have today's teens to personal computers.

11   Since 1989, when America Online burst onto the scene with chat rooms and instant-messenger systems, teens flocked to them by the millions. Traffic soared in the mid-1990s when AOL developed a "buddy list" for the instant-messenger system, enabling teens to know when friends were online, and then start a conversation. If all the buddies wanted to e-mail at once, they could enter their own chat room.

12   Teenage use of computers grew even more over the last two years, thanks to the steep drop in prices of personal computers. About 40 percent of U.S. households now have a computer, and nearly 70 percent with incomes more than $50,000 have them, according to the Yankee Group, a Boston-based technology research firm.

13   Not surprisingly, AOL reports a spike in instant-messenger traffic in the mid-afternoon, just after school lets out. Teens say it's little different than the rush at McDonald's after 2 P.M. as adolescents look for ways to unwind.

14   "School is stressful and busy. There's almost no time to just hang out," said Parker Rice, 17, of Newton South High School. "Talking online is just catch-up time."

15   Many teens acknowledge there's an unreal quality to their cyber-space communication, including their odd shorthand terms, such as POS (parent over shoulder) or LOL (laughing out loud). Psychologists see this code as part of the exclusive shared language that teenagers love.

16   When it comes to e-mail exchanges, teens also show a remarkable tolerance for each other's fudges or deceptions. Nor are they surprised when a mere acquaintance unloads a personal secret through e-mail. Nobody seems to expect the online world to be the same as the real world.

17   While waiting outside school recently, Rice recalled a timid boy in class who recently got up the nerve to send her an e-mail. At the end, he issued an uncharacteristically macho send-off, "Later, Babe."

18   "He'd never say that to me face to face in school," said Rice, more amused than annoyed. "Sometimes people try to seem more self-confident online."

19   And consider the fact that Jonathan Reis, 14, of Somerville, didn't seem the least bit put off when a girl who had described herself online as slender turned out to be quite heavy. "I know it's likely they'll say they look better than they are," he said while shopping at the Cambridge Side Galleria.

20   Teens say they also appreciate the ability to edit what they say online, or take the time to think about a response. As cowardly as it may seem, some teens admit that asking someone for a date, or breaking up, can be easier in message form.

21   But they insist there's no harm intended, and cyberspace has become just another medium—like the telephone—in the often-clumsy, experimental world of adolescence.

22   Echoing the view of these youths, Turkle, an MIT specialist in the computer's impact on human behavior, sees cyberspace as the new elec-

tronic "playspace" for adolescents, an escape from the pressure of everyday life.

23   While she worries about some safety issues, Turkle said the anonymity and distance of cyberspace allow young people to try out new identities. For instance, an artistic boy can admit to an interest in fashion or an awkward girl can reach out to some new friends with little fear of rejection. Shaping their own identities and forming strong peer groups are among the most central themes of adolescence, she said.

24   "The Web is the location where much of the work of adolescence is being done these days," said Turkle.

25   But other researchers don't think everything is so benign, worrying that some teens will mistake the "weak social ties" so easily found among e-mail buddies for genuine friendship.

26   "These are not the kind of relationships that will sustain you if you have a personal crisis or a death in the family," said Harry Waxman, a psychologist and chair of the Project on the Internet and Human Behavior at Harvard Medical School.

27   Waxman and others worry about raising a generation of teens who, as adults, would rather solve a dispute through e-mail than in person. In some ways, the Internet exacerbates the trend toward isolation and away from community that Harvard government professor Robert Putnam has described as "bowling alone."

28   Beyond the issue of social isolation, a small group of researchers speculates that the developing neural connections in the brains of teens could be affected by such intense involvement with the computer screen.

29   "If you restrict your experience to staring in front of the screen, you may be short-changing your brain," said Dr. Martin Teicher, head of developmental biopsychiatry at McLean Hospital.

30   In fact, McLean Hospital has already set up an Internet Addiction Center for teens as well as adults who fear computers are harming them psychologically.

31   Maressa Hecht Orzack, its coordinator, said she gets many teenage patients, often youngsters who are socially marginalized or among the "bright and bored." She's eager for more research to be done on the impact of online life on teens, saying the good and bad of the medium are not yet fully known.

32   "These young people may be losing connections to real objects," she said.

Analyze the Reading

1. What was the topic of e-mail narrowed to?

_____

_____

2. Highlight the thesis in green. Highlight the main supporting details in blue and the examples in yellow.

_____

_____

Here are the introductory paragraphs from another newspaper article on
e-mail. Notice how, although the topic is e-mail, it has been narrowed to
another aspect of e-mail. As you read, determine the narrower topic.

E-Mail Activism

Siona LaFrance

1   E-mail, so useful for staying in touch with friends and family, has become an indispensable civic tool, helping neighborhood leaders and
community activists spread news fast, strengthen ties, and when the
need arises, quickly mobilize residents.

2   It already may have saved one piece of New Orleans history.

3   The Arts Council of New Orleans' plans earlier this year to raze the
Bradford Furniture Co. building prompted a firestorm of protest from
preservationists, especially after workers removed the 30-year-old alu-
minum panels that covered the structure, revealing a yellow brick
façade with fanciful terra cotta ornaments.

Source: Siona LaFrance, "E-mail Activism," *New Orleans Times-Picayune*, August 10, 2000,
p. E1.

Analyze the Reading

1. What specific topic within the overall subject of e-mail does this writer
    address?

When you reply to an e-mail message, you are writing a response. One
kind of writing is very helpful in narrowing a topic appropriately. It occurs
when you are writing in response to something, usually a piece of writing.
However, response writing also occurs in other circumstances, such as when
writing essay exam answers, writing a letter to an editor (or a congressional
representative), or writing a letter to an employer discussing a concern.

Because you are writing in response, you are necessarily narrowing the
topic to the specific issue you are responding to. This makes *response* one of the
easiest types of writing.

In the following reading selection, you can see how differently people can
respond to one topic and also see the differences in how males and females
might communicate. This "story" was written by two authors. The first author
wrote a paragraph and gave it to the second author. The second author continued the story by writing the next paragraph and then returning the paper to
the first author to continue the process. This is supposed to be a real piece of
writing that came out of a university writing classroom similar to your classroom.

This assignment was actually turned in by two of my English students:

Rebecca <last name deleted> and Gary <last name deleted>
English 44A
Creative Writing
Prof. Miller
In-Class Assignment for Wednesday

Today we will experiment with a new form of writing called the tandem story. The process is simple. Each person will pair off with the person sitting to his or her immediate right. One of you will then write the first paragraph of a short story. The partner will read the first paragraph and then add another paragraph to the story. The first person will then add a third paragraph, and so on back and forth. Remember to reread what has been written each time in order to keep the story coherent. The story is over when both agree a conclusion has been reached.

1   At first Laurie couldn't decide which kind of tea she wanted. The chamomile, which used to be her favorite for lazy evenings at home, now reminded her too much of Carl, who once said, in happier times, that he liked chamomile. But she felt she must now, at all costs, keep her mind off Carl. His possessiveness was suffocating, and if she thought about him too much her asthma started acting up again. So chamomile was out of the question.

2   *Meanwhile, Advance Sergeant Carl Harris, leader of the attack squadron now in orbit over Skylon 4, had more important things to think about than the neuroses of an air-headed asthmatic bimbo named Laurie with whom he had spent one sweaty night over a year ago. "A.S. Harris to Geostation 17," he said into his transgalactic communicator. "Polar orbit established. No sign of resistance so far . . ." But before he could sign off a bluish particle beam flashed out of nowhere and blasted a hole through his ship's cargo bay. The jolt from the direct hit sent him flying out of his seat and across the cockpit.*

3   He bumped his head and died almost immediately, but not before he felt one last pang of regret for psychically brutalizing the one woman who had ever had feelings for him. Soon afterwards, Earth stopped its pointless hostilities towards the peaceful farmers of Skylon 4. "Congress Passes Law Permanently Abolishing War and Space Travel," Laurie read in her newspaper one morning. The news simultaneously excited her and bored her. She stared out the window, dreaming of her youth—when the days had passed unhurriedly and carefree, with no newspapers to read, no television to distract her from her sense of innocent wonder at all the beautiful things around her. "Why must one lose one's innocence to become a woman?" she pondered wistfully.

4   *Little did she know, but she has less than 10 seconds to live. Thousands of miles above the city, the Anu'udrian mothership launched the first of its lithium fusion missiles. The dim-witted wimpy peaceniks who pushed the Unilateral Aerospace Disarmament Treaty through Congress had left Earth a defenseless target for the hostile alien empires who were determined to destroy the human race. Within two hours after the passage of the treaty the Anu'udrian ships were on course for Earth, carrying enough firepower to pulverize the entire planet. With no one to stop them, they swiftly initiated their diabolical plan. The lithium fusion missile entered the atmosphere unimpeded. The President, in his top-secret mobile submarine headquarters on the ocean floor off the coast*

of Guam, felt the inconceivably massive explosion which vaporized Laurie and 85 million other Americans. The President slammed his fist on the conference table. "We can't allow this! I'm going to veto that treaty! Let's blow 'em out of the sky!"

5   This is absurd. I refuse to continue this mockery of literature. My writing partner is a violent, chauvinistic, semi-literate adolescent.

6   _Yeah? Well, you're a self-centered tedious neurotic whose attempts at writing are the literary equivalent of Valium._

7   You total jerk!

8   _Stupid airhead!_

Analyze the Reading

1. What was the overall topic of this writing?

_____

2. How did the two writers handle their topic differently?

_____

_____

3. Could you have told the two writers apart by their writing even if the same typeface had been used? Explain.

_____

_____

4. As they continued to write, the writers stopped responding to the story and began responding to each other. Why do you think that happened?

_____

_____

OPTIONS ▶ Customize

You may want to do the following activities in class and end the homework assignment here. If you choose any of the items from **Options:Customize,** you may want to begin class with them.

1. Choose a writing partner. Via e-mail or by handing a piece of paper back and forth, write a story *in tandem.* One of you will write the first paragraph and the partner will respond by writing a second paragraph based on what was written in the first paragraph. This will continue until time runs out or the story is finished to the satisfaction of both writers.

2. If you don't have access to e-mail in class, you can use paper or overhead projector blanks to create your tandem story. Just write your part of the story on the paper or overhead blank and pass it on to your partner, continuing until you come to a conclusion.

3. Another twist to this assignment is to have a partner or partners in another class. You can hand in your first paragraph to your instructor, who will keep it until a later class. The instructor will then hand the papers out to those students, collect their additions, and return them to you. You can do this project over several weeks until your story is finished.

4. If your instructor has a contact at another school, you might be able to establish an e-pal relationship. Partner with a student from another school to do your tandem writing.

FILE ▶ Create

00:45

It is helpful to do the following exercise in class as a prewriting activity.

The more ideas generated by the class that can be used by the students in writing the individual essay, the better. The more scaffolding students get at this point, the more they will learn and the better the work they will be able to do later, independently. If many of the essays students write are making similar points or using the same examples at this point, that is fine. Students will become more independent as the process continues.

Response Essay

1. Break into small groups. Select a group member to keep brief notes and discuss your responses to "Researchers Worrying as Teens Grow Up Online." Explore how others agree or disagree with the points made in the article. Let those group members with e-mail experience share their experiences. Determine if you have any parents of teenagers in your group who may have something to relate on this subject. Is there much disagreement within your group?

2. Review the notes from your discussion. As a class, share the notes. What are the similarities and the differences in the responses from group to group? Is there much disagreement between groups? Discuss whether there is enough material in the group notes to generate an interesting essay. Is there enough material to support two sides of the argument?

3. Individually, take notes on the in-class discussion from number 2 above, jotting down points that support your views. Add any additional examples that have come to mind as a result of the class discussion.

4. Cluster as a prewriting activity to see if you can generate any more ideas in response to "Researchers Worrying as Teens Grow Up Online."

Now you are ready to turn your cluster into a rough outline so that you know where to begin writing. You may want to use a highlighter first to identify the ideas in your cluster you want to use. You can color code to organize these ideas.

In the next chapter, students move from the paragraph to the essay—from one paragraph on a topic to three or more. Chapter 4 discusses adding detail and developing the essay further, so at this point students are just jotting down the details for these paragraphs as best they can. If you feel your students aren't ready to tackle a longer essay, you may wish to change this sequence. For now you may not want to give students a suggested length or number of paragraphs. You could just tell them to write down their ideas on the topic and to make sure that all of their ideas relate to the topic. You will be able to see what students do with this task on their own and to estimate their experience and expertise. Chapter 4 will help students make the transition to several paragraphs.

These outlines will become more detailed as students learn more about the writing process and incorporate more aspects, such as audience and purpose.

Name: _____   Date: _____

Write an outline:

Topic: _____

  I. First key point:

     Supporting details:

  II. Second key point:

     Supporting details:

  III. Third key point:

     Supporting details:

FILE ▶ Save As

You may want to begin the homework assignment here. In addition to assigning the writing, it is important to ask students to read the essay on pages 79–80 in the next chapter, so that they will be ready for the first Chapter 4 class activity.

Response Essay

Write an essay in which you respond to "Researchers Worrying as Teens Grow Up Online." First, decide if you agree or disagree with the author. Then formulate your assertion. By formulating your assertion, you narrow the topic. Now you are ready to draft your ideas. Use any of the ideas generated by group and class discussions. Pay careful attention to the topic and make sure that all of your supporting ideas relate to the specific topic as you have narrowed it.

Save your essay as a draft. In the next chapter you will learn some ideas about how to organize and expand your supporting ideas.

After you have written your essay, read pages 79–80 in Chapter 4.

Go To ▶ Go to one of the chat rooms listed on the *Writing Now* web site to observe how people respond to each other. Since the people in the chat room are "talking" to each other without benefit of body language, do they do anything special to let people know what feelings are behind their words?

C:\Prompts for Writing ▶

Any of these activities may be substituted for the central assignment. If it is too early in the semester for students to access the web site easily, or if they do not have timely access, you may go to the web site, print the articles mentioned, and distribute them to the class.

1. Select one of the other reading selections in this chapter and respond to it.

2. Write a one-paragraph response to each of three reading selections in this chapter. Notice how the responses are different, depending on what you are responding to.

3. You probably know what a dress code is. Does a dress code policy relate in any way to a speech code, as discussed here? Write about your experiences with dress codes, either on the job or at school, and discuss whether you believe they accomplished the purpose they were intended to meet.

4. In the article "Parent-Child Speaking Differentiated by Gender Early On" (found on the *Writing Now* web site), Michelle Trudeau asserts that "the way a child communicates largely defines that child, so it is critically important . . . that parents from the beginning be aware how they are speaking—for children are listening, imitating what they hear, and themselves talking the way that the language has been presented to them." Respond to this statement in three paragraphs.

CHAPTER 4
We Are Not Alone

Never doubt that a small group of thoughtful, committed citizens can change the world. Indeed, it is the only thing that ever has.

Margaret Mead

Chapter Contents

Log On ▶ **Reflection**

Write whatever comes to mind when you read the chapter title and opening quotation.

_____

_____

_____

_____

_____

_____

_____

_____

_____

_____

_____

_____

_____

_____

_____

_____

_____

_____

_____

_____

_____

_____

_____

Students should have read pages 79–80 before beginning this class session. This session consists primarily of analyzing an essay in detail. You'll want to allow sufficient time for that.

FILE ▶ Open

00:05

Even if you can allow only 5 minutes for **File:Open,** it is critical for activating students' schemas—for allowing them to make connections. Students need to begin with the familiar and experience giving "right answers" and success before experimenting with the unfamiliar. These questions prepare students for peer revision. They also prepare them for peer scaffolding in which stronger students help weaker students when working collaboratively.

Connecting with Previous Learning

▶ How would you describe your experiences working collaboratively in this class so far?

▶ Do you think you learned better working in a group or by yourself so far? Explain. List some advantages and some disadvantages of working in a group.

▶ How would it help if another student read your essay before you submitted it?

▶ Would you be able to help another student improve his or her essay? If so, how?

Connecting with Writing

▶ Why does an author add details after stating the main point?

▶ What do details contribute to a piece of writing?

Connecting with Experience

▶ What are the similarities between the words *skinny, slim, slender, scrawny,* and *thin?* What are the differences? What factors would determine the words you would choose to describe someone?

▶ How could you tell that a person was angry if all he or she said was, "Why are you doing that?"

▶ What are some possible interpretations of the statement: "Do you think you can handle that?" How would you know which interpretation was intended?

▶ What is meant by "tone of voice"?

▶ Could writing have a tone? If so, how would the writer get it across to the reader?

FILE ▶ New

If you want to begin with these activities in class, students should have been assigned to read pages 79–80 for homework. You may wish to spend the class period completing pages 80–82 as a class or in small groups. Students will work with topic sentences in the next chapter. This activity is introductory.

From Paragraph to Essay

Once you have decided on a topic and narrowed it, you need to identify what you want to say about your topic. What you want to say is partly determined by how you narrow the topic and by whether you are responding to someone else's position on the topic. A one-sentence statement of your main point about the topic is known as a *topic sentence.* It contains the main idea of the paragraph.

Usually the first or second sentence in a text makes the main point of the paragraph. That is the topic sentence of the paragraph. A clearly stated topic sentence helps readers understand and prepare for what is discussed in the paragraph. In some paragraphs, the topic sentence is the last sentence. It summarizes the information for readers so that they are sure to get the point.

Not every text, however, directly states the topic sentence. Sometimes the main point of the paragraph can be implied. You, the reader, are able to determine the main point of the paragraph through the *supporting details* and *examples* that are given. These details and examples support the *main idea* of the paragraph even though the main idea is not stated outright but is implied. In this chapter you will analyze supporting details and examples of paragraphs and learn how to turn one paragraph into an essay of several paragraphs by adding additional detail.

In summary, every paragraph has a main idea. If it is stated directly, that sentence is called a topic sentence. From now on, when you read texts in this course, you should highlight the topic sentence of every paragraph in blue. Doing this will help you understand the author's points and help you write in response to them. If the paragraph doesn't directly state its topic sentence, you can highlight the topic and key words that relate to the topic. The next chapter will help you develop further the skill of finding main ideas.

In order to write a good paragraph, you will find it easier, as a beginning writer, to begin with a strong topic sentence. The next chapter will give you more instruction on writing topic sentences. In doing the assignments for this chapter, just be sure that you are making a statement about the topic you have selected.

Have students focus here on the concept of *topic* and on sticking to their topic.

Examining Topic Sentences

1. Refer to your clusters on the writing process from Chapters 1 and 2. How do the circles in Level 2 of the clusters relate to the idea of topic sentences?

_____

_____

2. How do the ABCs in your outline relate to the idea of topic sentences?

_____

_____

After you write a topic sentence, your next step in getting your brainstormed ideas onto paper is to support it with details and examples that you brainstormed earlier. Again, you will continue to work on this skill throughout the book. For this chapter, concentrate on learning to expand and develop your ideas, making sure your ideas relate to the topic of the paragraph.

Up to this point, you may have written only one paragraph about a topic. Now you will learn to develop your ideas from those suitable for one paragraph to those suitable for a two-, three- or four-paragraph essay. In this chapter you will turn the central assignment into a longer essay on one topic.

As you learned in Chapter 3, each paragraph focuses on one central idea or topic. A writer includes in a paragraph only the ideas that pertain to the subject or topic of the paragraph. However, a writer can write several paragraphs on one topic. In this case, each paragraph focuses on a narrower aspect of the topic.

In other words, writing several paragraphs on one topic requires you to break your topic down into smaller parts. Each paragraph could either focus on a narrower part of your overall topic or provide a particular example to support the overall topic.

To understand how paragraphs are organized, it is helpful to examine how other writers organize their paragraphs. First, analyze the following text. This is a paragraph about the stereotype that women talk more than men.

1   Most people will say that they agree with the stereotype that women talk more than men. However, there are no studies to prove that this is true. Furthermore, although we may *say* that women talk more, inside we often know that it isn't the case. Although people often make stereotypical statements, if called upon to make a judgment, they can base their judgment on actual behavior rather than on a stereotype. Once people get to know a person, they tend to judge the person as an individual rather than according to stereotypes.

Read the following text on the same subject. Notice how the essay is based on the ideas given in the previous paragraph. However, the ideas stated in the single paragraph above have each been expanded into a full paragraph in the essay below that clarifies and gives facts and examples as support.

Talking Like a Lady: How Women Talk

Francine Frank
Frank Anshen

1   Perhaps the most common stereotype about women's speech is that women talk a lot. If we take "a lot" to mean more than men, we are faced with the surprising fact that there seems to be no study which supports this belief, while there are several which show just the opposite. One such study, by Otto Sonder, Jr., is particularly interesting. Sonder organized discussion groups which included women and men and assigned them specific topics. The discussions were recorded and transcribed, but in the transcripts, the participants were identified only by letters, as A, B, etc. Panels of judges who tried to identify the sex of each speaker from these transcripts were correct about fifty-five percent of the time, a result which is better than chance, but not overwhelmingly so. Closer examination of the data, however, reveals some interesting facts. A word count of the recorded discussions showed a clear tendency for the men who participated in the study to utter more words than the women. In other words, men, on the average, actually talked more than did women. Even more interesting is the fact that individuals of either sex who talked a lot were more likely to be judged as males, while taciturn individuals of either sex were more likely to be identified as females. Not only does this study suggest that men are more talkative, it also suggests that the judges "knew" this fact and used it to make judgments about the sexual identity of unknown speak-

Source: Reprinted from *Language and the Sexes* by Francine Frank and Frank Anshen, by permission of the State University of New York Press © 1983, State University of New York. All rights reserved.

ers. Although, consciously, they would probably subscribe to the cultural stereotype of the talkative woman, their judgments show that they knew that the real situation is the direct opposite of the stereotype.

2 How can we reconcile this apparent contradiction between our beliefs and our actions? It seems that people have an incorrect conscious stereotype of how much women and men talk, while at the same time having, at a less conscious level, the knowledge that men tend to speak more than women. When called upon to make judgments, they use their knowledge of actual behavior rather than the stereotype of presumed behavior. We are reminded of individuals in pre–Civil War America who thought slaves were lazy, in spite of the fact that they observed them doing backbreaking work from sunup to sundown.

3 Students of stereotypes believe that our preconceived notions influence our expectations and responses during initial contacts with strangers. However, when we get to know people even slightly, we usually treat them as individuals and ignore the stereotypes. This is commonly recognized as the "Some of my best friends are . . ." syndrome. We may, for example, believe that girls are, in general, more social than boys, even though that may not be true of our own children or, indeed, of any children we know well; or we may believe that women are more talkative than men, although members of our family or circle of friends do not act that way.

00:40

We introduce the topic of thesis here but cover it in more detail and expect mastery of it in Chapter 5.

Although we recommend that this activity be done in class since students need much scaffolding and explanation, students could possibly work in small groups if you feel that they have read the material and have sufficient ability to help each other understand it well. Later in this chapter students will become aware of the importance of group work and peer revision; after that, you will probably want students to work in groups as often as possible.

Point out to students that one long, detailed paragraph thoroughly explains and supports the authors' statement. Highlighting will help students see the relationship between the sentences. This practice will continue throughout the textbook, so it is important to establish its relevance early on. Not only does color enhance memory and learning, but it also models for students how much support is involved in each main idea. Consistency in the use of colors will help students keep the concepts straight. Don't let the fun of using different colors minimize the fact that students are doing something important. Of course, students could underline in these colors if they preferred.

Analyze the Reading

1. Highlight the first sentence of paragraph 1 in green. This is part of the *thesis* of the entire article. Although you will learn more about it as time goes on, for now it is important to know that the thesis is the main idea of the entire article. You will look for a thesis in everything you read and you will highlight the thesis statement in green. Like main ideas of individual paragraphs, sometimes thesis statements are implied and you won't find them stated directly in every text.

2. Highlight the second sentence of the first paragraph in blue. This is the main idea of the first paragraph, also known as a *topic sentence* for that paragraph.

3. What follows that main idea in that paragraph? If you find examples, highlight them in yellow. If you find facts, highlight them in pink. You will do this for all of the reading selections throughout the rest of this course. Sometimes you will find only one long example, explained in detail. Sometimes you will find a series of facts. Of course, there may be any combination of supporting material included in a paragraph.

4. Now compare the yellow and pink sentences to the blue one. Do the yellow and pink sentences relate to the blue one? How?

_____

_____

_____

5. Do you think the yellow and pink sentences help you understand the blue sentence? Explain your answer.

_____

Have students *attempt* to write a thesis statement here, but it is probably not necessary at this time to spend time to correct their thesis statements or teach about thesis statements. This task foreshadows the learning to come; it allows students to gain a little familiarity with thesis statements.

6. The yellow and pink sentences (facts and examples) should always support the blue sentence (topic sentence) or green sentence (thesis). Is that true in this case? Explain.

_____

_____

_____

7. Examine the last sentence of the first paragraph. This is an example of a main idea placed at the end of a paragraph. Highlight that sentence in green. This is another part of the author's overall *thesis.* The ideas outlined in green in every paragraph can be combined to give the overall *thesis* or main idea of the entire text. Now try to write the ideas presented in the two green sentences as one simple statement below:

_____

_____

_____

8. How is the first sentence of the second paragraph different from the others? (From now on, we'll use a number format, such as 2:1, to indicate paragraph 2, sentence 1.)

_____

_____

The thesis statement asks a question; the rest of the paragraph answers the question.

9. What does the rest of paragraph 2 do?

_____

_____

10. Turn 2:1 into a sentence instead of a question. Write the sentence on the following lines and highlight the sentence in blue—both below and in the text. You are writing a topic sentence for the paragraph.

_____

_____

_____

11. The author gives an example in paragraph 2. Highlight the example in yellow.

To answer the question . . . to explain the main idea in detail.

12. Notice the remaining sentences that are not highlighted. What is their function in the paragraph?

_____

_____

_____

However, it shows the contradiction between what is believed to be the case and what is actually the case. You may want to spend time explaining that what comes *after* the word *however* is the important part of the paragraph. Often students commit the error of thinking the first sentence is the main idea and then they have the completely opposite idea of what they should be getting from the paragraph.

13. Read 3:1 and 3:2. Circle the key word *however.* What does it do?

_____

_____

14. Which sentence states the main idea of the paragraph, the one before the word *however* or the one after? Highlight it in blue.

15. What does 3:3 do?

_____

_____

_____

16. Highlight the example in paragraph 3 in yellow.

17. Turn back to page 79 to reread the brief summary. Where did these ideas come from?

18. What have you learned about expanding a topic from one paragraph to three from this activity?

_____

_____

_____

_____

_____

In this chapter students are not spending much time on the concept of adding details. At this point, they are being introduced to the concept. When students become more experienced with the writing process, the work that focuses on adding details to support assertions will make more sense to them. Because writing is a recursive process, the introduction of steps can be done in a simplified version first and then in more detail later.

19. What have you learned about developing your ideas with facts and examples from analyzing this text?

_____

_____

_____

_____

20. Using the central assignment you drafted in Chapter 3, find your main ideas. On a separate sheet of paper, list them. List all supporting information under the main ideas. Add information as necessary to fully support each idea. Turn this outline into a second draft of your central assignment. This second draft will be more fully developed and better organized than your first draft.

Go To ▶ Go to a news site on the Web, such as CNN.com, and print an article about a current event. Highlight the thesis in green, main ideas in blue, examples in yellow, and facts in pink. How do topic sentences help you understand the story quickly?

TOOLS ▶ **Language**

Word Choice and Tone

In addition to improving your writing by adding interesting facts and examples, you will want to use specific and descriptive words that convey what you really mean. Again, the purpose of writing is to communicate. Sometimes you are communicating more than facts; you are communicating your feelings or attitudes toward those facts. Since readers cannot hear your voice or see your facial expression, you have to convey your attitude through the *tone* of your writing, which is similar to tone of voice in speaking. Tone can be conveyed through appropriate *word choice.*

For example, if you are sending an e-mail to a friend, complimenting her about how she looked at a party, you might want to say how trim she looked. All of the following words mean trim, but only some of them say it in a complimentary way. Circle all words that would be flattering to your friend. Underline the ones that would be insulting.

skinny, scrawny, thin, slim, emaciated, slender, petite

Now if you were writing an e-mail to your friend *about* someone else whom you did not like, which words would you use to describe the person you didn't like?

_____

Which words would you prefer people to use when they are referring to you?

_____

Are any of these words neutral in tone? Explain.

_____

This is the power of words. Therefore, you want to choose your words carefully. Many friendships have been lost over e-mail that was well intended but whose word choice conveyed the wrong tone. Read the following article about the perils of word choice in e-mail.

Be Careful of the Drawbacks in Hasty Use of E-mail

Stephen Wilburs

1 The problem with e-mail communication is that it is easily misunderstood. Its most attractive attributes—speed and convenience—are linked to its chief drawbacks. Operating within its culture of quickness and immediacy, writers tend to fire off hastily composed messages that are disorganized, incomplete and ambiguous.

2 Imagine, for example, that you have received an e-mail message from your boss requesting you to present a proposal at next week's staff meeting. You don't mind the assignment, but you're preoccupied with other matters at the moment, so you respond by simply typing "Fine" and hitting the Send button. On opening your message, your boss sees your one-word response and interprets your tone as sarcastic, as in "Fine. Just what I wanted. Another assignment. As if I don't already have enough work to do." The reason for the miscommunication? In your haste to respond promptly, you responded briefly, relying on your intended tone to convey your meaning. It's a common error.

3 By its nature e-mail communication encourages a personal, informal style of writing, a feature most people view as attractive. Writers get into trouble, however, when they assume that readers actually can hear their voices. Although e-mail may be more like oral communication than traditional forms of written communication, it's still writing, not speaking. Your reader cannot hear the inflection of your voice. To guard against this type of misunderstanding, take this simple precaution: Include a goodwill statement in every message you send.

4 Rather than write "Please come prepared to discuss the report," for example, add another sentence: "As always, I value your experience and insight."

5 Rather than "Fine," write "Fine. Happy to do it." Rather than "Well, you did it again. Would you mind adapting your presentation for our board?" write "Well, you did it again. Great job! Would you mind adapting . . ."

6 A goodwill statement is like an insurance policy. It protects you from being misunderstood. Including it reduces the risk of miscommunication when you are writing quickly.

7 Here are some additional tips to help you use e-mail effectively:

- Include a purpose statement. Although not always necessary in a rapid exchange between two writers, a purpose statement orients your reader to your message. If you find yourself beginning a message with one point in mind then adding three other points, go back to the top and add an introductory statement such as "I have four questions for you."

Source: Stephen Wilbers, "Be Careful of the Drawbacks in Hasty Use of Email," Minneapolis *Star Tribune*, September 3, 2000 is reprinted with permission of the author. Minneapolis consultant Stephen Wilbers offers training seminars in effective business writing.

- Write in short paragraphs. Nearly everything you write can be divided into three parts: introduction, body, closing; or—to use the three-step memo approach—purpose, background, proposed action. To communicate in chunks of unbroken text is discourteous to your reader.

- Stick to the point. When you ramble or express yourself incompletely, you increase the chances of being misunderstood. It's fine to be informal and playful, but always write with a sense of purpose.

- Don't write in anger. It's a lose-lose endeavor. You risk appearing foolish, and you are likely to elicit an angry response from your reader. Don't let the ease of using e-mail tempt you to fire off a hot one.

- Don't write anything you don't want the whole world to see. E-mail is notorious for the speed and ease with which confidential information can be disseminated—often to just the wrong person or persons. Remember, in online communication there's no such thing as privacy.

- Proofread your writing. Although occasional typographical errors might be tolerated by your reader, always read over what you have written at least once to check for clarity and accuracy.

8   In today's frantic workplace, where nano-seconds seem like hours, speed is a virtue, but sometimes slowing down a little is the surest way to reach your destination.

Analyze the Reading

1. What did you learn about *tone* from reading this text?

_____

_____

_____

2. What did you learn about the effect of word choice on your writing?

_____

_____

_____

3. Highlight the first sentence in green. It is the thesis statement of the entire piece.

4. How did the author support his point about miscommunication in e-mail?

_____

_____

_____

5. Highlight the examples that support the author's thesis statement in yellow.

6. Note that each tip begins with a topic sentence. Highlight the topic sentence in blue.

In an article about miscommunication arising from cultural differences in the meanings of facial expressions, Steve Emmons also illustrates the importance of communicating your tone when writing.

1 In face-to-face communications, it's the face that does the most important communicating, Mr. Tang says. Certain things are just understood. You understood my intentions by seeing my facial expression. It's efficient; I don't have to say it. It becomes a cultural norm. . . .

2 But when it comes to verbal communication, adding facial expression sometimes is vital. To avoid misunderstandings, smiling face images are often added to electronic mail to make sure the reader understands the statement is meant to be friendly or joking.

Analyze the Reading

Have you ever made the smiley face, : -) or ☺, in your e-mails? If so, why?

_____

_____

This is an opportunity to make students aware of the difference between passive and active voice and how it subtly changes the tone of writing. When looking at the reading "Words as Weapons," discuss which phrases are passive and which are active. Discuss the impact of both types of phrases.

Creating a tone can be achieved not only with word choice, but even with the use of a passive verb instead of an active one. If you aren't sure of the difference between passive and active verbs, see if you can figure it out by reading the following selection. As you read, notice how word choice and the use of passive voice affects tone.

Students enjoy responding to this essay. If you have time, you may want them to write an essay in response to it or e-mail each other with responses. This activity is given as an alternative under **C:\Prompts for Writing**, page 97.

Words as Weapons

Richard Mitchell

1 Imagine that the postman brings you a letter from the Water and Sewer Department or the Bureau of Mines or some such place. Any right-thinking American will eye even the envelope in the same way he would eye some sticky substance dripping from the underparts of his automobile. Things get worse. You open the letter and see at once these words: "You are hereby notified. . . ." How do you feel? Are you keen to read on? But you will, won't you? Oh, yes. You will.

2 Here comes another letter. This one doesn't even have a stamp. It carries instead the hint that something very bad will happen to any mere citizen caught using this envelope for his own subversive purposes. You open it and read: "It has been brought to the attention of this office. . . ." Do you throw it out at that point because you find it too preposterous to think that an office can have an attention? Do you immediately write a reply: "Dear So-and-so, I am surprised and distressed by the rudeness of your first ten words, especially since they are addressed to one of those who pay your salary. Perhaps you're having a bad day. Why don't you write again and say something else?" You do not. In fact, you turn pale and wonder frantically which of your misdeeds has been revealed. Your anxiety is increased by that passive verb—that's what it's

Source: From *Less Than Words Can Say* by Richard Mitchell. Copyright © 1979 by Richard Mitchell. By permission of Little, Brown and Company Inc.

for—which suggests that this damaging exposure has been made not by an envious neighbor or a vengeful merchant or an ex-girlfriend or any other perfectly understandable, if detestable, human agent, but by the very nature of the universe. "It has been brought." This is serious.

3   Among the better class of Grammarians, that construction is known as the Divine Passive. It intends to suggest that neither the writer nor anyone else through whose head you might like to hammer a blunt wooden spike can be held accountable for anything in any way. Like an earthquake or a volcanic eruption, this latest calamity must be accepted as an act of God. God may well be keeping count of the appearances of the Divine Passive.

4   Another classic intimidation with which to begin a letter is: "According to our records. . . ." It reminds you at once, with that plural pronoun, that the enemy outnumbers you, and the reference to "records" makes it clear that they've got the goods. There is even a lofty pretense to fairness, as though you were being invited to bring forth *your* records to clear up this misunderstanding. You know, however, that they don't suspect for an instant that there's anything wrong in their records. Besides, you don't *have* any records, as they damn well know.

5   Such frightening phrases share an important attribute. They are not things that ordinary people are likely to say, or even write, to one another except, of course, in certain unpleasant circumstances. We can see their intentions when we put them into more human contexts: "My dear Belinda, You are hereby notified . . ." conveys a message that ought to infuriate even the dullest of Belindas. Why is it then that we are not infuriated when we hear or read such words addressed to us by bureaucrats? We don't even stop to think that those words make up a silly verbal paradox; the only context in which they can possibly appear is the one in which they are not needed at all. No meaning is added to "Your rent is overdue" when the landlord writes, "You are hereby notified that your rent is overdue." What *is* added is the tone of official legality, and the presumption that one of the rulers is addressing one of the ruled. The voice . . . puts you in your place, and, strangely enough, you go there.

6   We Americans make much of our egalitarian society, and we like to think we are not intimidated by wealth and power. Still, we are. There are surely many reasons for that, and about most of them we can do nothing, it seems. But one of the reasons is the very language in which the wealthy and powerful speak to us. When we hear it, something ancient stirs in us, and we take off our caps and hold them to our chests as we listen. About *that* we *could* do something—all it takes is some education. That must have been in Jefferson's mind when he thought about the importance of universal education in a society of free people. People who are automatically and unconsciously intimidated by the sound of a language that they cannot themselves use easily will never be free. Jefferson must have imagined an America in which all citizens would be able, when they felt like it, to address one another as members of the same class. That we cannot do so is a sore impediment to equality, but, of course, a great advantage to those who *can* use the English of power and wealth.

7   It would be easier to see bureaucratic language for what it is if only the governors and bureaucrats did in fact speak a foreign tongue. When the Normans ruled England anyone could tell the French was French and English, English. It was the government that might, rarely, pardon you for your crimes, but it needed a friend to forgive you for your sins. Words like "pardon" and "forgive" were clearly in different languages,

and, while either might have been translated by the other, they still meant subtly different acts. They still do, even though they are both thought of as English words now. Modern English has swallowed up many such distinctions, but not all. We still know that hearts are broken, not fractured. This is the kind of distinction Winston Churchill had in mind when he advised writers to choose the native English word whenever possible rather than a foreign import. This is good advice, but few can heed it in these days. The standard American education does not provide the knowledge out of which to make such choices.

Analyze the Reading

1. How did this essay help you understand the concept of *tone?*

_____

_____

_____

_____

_____

2. What did you learn about word choice from reading this text?

_____

_____

_____

_____

He begins with examples and then makes his point.

3. Mitchell does not organize his essay in the typical fashion. Instead of presenting his topic first and developing it with facts and examples, he begins his essay differently. How is it different?

_____

_____

_____

4. Explain how the title gives you a clue to the topic of the reading.

_____

_____

_____

5. Highlight all of the examples in yellow.

The rest of the paragraph gives the example.

6. 1:1 introduces an example. What does the rest of the paragraph do?

_____

Changes the topic to another letter and number example.

7. The first sentence in paragraph 2 (2:1) does what?

_____

Gives the example.

8. What does the rest of paragraph 2 do?

_____

Introduces another example.

9. Look at 4:1. What does the sentence do in that paragraph?

_____

Blue for main idea. We know the statement gives away the answer, but this is a learning process, not a quiz. It teaches students while they are engaged in the thinking process.

10. Highlight 5:1 and 5:2 in the color that you think it should be: (overall thesis = green; main idea = blue; examples = yellow; facts = pink). Notice that it takes two sentences to create the main idea for this paragraph.

11. Highlight 7:1. Did the author explain that statement in the paragraph? Do you agree with that statement? Explain.

_____

_____

_____

12. In what other ways can words be used as weapons?

_____

_____

_____

This is the homework assignment. Students should come to the next class with a rough draft so that they can participate in peer revision during the class.

Using a different color ink, go through your draft of the central assignment, changing general words into more specific words that convey your tone. In the top right-hand corner of your draft, write a word that describes your overall tone. See the Tone box below for ideas for labeling tone.

Tone			
angry	controlled	formal	hypocritical
arrogant	cynical	grave	impassioned
bitter	decorous	happy	impersonal
casual	defiant	hateful	informal
cheerful	elaborate	hopeful	ironic
comic	factual	humorous	jovial

joyful	opinionated	reasonable	serious
light	optimistic	reserved	sincere
mocking	personal	sarcastic	somber
nostalgic	pessimistic	satirical	straightforward
objective	plainspoken	scornful	subjective
offhanded	playful	sentimental	

OPTIONS ▶ Customize

Students could make a mini-poster illustrating tone using their writing sample, labeling it, and highlighting key words.

1. Bring examples to class that illustrate tone. You can refer to the Tone box above to give you an idea of various tones used in the example you chose. You may use junk mail, letters to the editor of newspapers or magazines, or advertisements.

2. Rewrite an earlier essay from this class in a very different tone. Notice how changing the tone can affect your purpose, your message, and your audience.

3. Check out **<http://www.plumbdesign.com/thesaurus>**. This site describes itself as "an exploration of sense relationships within the English language." By clicking on words, you follow a thread of meaning, creating a spatial map of linguistic associations. Explore the site and describe what it does. Could it help you add detailed, descriptive words to your writing?

4. Before the next class, notice who talks more in a mixed-gender gathering—the men or the women. Be prepared to discuss your findings in class or use your findings as an example in a response essay.

Experiment with Tone

1. Refer to the tandem writing activity in Chapter 3, page 69.

   a. How did the "two writers" differ in their tone?

   b. How did their tone change as the writing continued?

   c. How was their word choice different?

00:45

You will probably want to devote the first half of class to discussing students' answers to the homework questions. The following activities are good for group work or general class discussion.

You may want to give students a set amount of time in small groups or individually to write as many words as they can. Then put all of the words on the board and, as a class, mark the positive and negative words. Encourage students to use more descriptive words in their writing.

2. Experiment with alternative word choices. For each of the following words, come up with as many alternatives (synonyms) as you can.

a. talkative friend

b. thrifty parent

c. persistent salesperson

d. modest home

e. budget motel

Now highlight the pleasant-toned words above in yellow and the unpleasant-toned words in green. Find three descriptive words that are neutral and highlight them in blue.

Have you noticed that some of the words on your lists are more interesting, more descriptive, than others? Try to use these words in your writing. Instead of saying, "She is a fun friend," you could describe your friend as "outgoing, vivacious, energetic, daring, creative, humorous," and so forth. These descriptive words will convey the intended tone in your writing and make your writing more interesting.

Go To ▶ 1. Go to the Capital Community College site, **<http://ccc.commnet.edu>** and click on: College Web Pages; Guide to Grammar and Writing; Essay and Research Paper Level; Tone; to read, "Tone: A Matter of Attitude" for additional examples to aid in your understanding of tone.

FILE ▶ **Edit**

`00:45`

Peer Revision for Details and Word Choice

In Chapter 3 you wrote a response to a reading selection, getting all your thoughts on the subject down on paper. At the beginning of this chapter, you organized your thoughts into main points and supported those points with facts or examples. Finally, you examined your word choice for appropriate tone. You now have a *draft* that you are ready to turn into a finished essay.

The procedure for turning a draft into a finished text is *revision*. One of the most important steps in revision is having another person read your text and make suggestions. When you write a text, you know what you mean, so what you write seems clear to you. When someone else reads it, however, the point may not be as clear to that person. Also, you don't notice all your mistakes when you read your own paper because we often see what we want to see, or what we think is there, instead of what is really on the page. This happens to everyone, including professional writers. The more experienced a writer, in fact, the more he or she seeks feedback at various stages in the writing process.

You are fortunate in that you are in a classroom with your *peers*—people like yourself or people in the same position as you. Therefore, you can take advantage of *peer revision*, seeking feedback from and giving feedback to classmates. You will gain some experience with peer revision now and continue to use the process throughout the rest of this course. You will find it a useful technique in future courses and in career writing as well.

Peer revision can be accomplished in many ways. The simplest way is for two people to exchange papers and give each other written and/or verbal feedback. A round robin lets you read the work of, and get feedback from, every member of a group. Peer revision can even be done via e-mail, attaching your text to an e-mail message.

In addition to various methods, peer revision has many purposes. You may want someone to read your paper to see if you have clearly supported your point. You may want your classmates to tell you if your explanation is clear. Peers often proofread the very last draft of a text for language conventions, spelling, and so forth. Sometimes, as in a writing classroom, peer revision accomplishes all of the above—you examine your classmates' paper in light of everything you have learned about writing to that point. You will make any helpful suggestions that your own experience enables you to give.

Keep in mind, however, that when you receive feedback, you must combine it with your own sense of what you have done and decide whether or not the feedback is helpful. You may prefer to keep your work as you have written it. Sometimes feedback is factual and sometimes it borders on opinion. You will make the final decision about how you use the feedback you receive.

In this chapter you will be seeking feedback primarily on those aspects of the writing process you focused on in this chapter: topic, adequate support of topic, word choice, and tone. Before submitting your paper for review by a classmate, read it once again and check for the following:

1. Do you have a clearly stated topic, with a different focus in each paragraph?

2. Does each paragraph support and elaborate on your topic?

3. Are your examples well developed, and do they help the reader understand your point?

4. Is your word choice interesting? Is it appropriate to the topic and your attitude toward the topic?

5. Is the tone of the paper clear? Can the reader determine your attitude toward your subject?

(*Note:* When you read your classmate's paper, you will also focus on the above questions and provide feedback on the questions. If you notice any other areas of improvement, please suggest them as well. But when offering suggestions, remember to keep your tone helpful.)

Your instructor will ask you to participate in some type of peer revision at this point. However, some basic considerations apply to all methods of peer revision.

Respect is the key word. Respect yourself first. If you respect the time and effort you are putting into succeeding in college, you will understand how you want to be treated. Also respect your classmates and their writing.

Know that most writers do not work by themselves. Friends, writing groups, and professional editors read and comment on their work. By happy

You may want to have students take their completed essay and engage in peer revision. During this editing section, students will focus primarily on strength of support (good examples to support points) and word choice (do the words convey the intended tone?). In the following chapters, students will focus on other aspects of writing, incorporating everything they have learned so far. If during peer revision students see other areas that need improvement or notice inappropriate language use, they should note and correct them in their revisions. But your expectations of the students' writing ability may want to focus on what has been learned and practiced so far—support and word choice.

coincidence, the more you help your classmates make decisions about their writing, the easier it will be to make good decisions about your own. In other words, you will learn to write better by helping others improve their writing.

Make sure you and your peers are, as the saying goes, "reading from the same page." After you read a classmate's work, answer the Peer Revision Worksheet questions on page 95. If your answers are similar to the writer's answers, you are on the right track and can begin revising. If your answers are vastly different, then you need to discuss what the writer meant the answers to be and where the essay misled you into coming up with different answers.

Try to start your feedback with something positive. Say what you like about the essay first, then ask questions about what you don't understand or need more information on. The writer should be making notes about your response now and deciding later what to include and what not to include in his or her essay. It's best not to say, "This part is wrong." If it looks wrong to you, try to find out what the writer intended by asking questions. Once you understand, work with the writer to change the wording so that it means the same thing to both of you.

Stay on task. You are revising a paper, not commenting on your peer's life. Don't say, "I like the way you handled the problem with your girlfriend." Instead say, "I like the way you *described* the way you handled the problem with your girlfriend. After reading about it, I can see clearly what you did and why you did it." Deal with how well the essay expresses the writer's thoughts and actions, not whether you agree with them.

If you work in a peer group instead of a partnership, discuss the roles of group members. You might want one person to warn members if someone gets off task, another to be the leader to say whose paper will be discussed next, and another to manage time if you have a specified amount of work to cover in a limited time period. You might even want a note taker so that the writer can interact in the discussion without having to stop to write things down. Trade roles so that everyone participates fully.

Help Screen

Revising Using a Word Processor

To change a font, move a section of text, or delete a section of text, you must first "select it." To select a section of text, hold the right mouse button down and move the cursor over the text you want to select—moving left to right and then down. You will see the selected text is now highlighted. After you have highlighted the text, you may do the following:

To change the font and type size of your essay, highlight the passage you want to change and then choose the font and size you want to use. You can change the font and size of the type by going to the toolbar at the top of your computer screen. Select Tools from your toolbar. When the drop down menu appears, select "font." There you can change the font and type size of your essay. If the font stays the same, you probably forgot to select the passage you wanted to change.

To move a passage, select and highlight the appropriate material, then cut it. You can cut by going to Edit, Cut; by using the Cut button on the toolbar (scissors); or by holding down the Control key and pressing the X key. Paste the material by selecting the space where you want it to go and choosing Edit, Paste; by using the Paste button on the toolbar (clipboard); or by holding down the Control key and pressing the V key. (*Memory trick*: The V is an arrow pointing down into the space where you want your text to go.) A slightly safer way to do the same thing is to copy the material (Control plus C key), paste it, then go back and cut it from its original location.

The Delete key (DEL) deletes forward, the Backspace key (BKSP) deletes backward. The Insert key (INS) is a toggle (on–off) key. If you start typing in the middle of a passage and the INS key is engaged, what you type will be inserted at the point of the cursor. If it is not engaged, then what you type will type over your existing text. If you are typing and what you wrote before starts disappearing, letter by letter, press INS to toggle back to Insert.

You may want to model this activity for your class by having a volunteer read his or her paper aloud; then having the class answer the questions together. Ask the writer if the class had the same answers as he or she did.

"While there may be no one-to-one relationship between peer comments and revision, these studies, particularly the qualitative ones, suggest a range of real and potential benefits for students participating in an effective community of responsive peers."

Andrea W. Herrmann, from the ERIC database. For the full text, see the bibliography provided at the end of the START section: **<http://ericae.net/ db/edo/ED307616.htm>**

PEER REVISION WORKSHEET

Reviewed by: **Date:**

Focus of review: topic sentence, support, word choice, and tone

Reviewing paper written by:

Peer Revision Questionnaire

Ask yourself the following questions about your draft. Then, if possible, ask a friend or classmate to read your draft and answer the same questions about it. If your answers do not match, you haven't succeeded in communicating what you think you did. Where answers don't match well, discuss them together and try to think of ways to make your essay clearer.

▶ What is this essay about? (topic)

▶ What is the event or situation that prompted the essay? (prompt)

▶ What do you have to say about your topic? (thesis or main idea)

▶ What personal experience (life, reading, TV, stories you've heard, etc.) have you had with this topic?

▶ Is there anything else the reader should know? Are there any questions in the reader's mind left unanswered by the essay?

FILE ▶ Save

You may want students to submit this worksheet with their essay. You can use the worksheet to give students feedback.

After carefully examining your topic, support, word choice, and tone and after making appropriate changes suggested by your peers, you are ready to do a final edit. Perform all the proofreading and revision techniques you have learned so far. Use this checklist to review your paper a final time. Print or rewrite a neat version of your paper and submit it to your instructor.

Revision Checklist

❏ I have arranged my ideas in an order appropriate to the topic.

❏ I had someone read and annotate my essay.

❏ I have an appropriate title.

❏ I have a clearly stated topic.

❏ I have developed a topic that is appropriate, neither too broad nor too specific.

❏ All paragraphs support my overall topic.

❏ Each paragraph has a different focus relating to my topic.

❏ Each paragraph has well-developed supporting examples and/or facts.

❏ I revised my word choice to use descriptive and appropriate words.

❏ My tone is clear and consistent throughout the essay.

Proofreading Checklist

❏ I have read each sentence aloud, starting with the last one first and working backward to make sure that each sentence is clear and uses appropriate language conventions.

❏ I used my proofreading frame to check for spelling.

❏ I asked a classmate to read my draft and to complete the Peer Revision Worksheet.

The exercises on this page are an important feedback for you. They allow you to see if learning is taking place.

C:\Prompts for Writing ▶

This can be a powerful assignment or class discussion to motivate students to learn as much as possible in this course.

Try to allow time to discuss 6:8 from "Words as Weapons" even if you do not have time for students to write about it.

This is an easy essay for students to write. They can easily recall situations in which words have been used as weapons against them, from name calling to threats to mockery.

1. Experiment with tone in a personal letter.

   a. Write a letter to yourself from your teacher, telling you how you are doing in this class. Write the sentences using a very unpleasant tone. Try using the passive voice, as illustrated in the reading by Mitchell.

   b. Now write a letter from your teacher using a very pleasant tone.

   c. Write two to four sentences explaining how you were able to create the two different tones.

2. Practice critical thinking. Examine 6:8 in "Words as Weapons." Write the sentence at the top of a sheet of paper and respond to it. What does it mean for you in terms of applying yourself in this course?

3. Write a response to "Words as Weapons." Each paragraph will be an example of how words can be weapons.

4. Write about a time when you were involved in a misunderstanding. Describe what happened; then explain how communication could have been clearer so that the misunderstanding would not have happened.

5. Use the Tone box for tone words to expand your understanding.

   a. Choose a word from the tone box on pages 89–90 to define for the class. Your definition should be descriptive enough so your classmates can guess the tone word used.

   b. Make a collage using photographs of faces cut from magazines. Label the photographs with tone words that characterize the facial expressions depicted in the photographs.

   c. Choose a tone word from the tone box on pages 89–90. Based on the word you select, write two or three sentences about a party you attended. Have classmates guess your tone from your word choice.

Log Off: ▶ **Review and Reflect**

Take some time to reflect on what you have learned about writing in this chapter. How has your writing changed as a result of the discussions, readings, and activities in this chapter?

_____

_____

_____

_____

_____

_____

_____

_____

_____

_____

_____

_____

Compare what you wrote in **File: Save As** in Chapter 3 to your final version in this chapter's **File: Save**. How are the two versions different?

_____

_____

_____

Which version is better, and why?

_____

_____

_____

_____

What surprised you in this chapter?

_____

_____

_____

_____

Chapter 5
I Know *This* about Computers . . .

I think there is a world market for maybe five computers.

—Thomas Watson, chairman of IBM, 1943

Computers in the future may weigh no more than 1.5 tons.

—*Popular Mechanics*, forecasting the relentless march of science, 1949

There is no reason anyone would want a computer in their home.

—Ken Olson, president, chairman, and founder of Digital Equipment Corporation, 1977

640K ought to be enough for anybody.

—Bill Gates, 1981

Chapter Contents

Log On ▶ **Reflection**

Write whatever comes to mind as you read the chapter title and opening quotations.

_____

_____

_____

_____

_____

_____

_____

_____

_____

_____

_____

_____

_____

_____

_____

_____

_____

_____

_____

_____

_____

FILE ▶ Open

Remember that it is important to begin a new lesson with a no-fail activity. Even if time is short, try to fit in a few minutes for at least part of the connecting exercises and the first activity.

In this chapter, you may want to select one or two items from the connecting exercises for freewriting. Then address all of the items in small groups or as part of a class discussion.

Different words used to signify the same concept can be confusing to students. Our objective here is for students to realize that subjects and topics are the same. If they already know about subjects, they already know about topics, too.

Connecting with Experience

▶ How has computer technology affected your everyday life?

▶ How has it affected your school work?

▶ List as many advantages and disadvantages of widespread computer use as you can.

▶ What are the advantages of the Internet?

▶ What are the disadvantages of the Internet?

▶ How has the Internet affected communication between or within groups of people?

Connecting with Previous Learning

▶ In Chapter 3 you worked with the concept of the topic. List as many subtopics of the topic *computers* as you can think of in 3 minutes. Turn each topic into a sentence expressing a personal opinion. For example, for the topic *e-mail,* you might say, "I spend too much time on e-mail."

Connecting with Concepts: Assertion

▶ What does it mean to be *assertive*?

▶ In the sentence, "Tanya asserted that she was not in the wrong," what do you think *asserted* means? Explain and then give a synonym.

▶ What do you think an *assertion* might be?

Connecting to Writing: Subject and Topic

▶ If you are the *subject* of a conversation, what are you?

▶ If you are the *topic* of conversation, what are you?

▶ Describe the relationship between the words *subject* and *topic.*

▶ Relate this to your understanding of the subject of a sentence.

▶ What else must a sentence have in addition to a subject?

▶ Based on your answer to the above question, what else might a topic have to have?

Connecting to the Topic

▶ Cluster the term *technology* on a separate sheet of paper.

Connecting to New Material

▶ In small groups, discuss your individual experiences and skill levels in working with computers. List the computer skills that each individual has and put the names of the students beside the skills they bring to the group. If you don't yet have computer skills, list the writing skills you may have, such as the ability to think of topics, write effective sentences, use conventional language, and proofread. Add those skills to the list. Copy the list so that everyone has a copy of this master list. If you have questions or need help with the computer, you can refer to the master list for the appropriate contact person.

FILE ▶ New

Topic/Assertion = Thesis Statement

Most academic essays have a thesis. A thesis consists of two parts: a topic and an assertion. The *topic* is the subject of the essay. The *assertion* is the key point being made about the topic. For any given topic, a variety of assertions could be made.

For example, if the topic were *a college education,* the following are just some of the possible assertions that could be made. A college education

▶ is very expensive.

▶ is critical to getting a good job.

▶ is overrated.

▶ is different today from twenty years ago.

▶ changes people.

If you wrote one paragraph for each assertion listed above, each of these paragraphs would be very different from each other. Each paragraph would require a different set of details to develop its assertion. Can you see how the assertion controls the paragraph or the essay?

The *thesis statement* in an essay is the author's topic *plus* his or her assertion about the topic. The rest of the essay develops and supports the author's thesis by developing and supporting the assertion made about the subject.

Beginning writers often encounter difficulties when they choose a topic and begin writing without first formulating an assertion about that topic. Since they don't know what to say about a topic that, without an assertion, is probably far too general, what they write is vague and uninteresting. You may have already discovered this problem in your own writing.

If you consciously formulate an assertion about your subject, however, you are narrowing your topic and giving it direction—both steps that make for a much more interesting essay.

Experiment with Assertions vs. Topics

1. This exercise will help you see how the topic is different from the assertion. For each of the following topics, select an appropriate assertion from the list provided on page 106.

00:25

We believe it is important to do the next assignment as a class or in small groups so that students have some positive, successful experience in working with assertions.

a. Children

_____

_____

b. Medical information on the Web

_____

_____

c. Libraries

_____

_____

d. Teenage hackers

_____

_____

e. Online relationships

_____

_____

f. Parents who let children surf the Web unsupervised

_____

_____

g. Censorship on the Web

_____

_____

h. The elderly

_____

_____

i. College students on the Internet

_____

_____

j. Chat rooms

_____

_____

k. Privacy on the Web

_____

_____

Assertions

• Improve the lives of the lonely, disabled, or shut-in.

• Are simply curious.

• Can cause problems in marriages.

• Can be dangerous.

• Can be harmful to other relationships.

• Should be prosecuted.

• Can seem real.

• Will promote better health.

• Should block access to certain sites.

• Can keep in touch with family to a better degree than before.

• Should allow minors to surf the Net.

• Are taking risks.

• Can become addictive.

• Benefit by searching for medical information and by making friends online.

• Undermines our freedom.

• Can help each other with homework.

• Are failing in their duties.

• Can save time doing research.

• Is a necessity.

• Can cheat by plagiarizing from the Net.

• Spend too much time on the Net.

• Is a false security.

• Benefit from early exposure to computers.

• Should use computers but not get online.

Every assertion begins with a verb.

2. What does every assertion begin with?

_____

3. Choose three of the topics listed on pages 105–106. Write a sentence using each of the three selected topics, creating your own assertion about a topic. Next, pair up with those who selected one of the same topics as you. Compare how different your assertions are.

4. Individually or in small groups, write assertions about each of the following topics found on pages 105–106. Then, as a class, compare assertions. Notice how many different assertions were written for each topic. Discuss how each assertion would change the kind of detail that would go in a paragraph.

    • Word processing

    • The Internet

    • Cell phones

    • Video games

    • Fax machines

    • E-mail

    • Web cams

    • Chat rooms

    • Internet blocking devices in libraries

This activity becomes part of the central assignment. You may want students to begin it in class or do it as a homework assignment.

5. Choose one of the four topics on pages 105–106 about which you would enjoy writing. Brainstorm on this topic, coming up with as many details as possible. This will be part of the central assignment for this chapter, so choose a topic about which you have something to say.

Go To ▶ Go to the *Writing Now* web site, to find links to online writing labs (OWLs). Choose two or three sites, and see how the links present the idea of a thesis. Write a statement in your own words to remind yourself what a thesis is.

OPTIONS ▶ **Customize**

To compare your assertions with those of other groups in the class, you may write your assertions on the board. Computers, however, offer many other ways for groups to communicate with each other.

▶ **E-mail options:** You can create a *group mailing list* in your e-mail address book. Messages sent to the group you create will go to all members at once. Each e-mail program does this a bit differently, but if you go to the Help screen in your e-mail program and look for help under *group* or *list*, you should be able to figure it out.

You can create a *mailing list that people can subscribe to* (for free). Every subscriber receives all messages. If you create a mailing list, you'll want to remind subscribers to pay special attention to creating a subject line so that readers can scan and delete messages pertaining to subjects that don't affect them. You can find links to mailing list hosts at the *Writing Now* web site.

You can also set up a *threaded forum*. As with a mailing list, all subscribers can read all messages. The messages, however, don't go directly to subscribers. Subscribers have to go to a web site to read the messages. This kind of program works like a bulletin board, but messages are grouped by topic. The subject line for the first message in each *thread*, or subject, is very important. Readers can choose to respond to a message that starts a new thread, they can respond to another response, or they can start a new thread. You can find links to threaded forum hosts on the *Writing Now* web site.

If you use one of these e-mail options, remember to treat it as a professional or academic space, and do not e-mail the entire class with junk e-mail messages, known as *spam*.

▶ **Courseware,** such as Blackboard, WebCT, Norton Connect.net, or Daedalus is a kind of educational software that offers a variety of ways for groups to communicate. If you are already using one of these programs, now is a good time to explore the options they offer for group communication.

▶ **Chat rooms** and **MOOs** offer spaces on the Web for groups to meet, as well as a variety of options for recording and displaying the discussions that take place. Chat rooms and MOOs are introduced in the next chapter, and more detailed information can be found on the *Writing Now* web site.

▶ **Document-sharing software** is more often found in business settings than in classrooms. If your school has purchased such a program and makes it available to students, it might be worth a try. Courseware often has a document-sharing option that allows all students to see a document and make suggestions to change it.

▶ **What other options are there?** On the Web, you can probably find *white-board* sites, where people can write notes to each other; *graffiti* sites or software that allows graffitilike writing; and even guestbook programs, where people can sign in and leave messages. Share ideas with your classmates and with us by e-mailing *Writing Now.* If you come up with a new idea we can post to our web site, we'll let everyone know it was your idea.

This is a good place to begin the homework assignment. You may want to end the assignment on page 112. As part of the homework assignment, assign students to bring to class their brainstorming list or map for the topic they selected in activity 5, page 107.

Begin your study of assertions by reading the following essay, "What Computers Can, Cannot, and Should Not Do," and identifying its assertions by highlighting them in blue.

What Computers Can, Cannot, and Should Not Do

Timothy Trainor
Diane Krasnewich

Computers exist to benefit and assist people, not to replace them. Computers cannot, for example, make emotional judgments, disobey instructions entered by humans, read people's minds, or replace interpersonal relationships. On the contrary, people must be extremely explicit in instructing a computer to perform even the simplest commands. What computers can do, however, is extremely helpful. They can

- Store data in vast amounts
- Process data quickly and accurately

Source: Timothy Trainor and Diane Krasnewich, "What Computers Can, Cannot, and Should Not Do." *Computers,* McGraw-Hill, 1994, pp. 12–14. Reproduced with permission of The McGraw-Hill Companies.

- Simulate possible outcomes based on a given set of conditions

- Recommend or take action based on output

2   Computers cannot be effective unless the people using them are able to identify what results they need and how to achieve those results. Ultimately, computers are dependent upon people.

3   Accordingly, people should not relinquish their decision-making responsibilities to computers. Humans need to be on hand to interpret conditions reported by computers, particularly if medical treatment, national defense, air traffic control, or even loan processing is involved. Nonprogrammable, human factors must complement computer readouts for a complete and fair analysis.

4   At times computers may appear to make decisions. In monitoring a refinery, for example, a computer might trigger a fire-extinguishing system. Another computer, used for monitoring vital signs, might regulate the flow of oxygen to a patient. In both cases, however, although the computer initiates action, it does not make a decision. Rather, the decisions of these process control systems were made by the human beings who programmed the machines to respond to a particular set of conditions. Therefore people must take complete responsibility for a computer's actions. They must anticipate all potential problems and direct computers to avoid them.

5   While computers may be able to enhance a person's capabilities, they can never adequately replace interpersonal relationships. Even the most sophisticated computing machinery cannot supplant parent-to-child and teacher-to-student relationships. Similarly, the rapport between physician and patient is essential for successful treatment.

6   People, then, are an integral part of any computer system that accepts input, processes it, and delivers output. People control computer systems through program design, by monitoring operations, and by making final decisions based upon computer output. They should not give up decision-making responsibilities because the human qualities of analysis, reasoning, and compassion are required to interpret computer-delivered results.

Analyze the Readings

1. Highlight the topic sentence of each paragraph in blue. Underline the topic once and the assertion twice in each highlighted sentence.

2. Which assertion is the main one—the thesis statement—for the entire essay?

For the following excerpts, highlight the topic sentence in blue. Underline the topic once and the assertion twice.

E-mail in the Workplace

Barry Reece and Rhonda Brandt

1 The telecommuting trend is increasing dramatically. The greatest boost to this trend has been the expansion of electronic mail, often referred to as E-mail. E-mail is a message you send or receive through a computer and its modem (the computer's connection to a telephone line). During recent years, most companies have added E-mail capabilities to their computer networks. In such companies, a salesperson calling on a customer can receive up-to-date information on the status of the customer's order by means of a quick E-mail message to the shipping department. An executive could convene an emergency meeting of all department managers by transmitting an E-mail message directly to their computer monitors. With the inception of the Internet, the service that links computers and databases of libraries, universities, and government agencies throughout the world, E-mail can now travel on a massive global communications "superhighway."

2 As E-mail use expands, subtle advantages are beginning to surface. E-mail is now referred to as the "great equalizer." Because the sender's gender and skin color are not immediately obvious, prejudiced attitudes are less likely to alter the message. Before E-mail, lower-level workers had little access to the president or CEO of their organizations. Now they can contact these individuals electronically without anyone in between misinterpreting, sabotaging, or blocking the message. In addition, electronic messages are a wonderful alternative for those individuals who are painfully shy and find it difficult to express themselves when communicating with others face to face.

3 Despite all these advantages, E-mail has some disadvantages you should be aware of if you are going to be using it. Because E-mail is used to speed up the communications process, many people compose and send hastily written messages, which can be confusing. If you have to send a second message to clarify your first message, E-mail does not save you any time.

Source: Reece, Barry L. and Rhonda Brandt, *Human Relations: Principles and Practices.* Copyright © 2000 by Houghton Mifflin Company. Reprinted with permission.

Hint: The assertion in the following paragraph is *implied*. This means that it is not specifically stated in one or two sentences. You must read the entire paragraph and formulate the assertion in your own words. Instead of highlighting the assertion, write it on the lines below. Then underline the topic once and the assertion twice.

Problems with E-mail

William M. Pride, Robert J. Hughes, and Jack R. Kapoor

1   Spam does not always come in a can. When *spam* is used in reference to e-mail, it means the electronic version of unsolicited junk mail flowing into the more than 90 million e-mail addresses in operation around the world today. "Spamming" has become so bothersome that a district court in Ohio recently upheld CompuServe's right to block what it calls "trespassing." In addition, web sites have been established to help users delete their names from spam lists, and computer software companies are developing e-mail filters to screen out the clutter spamming creates.

_____

_____

_____

2   In addition to e-mail clutter, legal issues surrounding the misuse of e-mail are a bigger problem than ever before. A federal court recently ruled against an employee who sued because he had been fired after his employer read his e-mail. Two employees of another company are suing other employees for messages they construe to be racist and creating a "hostile environment." Since invasion of privacy laws involving e-mail messages are not clearly defined at the state or federal levels, firms are beginning to establish their own policies for employees' use of e-mail on company computers.

From William M. Pride, Robert J. Hughes, and Jack R. Kapoor, *Business,* Sixth Edition (Boston: Houghton Mifflin, 1999), p. 427. Copyright © 1999 by Houghton Mifflin Company. Reprinted with permission.

Sometimes an author takes several sentences to state an assertion, or thesis, and several paragraphs to explain it fully. Read the following excerpt of several paragraphs and find the assertion. Highlight the assertion and underline as the topic once and the assertion twice.

Unfair Access to Technology?

Michael N. Milone, Jr., and Judy Salpeter

1   Among the issues that face educators in the next decade, perhaps none is more important than providing all students with comparable educational opportunities, particularly with respect to technology. To understand how important schooling—and indirectly, exposure to technology—is to a student's future, one need look no further than the U.S. Department of Labor's 1992 publication, *What Work Requires of Schools: A SCANS Report for America 2000.* In the report, the authors assert that "More than half of our young people leave school without the knowledge or foundation required to find and hold a good job." The report was not addressing technology specifically, but given the rapid infiltration of technology into all careers, the inference one can draw is that today's young people are not being prepared as well as they should be to succeed in tomorrow's highly technical careers. . . .

2   If we begin with a look at the home scene, it becomes clear that there is a serious gap between higher-income students, many of whom have access to personal computers, and children from families that lack the resources to purchase such hardware.

3   The Link Resources Home Media Consumer Survey found that, in 1995, almost 42 percent of households with children had a personal computer. As computer prices drop, middle-income homes are gaining greater access. For example, a new study from Dataquest indicates that 52 percent of the people planning to buy a home computer during the next year have household incomes of $40,000 or less. Nevertheless, this leaves a sizable group of children whose families still cannot afford a home computer.

4   How can schools deal with this inequity? As T&L columnist Daniel Kinnaman pointed out in his April 1994 "Leadership Role" column, some educators might be tempted to respond by forbidding students to use home computers to complete assignments. After all, he quotes one teacher as saying, "Not every student has a computer at home, so it's unfair for those that have computers to use them." Kinnaman's response: "That's not equity. That's foolishness. Not every child has two parents at home either. Should we tell those who do that they can get help from only one parent?"

5   Taking away access from one group is clearly not the solution. But the inequality of home access does place a greater burden on schools to provide technology resources to students (and families) with the greatest need for them. How are we doing with this difficult task?

Source: From Michael N. Milone, Jr., and Judy Salpeter, "Technology and Equity Issues," *Technology and Learning*: January 1996, 38–47. Copyright © 1996 CMP Media, Inc. Reprinted by permission of *Technology and Learning* magazine (800-607-4410).

Perhaps after a brainstorming session on your topic you still aren't sure of your assertion. You just have a list of details. How can you examine this material in a way that will help you formulate an assertion? One technique, called *grouping,* works well after a brainstorming session in which you list facts and ideas. Here is a list of details one student developed as a result of brainstorming. (This student used listing instead of clustering, so the details appear in no particular order.) The topic the student brainstormed was *telecommuting.* Telecommuting means that instead of actually commuting to the office in a car or other means of transportation, the employee works from home and communicates with the office using electronic devices, usually computer, fax, and telephone. As you review the list, look for logical groupings and think of possible assertions that some of the details could support.

Telecommuting

Highway congestion	Global connectivity
Desktop computers	Flexible work hours
Less wear and tear on the car	Take work on vacations
Cable modems	Appearance matters less
Company Intranet	Work in comfortable clothes
Networking	Fewer sick days
High cost of office space	Reduced workforce
Frequent interruptions	Reduced office space costs
Longer work hours	Online chat
Fewer transfers to another location	Videoconferencing
Multiple phone lines	Slow connections
Document-sharing software	ADSL connections
Less interaction with coworkers	Reduced road rage
Lifestyle needs	Increased productivity
E-mail	Fax machines
Isolation	Laptop computers
Interruptions of family life	Federal clean air laws
Child care problems	Less supervision

Analyze the details

1. Underline all of the details that would support the assertion: *Many factors contribute to the growth of telecommuting.*

2. Circle all details that support this assertion: *Technology makes telecommuting possible.*

3. Highlight in yellow all details that support this assertion: *Telecommuting can increase flexibility and enhance productivity.*

4. Highlight in pink all details that support this assertion: *Telecommuting has some drawbacks.*

5. Highlight in blue all details that support this assertion: *Telecommuting offers many benefits for corporations.*

Some details work with more than one assertion.

6. What did you notice about the details you selected?

_____

_____

_____

7. Write an assertion of your own about telecommuting.

_____

_____

_____

_____

8. Write three details to support your assertion.

a. _____

b. _____

c. _____

9. Reflection: What did you learn from this exercise?

_____

_____

_____

_____

_____

_____

_____

_____

_____

It is a good idea to organize the material from a brainstorming session into a map. If you mapped or clustered as you brainstormed, then you will want to rewrite your material into a neatly organized map. (Remember, when you are generating ideas, you don't want to focus too much on the organization. It is better to organize your ideas after you have finished your creative, idea-generating session.)

Examine how mapping affects your list of details by completing the following:

1. Using the cluster diagram below, cluster the information from the *telecommuting* list on page 114 into an organized map. Notice that the diagram has several levels. Level 1 is the topic: *telecommuting*. Level 2 (main ideas) has five circles shooting off the central topic of telecommuting. These five circles each has details shooting off them (Level 3). Additional levels can be added by shooting off the Level 3 circles.

   As you can see, the cluster diagram has been started for you. Continue filling in the diagram until you have added all the details from page 114. Add additional circles as needed to place all the information into the diagram.

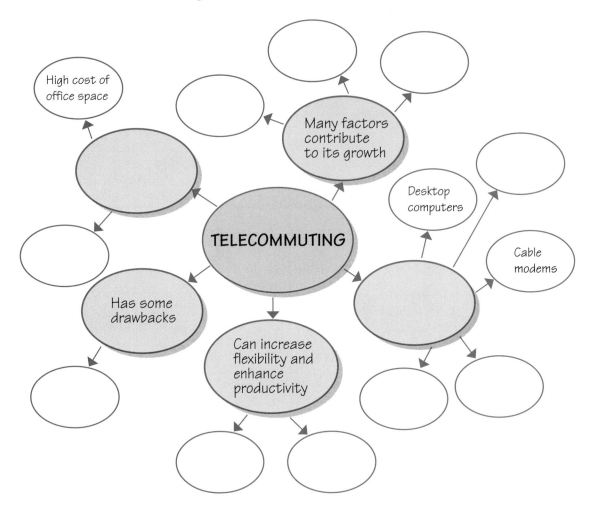

2. Using information you have brainstormed that was not included in the original list on page 114, add additional information (circles) to the cluster diagram.

3. Determine an assertion about telecommuting. What is your point of view? Write your thesis statement here:

_____

_____

4. While you have brainstormed many ideas about telecommuting, all of them will not support your individual assertions. You must decide which information will be the most effective to include. Cross out any information from your list that you know you will not include in your cluster.

You may want to do these activities on the board. See **Options:Customize** for alternative methods of doing these activities.

This activity is critical if you are using the central assignment as given in this chapter. Students are continuing to work with the central assignment in preparation for writing paragraphs on these assertions.

You will probably want to begin the homework assignment with the mapping and organizing practice activity here and continue through these readings, ending on page 124.

5. The next step is to examine your groups and decide how you are going to group your ideas most effectively to support your assertion. You may decide to leave the groups as they are, with each Level 2 becoming a separate paragraph. However, you may notice that some clusters have much more information than others. You may decide to group two Level 2 clusters into one main idea because they are more similar to each other than to the rest of the groupings. If you have a cluster without much detail, you may decide to eliminate it or put it with another cluster and broaden the topic. Which groups interest you the most? Which groups will be of most interest to your audience? Which ones have the best or most relevant idea? Keeping in mind that each group will become a paragraph, highlight each group (main idea and supporting details) with a different color.

6. Write a topic sentence for each group. You may revise this later when you are writing your draft, but for now it will help you focus.

Practice mapping and organizing your details by working with your selected topic from pages 105–106:

1. Using your brainstorming on the topic you selected from pages 105–106 in this chapter (or whatever central assignment your instructor gave), turn the brainstorming details into a map.

2. Highlight and group the details as you did in the previous practice. Make sure you have at least two groups with three or more ideas each.

3. Write an assertion for each grouping.

 **Go To** ▶

1. Go to the Telecommuting Jobs web site, **<http://www.tjobs.com/>**, to find out what kinds of jobs are available to telecommuters and to get a better idea of what telecommuting involves. Then, using a search engine, do a quick web search on telecommuting to see how popular the idea is now.

2. Go to your own college's web site to see what courses are offered online. Taking a course online is, in many ways, similar to telecommuting to a job. Brainstorm or cluster ideas about "telecommuting" to school.

Once supporting details are grouped, they are arranged into a paragraph to support the assertion of the paragraph, the *topic sentence.* Examine how some authors present many of the details about telecommuting in their texts. Notice that the details are arranged to support assertions. Many of the details listed above are included in the article "Telecommuting: Technology Instead of Traffic," excerpted from the textbook *Business.* As you read the article, look for the assertions.

Telecommuting: Technology Instead of Traffic

William M. Pride, Robert J. Hughes, and Jack R. Kapoor

1 In cities all over the United States, workers spend several hours a day in cars crawling along in traffic to get to offices many miles from home. They experience stress, waste time, and pay a lot for gas, car maintenance, and parking. Once they get to work, they make their way through a maze of cubicles, each with its computer, phone, and file cabinet. Nancy Alley, human resources manager at TBWA Chiat/Day, doesn't. She stays at home in her pajamas with a pile of résumés, talking with managers over the phone and faxing in paperwork. Instead of walking down the hall to chat with coworkers, she E-mails them. Nancy is a telecommuter, someone who works some or all of the time at home, and she is part of a trend. Since 1990, the number of U.S. telecommuters has grown from 4.2 million to 9.2 million, and experts predict that by the turn of the century, 55 million people worldwide will be telecommuting.

2 Highway congestion, the high cost of office space, federal clean-air laws, reduced work forces, and lifestyle needs—all these factors contribute to the growth of telecommuting. What makes it possible is technology. Desktop and laptop personal computers, networking, videoconferencing, fax machines, E-mail, and multiple phone lines provide the fast and efficient communication required for telecommuting.

3 The experiences of many companies suggest that telecommuting can increase workplace flexibility and enhance productivity. At Georgia Power Company, for example, a pilot telecommuting project was so successful that the company decided to triple its number of telecommuters. The company reduced the cost of leased office space by $100,000 a year, increased productivity among the telecommuting employees of its customer service center, and saved the workers a combined 750 commuter miles a day.

4 Telecommuting, however, is not without its obstacles. At one computer software firm, the information systems manager offered telecommuting as an option to her 100-person staff. After three months, the staff members reported that being away from the office was counterproductive to their work. Programmers missed being able to drop by analysts' cubicles with questions, and everyone reported they were interrupted at home more often. As part of its cost-cutting initiative, Nestlé required 140 sales employees to telecommute. Facing many technical problems with telephone lines and frustratingly slow computer networking, most

From William M. Pride, Robert J. Hughes, and Jack R. Kapoor, *Business*, Sixth Edition (Boston: Houghton Mifflin, 1999), 239. Copyright © 1999 by Houghton Mifflin Company. Reprinted with permission.

of these telecommuters found it an aggravating experience. Telecommuting also makes many employees feel isolated and out of touch, leading to decreased motivation and less, not more productivity. By blurring the barriers between work and family, telecommuting often leads to more work hours and more interference with family life.

5   Telecommuting is not universally applicable. Jobs and individuals must be suitable, and staff must be capable of managing telecommuters. In addition, technological improvements, such as high-speed modems, are crucial. Few people expect to conduct business regularly from a tropical island or mountain resort any time soon.

Analyze the Reading

1. Underline the assertions. Highlight the facts in pink and the examples in yellow.

2. Carefully examine the conclusion. How does it help you determine the overall assertion (or thesis) of the article?

_____

_____

_____

In the following article, "Telecommuting: This Life of Leisure May Not Be for Everyone," author Ruth Pennebaker uses humor to make some serious points about the problems a telecommuter faces. As you read the article, look for Pennebaker's assertion.

Telecommuting: This Life of Leisure May Not Be for Everyone

Ruth Pennebaker

1   Telecommuting is the wave of the future. I know that because I have read it everywhere. (All right, all right. So I have just read it twice, and I have forgotten where it was exactly. The point is, I know a trend when I see it.)

2   No more clogged freeways teeming with overheated cars and enraged drivers! No more office wardrobe expenses! No more wasted time hanging around the water cooler, listening to boring old office gossip about who is getting . . . well, never mind. No more long, tedious meetings where the boss drones on and on about being a team player, multitasking and brainstorming! You are going to be a telecommuter! You are on the cutting edge! Get ready to love your life even more!

3   And so on.

4   Listen, I really hate to rain on anybody's tirade. But I am pretty sure that all these prognosticators are nuts. They have stars in their eyes and large, vacant spaces where their brains should be. They are people who

Source: Ruth Pennebaker, "Telecommuting: This Life of Leisure May Not Be for Everyone" from the *Dallas Morning News,* August 29, 1999. Reprinted by permission of the author.

never have telecommuted in their lives, since they are too busy brainstorming, multitasking and hanging around the water cooler at work. But they think telecommuting is a great idea for everybody else.

5   Well, I am one of those everybody else people. I have telecommuted, more or less, for years, writing, faxing, and e-mailing from my home office, and I think these soothsayers should get a few clues from people like me. Working from home isn't as easy or as purely wonderful as they like to think.

6   Here is what I have learned after several years:

1. Some days, you will miss your old job, no matter how terrible it was. That is because you can get a tiny bit strange, staying at home and being by yourself all the time. Remember Jack Nicholson in *The Shining?* He was a telecommuter, sort of.

7   If you find yourself looking forward to telemarketers' calls, desperate to hear your name mangled and mispronounced, you aren't becoming a kinder and gentler person. You are becoming deranged. (That also may explain why you recently have begun to have long, intimate conversations with your cats, asking their advice about your love life.) Try to get out for lunch more frequently.

2. You won't miss those long, drawn-out meetings at work, but you will miss the office gossip like crazy. So what if the stories weren't true? At least they were interesting. And let's face it. You and the cats don't do anything that is nearly that interesting.

3. Step outside your office door, and you will find your kitchen. Yes, you are right. It still is dirty.

4. Sure, you won't have to invest in a snappy office wardrobe, and it really doesn't matter how you look, since you are by yourself all the time. But there will be days when you will get totally demoralized just looking at yourself. Uncombed hair, tattered T-shirts, ragged cutoffs and sandals? This is you?

8   Not everybody feels this way, of course. I have friends who even work in their pajamas, and they tell me it is wonderful. But I couldn't do it. I could be sitting at the computer, channeling the genius of Herman Melville and writing a sequel to *Moby Dick* or something and if I looked down and saw myself working in pajamas, I would die. I am sure great works of art have been created in nightclothes, but it never is going to happen to me. If it is 9 a.m. and I still am not dressed, I am a failure.

5. By the way, if you step outside your office again, the laundry room is pretty close, too. And, no, those clothes haven't folded themselves.

6. When you work at home, no one ever thinks you really are working. That explains why they don't mind calling you to talk for hours or asking you to do a favor, since you already are at home and have loads of free time on your hands.

7. Whenever there is a school holiday (and these times occur constantly, to my mind), you will find you are much less lonely. That is fine for about five action-filled minutes or so. After that, the constant battering of your office door, garbled screams and wrestling matches over the remote control and shrieked insults may interfere with your concentration.

9   If you find you have developed the ability to work through a maelstrom like that, it isn't necessarily good news. Your zen-like state may be a symptom of dementia. Consult your yoga teacher or therapist, as applicable.

    8. Finally, at some point, something truly dramatic will happen. You will be offered a regular job. You can return to the office, look nice everyday and have regular office hours and normal office friendships, and you never will be lonely again! You can stop all this telecommuting stuff and end all this isolation you have been complaining about!

10   You turn the offer down, of course. What do they think you are, a moron? You are a telecommuter! The wave of the future! Besides, how could you possibly give up all this freedom?

Analyze the Reading

1. Underline the assertions. Highlight the facts in pink and the examples in yellow.

2. Carefully examine the conclusion. How does it help you determine the overall assertion (or thesis) of the article? (*Hint:* In this case, look for the words to carry an *ironic* or sarcastic meaning. *Irony,* often used in humor, means that the words really mean the opposite of what they ordinarily mean. Ask yourself if the questions are meant to be serious or ironic, based on what the writer says in the rest of the article.)

_____

_____

_____

_____

_____

_____

3. Describe the difference in tone between the two articles.

_____

_____

_____

4. Both of these articles have the same topic and a similar assertion. What is the assertion they share?

_____

_____

_____

5. If the topic and assertion are similar, why are the two texts so very different?

_____

_____

_____

_____

_____

You have seen that most paragraphs have an assertion, a statement about the topic. This is usually referred to as the topic sentence. Sometimes the assertion is developed over several paragraphs. Often the author will not state the assertion directly; it is only implied. You draw conclusions about an implied assertion based on the content of the supporting paragraph(s).

Just as a paragraph has an assertion, or topic sentence, so does an entire text. All of the individual assertions in a text work together to support an overall assertion, known as the author's thesis. The thesis is the main assertion the author is making about the topic. For everything that you read in the remainder of this textbook, you will determine the author's thesis. The author's thesis statement consists of his or her topic and overall assertion about that topic. All of the paragraphs in the text will support the thesis statement.

Finding the thesis statement in a text is a skill you will need not only for this course, but for other courses, as well as for general reading. If you aren't able to determine the author's main point, then you really haven't understood the material.

To be sure you have understood the text thoroughly and determined its thesis statement, review the following after you read a text:

Effective Reading Skills

- Examine the title for clues to the thesis.

- Look for pictures, captions, graphs, or subheadings. These materials are clues to the author's thesis.

- Review the introduction and conclusion. Authors often state their main idea directly in one or both of these places.

- Highlight the topic sentences in paragraphs. Then look for a bigger idea that encompasses all of the topic sentences. This is especially helpful if the thesis is implied rather than stated directly.

- After you determine what you believe to be the thesis, review the steps here and check everything against your statement.

You will work with this concept more thoroughly as you continue to work through the chapters, particularly in Chapter 11. For now, practice finding the main assertion, the thesis statement, in this article written by a student at Michigan State University. As you read, think about whether you agree with the student's views on the topic of technology.

Someday Technology May Blow Up in Your Face

D. Rees Mills

1 The Internet, my friend. Yes, we MSU students couldn't get through a single day without logging on to our Pilot e-mail accounts or surfing the World Wide Web.

2 The Internet is an amazing thing with tremendous capabilities, a positive force in our society that allows better, faster communication.

3 I get all my test grades and keep in touch with high school friends through e-mail, and print lecture supplements off my courses' home pages, so I am a definite proponent of the Internet and computers in general.

4 But there lies a danger in basing everything on the function of machines—that is, after all, what computers are. They can't eat, breathe, sleep or tell when we are swearing at them. So, those who depend on computer technology for all their lives' needs are in for a big surprise when technology blows up in their faces.

5 All things break after so much use—even people. Because of this simple truth, I remain skeptical of the technological advancements of our modern world. When the Internet and other computer networks "break" some day, how many people will be standing in the street crying about how their whole life is in shambles because they can't get onto ESPN's home page?

6 Will we be able to fix the problem if a massive computer network shuts down unexpectedly? Probably, I figure, but that will take a great deal of effort and time.

7 If all the computers in this country shut down right now, we probably couldn't even buy groceries at Meijer—especially not in those checkout lines where you scan your own groceries, instead of the store paying an employee to do the job.

8 That seems to be the attitude in the United States, though: Why have a person do a job that a computer can do just as well? Well, wait until your technology shuts down and you're all standing around crying about how you can't buy cream cheese.

9 "But that would never happen—all the computers in the country would never break down!" I hear the idealistic computer aficionado screaming.

10 Stop being so arrogant—some of the most solid foundations in history have crumbled with time. Remember the Roman Empire? It eventually fell. No plantation owner from the early nineteenth century ever thought that slavery would end, but he was proven wrong. And do you think the investors of the Jazz Age expected the stock market to crash?

Source: D. Rees Mills, "Someday Technology May Blow Up in Your Face," *University Wire*, October 7, 1998. Reprinted with permission of the author.

11   Plus, almost everyone has heard of a computer virus and how it can adversely affect computers and networks. Well, I put forth the prediction that it will be an unstoppable virus—larger and more complex than we have ever seen—that interrupts our vacation in technological heaven.

12   And even if you balk at that idea, consider this: Do we know everything there is to know about computers? I mean, could we possibly know of every problem that may cross a computer's path?

13   Nothing is invincible, so we should stop basing so much on computers' functions.

14   A perfect example of relying too heavily on computers is the publication of MSU's Description of Courses and Schedule of Courses on the Internet.

15   When I first arrived at MSU, I could look at the hard copies (you know—printed on paper, able to be picked up) of these publications, without having to dial into the Internet, and plan which sections of courses I could possibly take before I started to enroll.

16   Well, we all know that's history, and I sure hope the MSU home page doesn't crash some day when everyone is trying to enroll.

17   If I don't catch myself, even I can fall victim to computer stress. Last week, I had to print one of my e-mail messages, because it was full of important review material for an exam I had the next day.

18   A problem arose—I couldn't connect to Pilot, and neither could anyone else I spoke with. By 11 p.m., I was getting upset, swearing at the computer and worrying about the exam that was rapidly approaching.

19   Luckily, I finally got through to my e-mail and got the information I needed. If I hadn't, I probably would have done very poorly on my test.

20   Now, multiply that small problem by every person who uses e-mail and the Internet, most of whom have much more serious things to do than I. That's a lot of swearing and broken office supplies.

21   When that happens, and everyone's going nuts, I won't be bothered, because I was humble enough to admit that it was going to happen.

I'll probably go do something that doesn't require a computer—like reading or fishing. In fact, when all this blows up in our faces, you can find me reading a book (a nice hard copy on paper) next to a remote river, away from e-mail and all the computer networks.

You may want to end the homework assignment here. It is a good idea to begin the next class session by reviewing the answers to questions 1–8 on pages 117–125.

Analyze the Reading

1. Write the author's thesis (overall assertion) on the lines below:

_____

_____

_____

2. How did the title help you to discover the thesis?

_____

_____

_____

3. Examine paragraph 4. What word gives a clue that an important assertion is coming?

_____

_____

_____

OPTIONS ▶ Customize

1. Write a response that you would want to e-mail to the author of the preceding text. As a class, select one to actually e-mail. If you like, you could write one as a class to e-mail instead of writing individual ones.

2. Earlier in this text, you acquired the e-mail addresses of some of your classmates. Refer back to that list and send an e-mail to the first name on your list. In the subject line of the e-mail, fill in a topic of your choice, but leave the body of the e-mail message blank. For example, you may want to fill in the subject line with the topic, *movies*. Upon receipt of a topic, the student should add an assertion about that topic and e-mail it to another student. If your topic is *movies*, an assertion about movies might be, "Movies are getting too violent." This process should continue until three assertions have been added, at which point the student adding the third assertion should send a copy back to all four participants and the instructor.

3. If you do not have access to e-mail, do a round robin of topic/assertion: The first student announces a topic. The next three students in the row each creates an assertion about the topic. The fifth student announces another topic, and the next three create assertions for that topic. Go around the room twice so that students who initially gave topics will be giving assertions on the second round.

4. Because mapping is such a useful tool for both readers and writers, software developers have created programs that allow users to create maps on the computer. Often these programs offer users several ways of looking at their ideas. The *Writing Now* web site has links to some of the mapping programs available.

Put a topic in the center of the board. Then write an assertion about the topic as soon as students can think of one. You can then ask students to come up to the board and add an assertion. Those who go to the board later will find it harder, since they cannot duplicate any topics already there. This increasing difficulty will enable them to "dig deep" to formulate creative assertions. When all possible assertions are on the board, circle the ones that seem most interesting. Each student can write on the topic of his or her choice, or the class (or small group) can select a topic for all to write on.

FILE ▶ Create

00:45

You may want students to work in groups to get started.

Paragraphs with Clear Assertions

1. Refer to the brainstorming activity that you started in **Connecting with Previous Learning** on page 103. Break into groups. Compare your assertions and details with members of the group.

    a. Are your assertions clearly stated?

    b. Do the assertions indicate the author's opinion?

    c. Do the details or examples listed with an assertion clearly support the assertion?

    d. Is there enough detail for the chosen assertion?

2. Now that you have seen how your classmates handled the topic, details, and assertion, you may want to improve your work by regrouping, adding, or deleting where necessary. Make your corrections in another color of ink.

3. Make a new outline or cluster of your assertion and details for two of your groups.

4. Brainstorm again to further develop each assertion. Write new ideas in another color of ink.

Name: _____

Date: _____

Before drafting a paragraph for two assertions, write an outline for each proposed paragraph.

I. Topic: _____

   Assertion: _____

   A. First detail:

   B. Second detail:

   C. Third detail:

   D. Fourth detail:

II. Topic: _____

   Assertion: _____

   A. First detail:

   B. Second detail:

   C. Third detail:

   D. Fourth detail:

FILE ▶ Save As

Write two paragraphs on one topic using your plan on page 127. Each paragraph will have the same topic but a different assertion. The different assertions will require different supporting details. Be sure that everything you include contributes to a reader's understanding of your assertion.

Your teacher may instruct you to submit these paragraphs for evaluation and feedback or to hold for further work in Chapter 6. Either way, be sure to save a copy of your draft for yourself.

C:\Prompts for Writing ▶

1. Refer to the excerpt written by Michael N. Milone, Jr., and Judy Salpeter on pages 112–113. Write on one of the following assertions:

   a. Computers create more equality.

   b. Computers create less equality.

2. Brainstorm on the idea of telecommuting to school—that is, taking courses and submitting work via the Internet instead of attending classes. Write an assertion reflecting your attitude toward going to school that way instead of attending in person. Write an essay supporting your assertion.

3. The entire class will write on one topic from the list on pages 105–106. Write a paragraph on that topic and prepare to read your paragraph aloud in the next class session. As you listen to your classmates' papers, note how many different ways a topic can be developed. List on the board some effective assertions that students wrote.

4. Respond to the essay "Someday Technology May Blow Up in Your Face," or write about technology problems you have encountered.

5. Write an assertion and supporting paragraph on one of the following topics:

   ▶ Violence in video games

   ▶ Medical advice on the Web

   ▶ Internet controls on library computers

Go To ▶ Go to the *Writing Now* web site for links to demo versions of mapping software. If your school allows you to do so, download a demo and try it out. What, if any, are the advantages of using mapping software over drawing a map by hand?

CHAPTER 6
Are You Talking to Me?

"On the Internet, nobody knows you're a dog."

Chapter Contents

Log On ▶ **Reflection**

Write whatever comes to mind when you read the chapter title and study the cartoon.

_____

_____

_____

_____

_____

_____

_____

_____

_____

_____

_____

_____

_____

_____

_____

_____

_____

_____

_____

_____

FILE ▶ **Open**

`00:45`

Connecting with Experience

▶ What kind of language do you use when you are talking to your friends? Do you use formal or informal language? Why?

▶ Do you use the same language around your friends as you do around your older relatives? At work? At school? At church? Explain the differences.

▶ Why might you change your language under different circumstances or for different "audiences"?

▶ What does it mean to "show your true colors"?

▶ Does your grammar affect how people see you? In other words, does it affect your audience and the way they "see" you?

Connecting with Writing

▶ Do you write the same way that you speak?

▶ Cluster *audience,* using everything you can bring to mind on the topic.

▶ Can you think of any way *audience* can relate to writing?

▶ How, if at all, does *audience* affect your writing?

▶ How does the cartoon relate to *audience* and writing?

▶ What does it mean to "be consistent"?

FILE ▶ **New**

Audience

The person or persons to whom you are addressing your writing are your *audience.* It is a good idea to have a specific audience in mind when you begin to write, because you will need to write differently for different audiences. Let's see how this works.

Explore the Difference Audience Can Make in Your Writing.

1. Visualizing your best friend as your audience, write one paragraph of at least five sentences describing the most exciting party you have ever attended. Make your sentences detailed and descriptive.

_____

_____

_____

_____

_____

_____

_____

_____

_____

_____

_____

_____

_____

_____

_____

_____

The more emotion you can inject into a learning activity, the more learning occurs. Laughter and pleasure are great motivators and enhancers of learning.

To stimulate these emotions, students play with what they write. Ask students to read one of their two paragraphs aloud, and then have the rest of the class guess which audience the student was addressing.

2. Now, change your audience to your grandmother, mother, or aunt. Visualizing that person, write a new paragraph of the same length describing the same party to her.

_____

_____

_____

_____

_____

_____

_____

_____

_____

_____

_____

_____

_____

_____

3. How are your two paragraphs different? Explain in detail.

_____

_____

_____

_____

_____

_____

4. Why are your two paragraphs different?

5. Are your two paragraphs alike in any way? Would, for example, a class-mate recognize the two descriptions as describing the same party?

6. What can you conclude about audience and writing?

Go To ▶

These Go To exercises are a good place to begin the first homework assignment. You may want to assign through page 142.

1. Go to the *Writing Now* web site, for directions to some chat rooms. Visit one of the chat rooms we suggest. Some chat rooms allow participants to represent themselves with *avatars*—graphic images of cartoon characters, famous people, or created characters that chat-room participants select to represent themselves in a given session. Does the chat room you are observing allow avatar use? How can a participant's choice of avatars influence the way an audience responds? Why is it important to know your audience when you choose an avatar to represent you?

_____

_____

_____

_____

_____

_____

2. Go to the *Writing Now* web site for directions to some academic MOOs (see **Help Screen** below). Visit one of the MOOs we suggest. In a MOO, participants can choose to name and describe the characters they will play. Use the Look command for several characters. Do the descriptions you read seem to be realistic or fantasy-like?

_____

_____

_____

_____

_____

Help Screen

Chat Rooms and MOOs

If you want to do the preceding **Go To** exercises but have never been to a chat room or MOO, the *Writing Now* web site will show you how to get connected to this kind of site.

If you've used the Web before this class, you probably are already familiar with chat rooms. Chat rooms are usually social places where people go to have online conversations about a variety of topics. Chat rooms are often designated for users with special interests or for special groups. Some are intended for young people. However, it is wise to be cautious. Some people may misrepresent themselves to fit in with the group just to create problems.

It is less likely that you are familiar with MOOs. At their most basic level, MOOs are like chat rooms in that they allow "real-time" chat—that is, communication with others who are online at the same time you are. In a MOO, however, participants can create characters and roles they play over a long time. Through description, they can create spaces that will remain in place and into which they can invite others. And through verbs, they can bring virtual action into the space. With a little practice and patience, you too can create spaces into which you can place your ideas, then invite others to interact with you and your ideas in ways impossible in a plain chat room.

MOO stands for MUD, object-oriented; that is, it is an object-oriented version of a MUD. A *MUD* is a multi-user dungeon/dimension. Originally created for role-playing games such as *Dungeons and Dragons*, MOOs are now also used by some English teachers because these "cyberspaces" require careful attention to the existing text and creative use of language in building spaces and inventing actions. Fully participating in a MOO requires more sophistication than does communicating in a chat room, because MOO participants must issue commands to create what they want.

Several MOOs are designed primarily for educational use. Even so, you should be careful about what you say and to whom you say it. As in a chat room, someone wishing to cause trouble may show up; although there is no physical threat to participants, people who want to be disruptive can have a negative effect, even in a virtual space. In a MOO, however, you will get some help. *Wizards*—practiced users who volunteer to make sure things run smoothly—generally keep watch to help those who seem confused and to warn newcomers if it looks as if trouble is near—if, for example, they have been approached by a known troublemaker.

The *Writing Now* web site offers suggestions on reliable MOOs and gives detailed instructions on visiting some MOO spaces designed by English students for class projects.

In the following reading selection, Angela Bouwsma describes a regrettable incident in which someone unaware of his audience showed "his true colors."

Showing His True Colors

Angela Bouwsma

1   I was ecstatic when my mother finally turned off the information dirt road and bought a PC a couple of years ago. Last summer she went all out and signed up for America Online. She subscribed because she wanted access to the Internet, not because she wanted to make friends. But as a result of the distinctive name she chose for herself, she often logs on and receives messages from strangers who are intrigued by her AOL handle.

2   Not long ago, my mother told me about a conversation she'd had online with a stranger, a computer engineer from the Midwest. They discussed a variety of topics, and toward the end the subject of beauty came up, followed by race. The man, feeling comfortable after almost an hour of chitchat and not knowing that my mother was black, went on to give her his honest impressions of her kind.

3   She couldn't recall precisely what he said, but the key words were "ignorant," "lie," "cheat," and "smell." My mother, stunned but in the comfort of anonymity, gathered herself and tried to reason with her new friend. He found her efforts to defend black people noble but incredibly naive. "One of these days you'll find out how black people really are," he wrote.

4   With that, my mother gave up reasoning and resorted to the easiest tactic to convince him that his beliefs were based on ignorance; she revealed that she herself was black. The man professed shock and endlessly apologized. Giving her what I suppose was intended as a compliment, he expressed his happy surprise at finally meeting an intelligent black person.

5   I won't recite my mother's academic and professional accomplishments here. Although her achievements and those of many other black Americans would make her friend look like a sheltered fool as well as a bigot, they're beside the point. The man, relying only on words as clues, assumed my mother was white, someone who would be sympathetic and to whom he could speak freely.

6   What my mother did not ask her computer acquaintance was whether he regarded himself as a racist. He was extremely contrite, even embarrassed, when she revealed her ethnicity. I'll speculate that because he was apologetic and didn't type "You're a lying cheat," he congratulated himself that he'd judged fairly. He might say that his ideas were based on experience. Once he saw how normal she was, the many interests they shared, he was willing to acknowledge her as someone deserving respect.

7   Stories like this have always infuriated me, but my mother's made me sad. She told me that all she could think of as she responded to this intelligent, college-educated man was me. Her talented, educated daughter, to whom she believed she'd given every advantage, for whom she had so many hopes, might be seen on the street by this man and reflexively judged as a stupid, lying cheat.

Source: Angela Bouwsma, "Showing His True Colors." From *Newsweek*, February 24, 1997. All rights reserved. Reprinted by permission.

8   For a large group of black Americans, particularly those of us trying to make it in corporate America, racism is not experienced the way it's depicted in movies: rednecks brandishing six-packs, bad haircuts and baseball bats. It's better explained by the absence of minorities in certain areas of life—boardrooms, film directors' chairs, or editors' desks. In these instances, black Americans are generally denied the opportunity to participate—with a few heralded exceptions—where they are not explicitly required. That kind of racism is subtle and insidious, not something that can be photographed, like a corpse swinging from a tree or a burning cross. It's a racism that smiles at you, shakes your hand, and wishes you luck. But its effects are clear and measurable.

9   To say that affirmative action should be scrapped because racial preferences are ideologically intolerable is alarming and insulting. It spits in the face of the reality we all share, one where implicit racial- and gender-preferences not only exist but, at the highest echelons, are the rule of thumb. As a result, more often than not, being black or being a woman pulls a little farther from your reach the top levels of success.

10   Last November my home state of California abolished affirmative action in state-run agencies and schools. Despite the temporary restraining order issued against it by a federal judge, Proposition 209 scares me a great deal. I'm convinced that, as the mood of the nation dictates, the Supreme Court will uphold it.

11   If that happens we'll begin a slide backward after 130 years of slow, painful progress. Such a decision will further polarize us into two separate Americas, one in which racism effectively disappeared the day the Civil Rights Act was signed, and another where it is as much a part of life as breathing. And though I'll urge her to pursue whatever success she desires, as I do, I'll be wondering whether strangers are dismissing my daughter the way my mother wonders today.

Analyze the Reading

1. In what way did the man Angela Bouwsma's mother was e-mailing misunderstand his audience?

_____

_____

2. On what basis did the man form his opinion of Bouwsma's mother?

_____

_____

_____

3. Bouwsma relates this story to make a point about something else. What is her thesis? Highlight it in green. Highlight any examples in yellow and facts in pink. If you are having trouble finding the thesis, highlight the facts and examples first.

4. Who is Bouwsma's audience meant to be?

_____

_____

5. Where was this article originally published?

6. Does the answer to question 5 tell you anything about the audience? (Check out **<http://www.msnbc.com/news/NW-front_Front.asp>** if you need more information on what this magazine is like.)

People who write personal ads, in which they describe themselves and/or the kind of person they want to meet, are acutely aware of their intended audience. As you read the following article by Patricia Wen, think about the impact of audience on specific writing situations. The paragraphs are numbered so that you can work with them in a later exercise.

The Data Game

Patricia Wen

1   Falling in love has never been rational. Humphrey Bogart just couldn't resist Lauren Bacall's sharp blue-green eyes. For Katharine Hepburn, Spencer Tracy was "irresistible" at first sight.

2   But these days, millions of single Americans, many already tied to their computers for most of their working hours, are taking a rational approach as they seek love via the magic of modems. And besides, who's got the time now for person-to-person courting?

3   It's not a new phenomenon. But if the volume of people seeking companionship via the Internet even approaches the numbers claimed by online dating companies, it indicates the industry is evolving from a fringe lonely hearts business to a legitimate Web service. It could also upend society's unwritten rules about how people meet, mingle and couple. For one thing, it's a world where spelling, punctuation and grammar, not clothes, can make the person.

4   Cerebral as this all sounds, many singles say it's an efficient way to screen others. "You get a lot more information about the person before meeting," said Ethan Brown, 28, a lawyer from Weston, Mass. "You can e-mail them and correspond for a while. It's easier."

5   Brown met Jodi Constantine, 29, a post-doctorate researcher at Harvard through Boston-based *People2People.com*, and they've been dating for six months. *People2People*, and two other big sites, *Match.com* and *Matchmaker.com*, boast of anywhere from 1 million to 4 million members each, hooking thousands more each day with free trial offers. Industry officials say most members are young professionals in their 20s and 30s without the time to look for other singles in bars or other places they might gather, and older never-marrieds, divorced or widowed men and women who don't want to.

6   Cyber-dating is more intellectual than physical, more rational than emotional, yet some say more intimate. In most cases, members type and edit their minibiographies (including data such as age, hometown, religion, education and sometimes income level), as well as write a short essay.

Source: Republished with permission of *The Boston Globe* from Patricia Wen, "When Two Click: Net Gives Singles Screening Room," *The Boston Globe*, April 5, 2000. © 2000. Permission conveyed through Copyright Clearance Center, Inc.

7   Using fictitious code names, they also enter qualities they want in their would-be lovers. Few are bold enough to offer a picture. The computer synthesizes the data, then delivers "matches," often hundreds within a short distance from where the member lives.

8   Though the sites claim a formidable success rate, others think people like Brown and Constantine just got lucky. Some psychologists and sociologists who study romance don't see e-dating as a promising method. First, early on, there's no context of voice or accent, face or expression. In anonymous exchanges, it's easy to lie. And the mind doesn't always know what the heart wants.

9   "It flies in the face of how romance works," said Thomas Lewis, a psychiatrist and co-author of a book, *A General Theory of Love,* published this year.

10   "Most people don't know what they want," said Lewis, who is also an assistant clinical professor of psychiatry at the University of California in San Francisco. "They may put in the criteria that match what their thinking brain says, but their emotional brain operates with a different set of operation instructions that are not rational."

11   In his book, Lewis talks about three sections of the brain: the "reptilian brain" that makes the heart beat and blood flow, the "neo-cortex brain" that does the intellectual work and scheming, and the "limbic brain" that is full of irrational emotion and guides our choices in love.

12   He said the limbic brain is shaped at an early age, affected largely by our childhood experiences about what types of looks, smells, gestures, strides and expressions we grew up with and are now likely to respond to on a visceral level. Humans often don't know what their limbic brain wants.

13   "Aren't we often surprised when we're attracted to someone who doesn't match what's on our predetermined list?" he said.

14   That may be true, but some singles contend they have some nonnegotiable requirements in a romantic partner, and computer power can be harnessed to screen and sort out these demands. Perhaps someone wants only a Christian, a nonsmoker, or someone who wants more children. Many sites also offer matches for gay men and lesbians.

15   If the information in the *Match.com* database is accurate, most members are open to meeting a wide variety of people. However, opportunities shrink for older women and shorter men, which is the brutal truth of the dating scene in general.

16   Singles who use these online sites say this method differs from print personal ads or singles clubs, the popularity of which has also exploded in recent years, because there's generally a prolonged period of e-mail exchanges before real names are given, phone numbers exchanged, or meetings set up.

17   With the blessing of executives at *Match.com*, the *Boston Globe* entered a number of fictitious profiles to gauge what sort of people the company's members were looking for. None of the matches was followed up with correspondence to members.

18   A fictitious woman, for example, seeking to date men within 25 miles of her home got anywhere from 350 to 500 "matches." (That's when both sides matched each other's criteria not all, but most of the time.)

19   That high bit rate held steady whether our woman was 25 or 45, from being agnostic to Christian to Jewish to Buddhist, turned from Caucasian to African-American to Asian, or transformed from heavy to slim.

20   Her prospects dropped when she turned 50; however, she still pulled 180 matches.

21 A fictitious bachelor also got anywhere from 300 to 500 matches under a similar variety of scenarios. What began to diminish a man's chances was the issue of height. Still, a guy who was 5 feet 4 inches got about 150 matches.

22 Seasoned members, however, say information in profiles—even pictures—can be unreliable.

23 A 35-year-old man who works in medical sales said he once met a woman through *JDate.com*, a site for Jewish singles, who didn't look anything like her picture.

24 "She said to me, 'By the way, I've gained 20 pounds since my picture,'" said the man, who gave his name only as Marc.

25 "There's a huge level of editorial shaping," said David Givens, an anthropologist who runs the nonprofit Center for Nonverbal Studies in Spokane, Wash. "That's the danger with words. They're conscious and you can manipulate them. Face-to-face, you might be able to choose your clothing or hairstyle. But otherwise, you're there. It's you."

26 Shaping image through the written word can have its benefits, said a 49-year-old single mother, who asked to remain anonymous. She likes the chance to take the time to express in writing who she is, though she acknowledges that this method favors the highly literate.

27 "If you saw me at a bar, you wouldn't walk in and say, 'Wow!'" said the woman, who is also a therapist. "But I can write a letter that will make you say, 'Wow!' It allows me to show how I think, how I write, and how I react to things."

28 For her, the biggest downside of Web matchmaking sites is that two people become vulnerable to quick intimacy, within the romantic "confessional booth" of private e-mail exchanges.

29 Sherry Turkle, a sociology professor at Massachusetts Institute of Technology, who specializes in technology's effects on human behavior, agrees.

30 "If you give someone small amounts of written information, the other person will construct the rest," she said. "Then when the two meet, there's this sense you already know each other."

31 Most singles say cyber-matchmaking works best if participants are aware of its pitfalls and use it as an extra, not only, method of meeting people. There's no shortcut to love, said James Gleick, a journalist and author of "Faster," which focuses on today's technology-driven hurried life.

32 "Sizing someone up is always time-consuming," he said.

33 And in e-dating, different prejudices are at play. Said Lori Orleck, a 38-year-old single woman: "If someone has misspelled words or bad grammar, I won't even look at them."

34 When rejection occurs, cyber-dating offers new ways of turning people away. You don't have to give a stammering excuse or turn your back.

35 One side hits the "delete" button instead of "reply," and the other side, perhaps mercifully, reads on the computer screen, "No messages."

Analyze the Reading

1. What is the topic?

_____

_____

2. What is the overall assertion about that topic?

_____

_____

_____

3. Who is the intended audience?

_____

_____

4. Are you a member of that intended audience? Why or why not?

_____

_____

_____

5. What does this article say about audience?

_____

_____

_____

This is a good place to end the first homework assignment.

When you begin the class activity in the next section, you may want to allow time at the beginning of class to discuss the homework.

Some instructors give the students a few minutes in small groups to go over the homework while the instructor takes roll and manages other classroom tasks.

Each group can report any questions that could not be resolved in-group. This technique puts the responsibility for learning on the student. Instead of just waiting until class to find out the answers, students have a responsibility to the group to complete their homework.

6. Reread paragraph 33. What does this paragraph say about a person's writing ability and audience?

_____

_____

_____

7. Are there circumstances in which *how* you say something can be as important as *what* you say? Discuss.

_____

_____

Analyze: Audience

Besides personal ads, as presented in the reading, name some other types of writing in which an understanding of the audience could be critical to the success of the writing.

_____

_____

_____

_____

TOOLS ▶ Language

`00:45`

Reminder: you may want to spend time discussing the homework assignment.

These activities are suitable for whole-class or small-group work.

Consistency in Subject-Verb Agreement

Did you notice in working with topics and assertions that topics tend to contain the subject and that assertions contain the verb? When you put a topic and assertion together to form a topic sentence or thesis statement, you will need to make sure that your subject (the topic) and your verb (the assertion) are in *agreement*. That is to say: if the subject is singular, the verb must be singular; if the subject is plural, the verb must be plural. This rule also applies to every sentence that you write. If you are writing and you aren't sure of the convention, you can use a handy tool as a guideline. Examine the following list of subject-verb pairs. What generalization (*inference*) can you make about the pairs?

Subject	Verb
1. he	takes
boys	take
2. plane	lands
planes	land
3. horse	races
horses	race
4. car	drives
cars	drive

_____

_____

_____

To add excitement and interest, give individual students or groups a set time, perhaps 5 minutes, to come up with as many subject-verb pairs as they can. Then have students write the pairs on the board. Can they find any exceptions? Move those to another column, or circle them with different-colored chalk. Have students copy the lists into their notebooks.

Again, you may want to give a set time, such as 3 minutes to see how many words students can come up with. Have students write the words on the board, then discuss the words and copy them into their notebooks.

Some evidence suggests that copying helps students focus on the mechanics of writing, particularly spelling, and also helps their reading.

This exercise helps simulate real-life editing by having the student look for errors in subject-verb agreement. It also avoids the negative activity of presenting students with incorrect examples to correct. (Research has shown that students are as likely to retain incorrect examples as correct ones.)

If you want to reduce the amount of time this activity takes, have the students simply make annotations on the article.

It is a good idea to do this editing activity in class and then have students take the last few minutes of class to compare their answers in small groups and resolve any questions.

Did you figure out that if you examine the subject and the verb together, you should not have more than one *s* ending per pair?

Generate as many more pairs like these as you can.

The "one-*s*" guideline is a handy proofreading tool. Before you turn in a paper, especially if you learn that subject-verb agreement is a problem area for you, check your subject-verb pairs. If you find more than one *s*, be sure to investigate. Sometimes there are exceptions to this guideline, however. For example, look at the first two items in the preceding list. Now look what happens when we use "They take." There is no *s* at all. You may find other exceptions. Determine whether you are using a true exception or whether you need to make a change.

Some subjects can be a little confusing. For example, is the word *class* singular or plural? We know that a class probably contains two or more people. However, we are referring to only one class, so the word is singular. Can you think of other subjects like this?

> *Example: The team plays* (many players on a team, playing together as one team)

Refer to "What Computers Can, Cannot, and Should Not Do," on page 108 in Chapter 5. Rewrite every sentence that contains the word *computers* in it, changing the word to *computer*. Sometimes the author uses the pronoun *they* instead of *computers*. You will have to rewrite these sentences also, making all pronouns singular to match the singular *computer*. Notice that you will also need to change the verbs when you change a noun from plural to singular to make the singular subject agree with the verb.

We've done the first one for you. What follows is the sentence in its original form: **Computers exist** to benefit and assist people, not to replace them.

When you rewrite the sentence using the singular form of the word *computer*, your sentence reads:

> **A computer exists** *to benefit and assist people, not to replace them.*

Notice in the example above that the *s* moved from the end of *computers* to the end of *exist*.

Now it's your turn.

Go To ▶ Go to the following URL: **<http://hotwired.lycos.com/cybrarian>**. You have read that people use the Web to meet people, but did you know that you can use the Web to find people, too? The *Hotwired Cybrarian* site links you to several search engines specifically aimed at helping you find people. Click on People Finder under References in the left-side menu. Search for yourself in some of the directories provided. Are you comfortable with the information available about you on the Web? You can also search for a friend you haven't heard from in a while. Enter in as much information as you have about your friend. Notice that the more information you have about the person you are looking for, the more accurate the hits (responses the search engine presents).

If you still have time, you might want to write a "fan" e-mail message to someone, or send an opinion on a political issue to a public official. Think about how else a people search might help you.

OPTIONS ▶ Customize

1. Refer to the list of topics and assertions that you wrote in FILE: NEW, pages 105–106 in Chapter 5. Highlight any subject-verb pairs that do not agree. Correct them in a different-colored ink.

2. You will find it helpful to keep a page in your notebook to list the words that you commonly misspell. You can review these words before and after writing. When you notice words that give you trouble as you or someone else proofreads your paper, add the words to a "Watch Out!" list. Eventually the words will no longer give you trouble. . . . Start right now to make this "Watch Out!" list.

TOOLS ▶ Language

You may want to assign this section as homework, allowing time at the beginning of the next class to review the answers.

Consistency—Parallelism and Balance

Just as you want to be consistent in subject-verb agreement, you need to be consistent in how you handle similar items within a sentence. This consistency is called parallel treatment or *parallelism.* As an example, notice the parallel treatment of the three list items in the following excerpt:

> In his book, *A General Theory of Love,* Lewis talks about three sections of the brain: the "reptilian brain" that makes the heart beat and blood flow, the "neo-cortex brain" that does the intellectual work and scheming, and the "limbic brain" that is full of irrational emotion and guides our choices in love.

In the preceding excerpt, the author lists and discusses three sections of the human brain: the reptilian brain, the neo-cortex brain, and the limbic brain. Instead of writing three separate sentences, the author writes a list in one sentence. Note that he is consistent in his presentation of these three list items.

First, the author uses parallel phrases to list and begin his discussion of each brain section: "the 'reptilian brain' . . ."; "the 'neo-cortex brain' . . ."; "the 'limbic brain'. . . " All three of these are adjective-noun phrases and, as you remember, a *noun* can be a person, place, or thing and an *adjective* describes a noun. Notice that the author also uses parallel structure in putting the name of each brain section in quotation marks.

Second, the author uses parallel structure to describe the function of each brain section. Each list item is followed by a parallel descriptive clause beginning with the word *that:* "the 'reptilian brain' *that* makes the heart beat and blood flow," and so forth. Notice that each description also contains a verb.

In the following activities, you will examine some of the readings in Chapter 5 and this chapter to see how the authors handle lists within a sentence. As you work, see if you can find any patterns in how these authors write their lists. Think about how the items in the list are *similar to* each other.

The following activities ask you to highlight *parallel units* within certain sentences in previous reading selections. Paragraph and sentence numbers tell you the location of these sentences within the selections. The number of the paragraph within the selection is given first, followed by a colon and the number of the sentence within the paragraph. For example, in activity 1a, the location numbers *1:2* refer to *paragraph 1, sentence 2* in the reading selection. Similarly, in activity 1b, the location numbers *1:5* refer to *paragraph 1, sentence 5* in the reading selection.

Note that some activities also ask you to underline parts of speech in the sentence. Underlining will help you to see patterns in parallel structure.

For Further Analysis

1. Refer to the following sentences in "What Computers Can, Cannot, and Should Not Do" on page 108 in Chapter 5. Highlight the parallel units (the lists) in these sentences. The first one is done here for you.

    Computers cannot, for example, *make emotional judgments, disobey instructions entered by humans, read people's minds, or replace interpersonal relationships.*

    As you can see, all four italic phrases list things that computers cannot do. The phrases also begin with a verb.

    a. 1:2   b. 1:5 (also underline the verbs)

    c. 3:2   d. 7:1 (also underline the verbs)

    Think about what you have highlighted and underlined in these sentences, then attempt to define the pattern for parallel structure used in each sentence.

    _____

    _____

    _____

2. Refer to the following sentences in "Telecommuting: Technology Instead of Traffic" on page 118 in Chapter 5. Highlight the parallel units in these sentences.

    a. 1:2   b. 2:1 (also underline the adjective/noun combinations)

    c. 3:3 (also underline the verbs)

    Can you generate a guideline?

    _____

    _____

    _____

3. Refer to "Showing His True Colors" on pages 137–138 of this chapter and highlight the parallel units. Note that two examples do not have the usual three or more items in a list. Instead, the parallel units each contain

two items. Find a way in which the two items in each of these units are parallel.

    a. 1:3   b. 2:3   c. 8:1   d. 8:2   e. 8:5

What do you notice?

_____

_____

_____

4. Turn to "The Data Game" on pages 139–141 of this chapter. Highlight the parallel units.

    a. 6:1   b. 8:3   c. 1:11   d. 12.1   e. 14:2   f. 27:3

Explain how your understanding of parallelism has changed as a result of your work in activities 1–4.

_____

_____

_____

Why would a writer want to use parallel construction?

_____

_____

_____

Now, turn to the paragraphs you wrote for the **File: New** activity. Somewhere appropriate in this paragraph, write a sentence using parallel construction. You may add a completely new sentence, or you may want to try combining two or three of your original sentences into one sentence using parallel construction. Look back at the sentences you have been working on in the previous activities if you need an example to follow. Be sure to use different-colored ink or to highlight the sentence so that your instructor can see your changes.

You may want to end the homework assignment here and discuss the answers in class.

You can spend this final class period putting some of the parallel structures on the board and helping students understand parallelism if they were not able to discover it for themselves. In addition, you have time available for students to begin writing the final part of the central assignment or to review any material in this chapter on which they need additional work. You may want to have students work individually or in small groups. Either way, you will probably want to allow time for them to share their work with the class.

Go To ▶ 1. Go to the *Writing Now* web site to examine the list of OWLs again. This time, look for the techniques different labs use to teach subject-verb agreement and parallelism. Pick one site and summarize what you found.

OPTIONS ► Customize

Consistency in Subject-Verb Agreement

1. Using the information you learned in this chapter, summarize the rules for parallel structure and keep them in your binder. Pick some sample sentences to illustrate your guidelines. You can do this on a word processor and print it out, or you can do a PowerPoint presentation by combining graphics and text.

2. Find examples of parallelism in magazines or newspapers. Cut out the examples and bring them to class, or make a poster of several examples.

EDIT ► Revise for Audience

You may want to begin the homework for the central assignment here or have students begin this work during class time.

Analyze your central assignment from Chapter 5.

1. Read the two paragraphs you wrote on a high-technology topic for the **File: Create** assignment on page 126 of Chapter 5.

2. Determine who might be an appropriate audience for each of your paragraphs, and write the name of each audience at the top of each paragraph.

3. Revise each paragraph as needed to fit its audience.

Now you are going to demonstrate your ability to write for more than one audience on a given topic/assertion. Select one of the paragraphs you wrote for the **File: Create** assignment on page 126 and which you labeled with an appropriate audience. Now rewrite it for a very different audience. Select an audience from the following list, or come up with your own:

● Someone who has never used a computer (or fax or cell phone)

● Someone who refuses to learn how to use e-mail

● Someone from a nontechnological society who is totally unfamiliar with the equipment in your topic

● A potential customer to whom you are selling the technology about which you wrote

See the C:\Prompts section for alternative assignments using audience.

● A young child to whom you are explaining the technology about which you wrote

Read your paragraphs aloud. Is it clear that they are written for two very different audiences?

Have a classmate complete your peer revision worksheet.

Peer Revision Worksheet

Reviewed by: **Date:**

Focus of review: topic assertion, subject-verb agreement, parallelism

Reviewing paper written by:

Peer Revision Questionnaire

Ask yourself the following questions about your draft. Then, if possible, ask a friend or classmate to read your draft and answer the same questions about it. If your answers do not match, you haven't succeeded in communicating what you think you did. Where answers don't match well, discuss them together and try to think of ways to make your paragraphs clearer.

▶ What are your paragraphs about? (topic)

▶ What is the event or situation that prompted the essay? (prompt)

▶ What do you have to say about your topic? (thesis or main idea)

▶ Who is your intended audience?

▶ What is your purpose in writing about this topic ?

▶ What personal experience (life, reading, TV, stories you've heard, and so on) have you had with this topic?

▶ What purpose does each paragraph serve? How does each support the thesis?

▶ Is there anything else the reader should know? Are there any questions in the reader's mind left unanswered by the paragraphs?

FILE ▶ Save

Paragraphs with Different Assertions and Different Audiences

After carefully reviewing your paragraphs for differing assertions and for differing audiences, you are ready to do a final edit. You will turn in three paragraphs: two with different assertions and one with the same assertion as one of the other two but written for a different audience.

Complete the following worksheet to indicate your writing plan.

Name: _____ Date: _____

Topic: _____

Assertion 1:

_____

_____

Audience: _____

Assertion 2:

_____

_____

Audience: _____

Assertion (Select number 1 or 2 above):

_____

Audience 2 (Same assertion but new audience):

_____

Perform all the revision techniques you have learned so far. The ones you learned in this chapter are given first on the following Revision Checklist.

Revision Checklist

☐ I have clearly stated assertions about my topic.

☐ I have a defined audience.

☐ I have arranged my ideas in an order appropriate to the topic.

☐ I had someone read and annotate my essay.

☐ I have an appropriate title.

☐ I have a clearly stated topic.

☐ I have developed a topic that is appropriate, neither too broad nor too specific.

☐ All paragraphs support my overall topic.

☐ Each paragraph has a different focus relating to my topic.

☐ Each paragraph has well-developed supporting examples and/or facts.

☐ I revised my word choice to use descriptive and appropriate words.

☐ My tone is clear and consistent throughout the essay.

Proofreading Checklist

☐ I have read each sentence aloud, starting with the last one first and working backward to make sure each sentence is clear and uses appropriate language conventions.

☐ I used my proofreading frame to check for spelling.

☐ I keep my subjects and verbs consistent—either both singular or both plural.

☐ I keep any items in a series parallel.

☐ I asked a classmate to read my draft and to complete the Peer Revision Worksheet.

C:\Prompts for Writing ▶

You may want to use this activity as an opportunity to discuss comparison/contrast paragraphs.

1. Write a personal ad of twenty to twenty-five words. Volunteers can read theirs to the class. Get feedback from the class as to whether the ad would appeal to your intended audience (the type of person you would want to respond to this ad).

2. After doing activity 1, write a description of yourself in twenty to twenty-five words that you would give to a potential employer. Write a paragraph explaining how the two different audiences in the two activities affected your writing.

3. Review "The Data Game" on pages 139–141. Then write two paragraphs about personal ads on the Web. In the first paragraph, you are someone offering a personal ad service on the Web, and your audience is people who would pay you to subscribe to your service. In the second paragraph, you are someone who has a personal ad in the newspaper, and your audience is a friend who has never placed an ad.

4. If you brainstormed or clustered on the topic of *telecommuting to school* in Chapter 5, use what you wrote as a basis for an essay comparing and contrasting telecommuting to work versus telecommuting to school.

5. Discuss the benefits as well as the drawbacks of taking a course via distance education delivery. Would you take a class online? What factors influence your decision to enroll in such a class? to succeed in such a class? What would be important to know about and plan for ahead of time?

Go To ▶ 1. Go to the Web to do a search for "predictions about computers" or "predictions about technology." Does it surprise you what people once thought about technologies that are now very successful?

2. Go to the Web and do a search on "computer humor" or "computer cartoons." Find a cartoon or joke that expresses something you know or feel about computers. We've reproduced one of our favorites.

"MY DAD DOESN'T KNOW A LOT ABOUT COMPUTERS. HE THINKS ISDN AND MP3 WERE THE ROBOTS ON 'STAR WARS'."

Log Off: ▶ Review and Reflect

To reinforce the concepts, it is a good idea to have students complete Log Off: Review and Reflect and turn it in with the assignment.

Take some time to reflect on what you have learned about writing in Chapters 5 and 6. How has your writing changed as a result of the discussions, readings, and activities in these two chapters?

_____

_____

_____

_____

_____

_____

_____

_____

Refer to the writing you did as the central assignment in Chapter 3. Did you have a strong assertion?

_____

_____

Was the writing directed to a specific audience?

_____

_____

In reviewing what you wrote, do you see any instances in which you need to make changes for consistency in subject-verb agreement or for consistency in parallelism? If so, what did you originally write, and how would you write it now?

_____

_____

CHAPTER 7
Seeing Ourselves, Seeing Others, Being Seen

A strong, positive self-image is the best possible preparation for success in life.
—Dr. Joyce Brothers

Chapter Contents

Log On ▶ **Reflection**

Write whatever comes to mind when you read the chapter title and opening quotation.

_____

_____

_____

_____

_____

_____

_____

_____

_____

_____

_____

_____

_____

_____

_____

_____

_____

_____

_____

_____

FILE ▶ Open

00:20

You may want to begin this unit with a class discussion and/or individual or small group activities. The timer icons on this page and the next divide the activities into suggested time segments that will allow you to complete these introductory activities within a 45-minute class session.

Connecting with Experience

▶ Think of a recent conflict you had with another person. Clearly visualize the conflict and write one paragraph telling your side of the story. You are explaining your viewpoint.

▶ Now visualize the other person in the conflict and imagine how he or she feels about the situation. Write another paragraph telling this other side of the story. You are telling the story from the other person's viewpoint.

▶ Think of someone who handles situations in a way that you admire. Visualize that person talking to you and giving you still another view of what was going on in the conflict. Write a paragraph pretending you are that person explaining to you how you should handle the situation. You are taking your role model's viewpoint.

00:10

This activity is suitable for either freewriting or class discussion.

Connecting with the Topic

▶ How do you picture yourself? What do you think are your most obvious characteristics or personality traits, both good and bad?

▶ Do you think your family sees you differently from the way you see yourself? If so, why?

▶ How do you think your friends see you?

▶ How does your friends' or family's viewpoint toward you differ from your own viewpoint toward yourself?

▶ Webcams are gaining in popularity, and video phone calls are now possible. Do you want people to be able to see you through a webcam or phonecam while you are talking to them? Why or why not? How important is it to you to be able to see the person you are talking to on the phone?

00:10

If there is time, either in this class period or the next, have some students read their three "conflict" paragraphs aloud to the class.

Connecting with Writing

▶ How could a piece of writing have a viewpoint?

▶ Whose viewpoint would it be?

▶ Examine the three paragraphs you wrote about a conflict in the Connecting with Experience section above. Why were they different even though they described the same conflict?

Copyright © Houghton Mifflin Company. All rights reserved.

00:05

This section helps students connect the key concept introduced in this chapter: *point of view.* The amount or quality of material students are able to contribute here is not important. This activity is meant to be experiential and exploratory. Students might examine either or both of these questions, individually or in small groups.

Connecting with New Material

▶ What do you think *point of view* means? Write a definition of *point of view.* To get some idea of the meaning of this concept, explore what you may already know. Cluster the concept *point of view.*

Go To ▶ 1. Go to the home page of a friend or an instructor at your school. The author of that page probably selected certain images to put there. What do those images say about the person and how he or she wants to be seen?

Assignment: Have students read pages 159–162 and pages 165–176 and answer the questions on those pages only. Save the rest of the questions to do in class. Remind students to highlight the essays, "Body Image" and "Controlling Others" in the ways directed by some of the questions. If desired, have students finish paragraphs on conflict if they were not able to finish in class.

How would/do you represent yourself on the Web? If you have a home page, do you use any kind of image of yourself? How did you choose that image?

If you were going to create a home page for yourself, would you choose a professional-quality photograph, a candid shot of yourself doing something you like, an image that you created or drew, or no image at all? What does your choice say about who you are? Would you use photo editing software to transform your web image into a vision that matches who you would like to be instead of who you are?

Start a section in your notebook for keeping a list of what you like or dislike about others' web sites. Add notes every time you use the Web and notice something about a home page.

FILE ▶ New

Point of View

In the **File: Open** section of this chapter, you looked at a conflict from several *viewpoints.* In writing, we use the term *point of view* when discussing the writer's viewpoint. A writer's point of view reflects the writer's attitude or way of looking at something, including his or her biases, assumptions, and beliefs. When we see another's point of view, we are seeing something through the eyes of that person.

Determining an Author's Point of View

A piece of writing is always written from a specific point of view. That point of view may be the author's own point of view, or it may be a point of view that author has created for the purpose of the particular piece.

Read the following article and answer the question, "From whose point of view is this article written?"

Body Image, Positive or Negative, Shapes People's Lives

Dennis M. Kalup

1 *Hey, Fatty Boobalatty!* No, Fatty Boobalatty is not the name of a cartoon character from by-gone years. It is me.

2 Well, it was me. It was the unfortunate moniker that my sister burdened me with as a child. I would hear it ringing in my ears every time I ate any slightly fattening yet delicious morsel.

3 It was not only my sister who chided my anti-svelte physique. Classmates, cousins, anybody who was anyone would get in on the derision. I remember the humiliation of having to go to the special store to buy "husky" clothes.

4 I remember when my friends and I went to see *Return of the Jedi* in the movie theater, and for days afterward they called me Jabba Jr. I just laughed right along with them, trying to hide the humiliation and self-loathing.

5 You can probably guess the rest of the story from here. I got older, I got taller, and I lost my baby-fat look.

6 I was still overweight, but by the time we got to high school, there were bigger fish to fry, so to speak.

7 So the chapter of my book entitled "Dennis Kalup, obese overachieving 10-year-old" comes to a close.

8 Or does it?

9 To be perfectly honest with you, I don't think it ever will. Deep down inside, I think there will always be a fat little 10-year-old boy cowering in a corner eating candy bars.

10 This part of me will always be a powerful influence over that subtle yet potent mystery of the human psyche: BODY IMAGE.

11 You may scoff at my apparent obsession.

12 Scoff not, I say. Body image is a very powerful force in our society. It affects people in many different ways, some positive, but most negative.

13 Most people I talk to are not happy with their bodies. I used to think only heavy people suffered from this social stigma. The people that I consider to be "in shape" and "thin" have things about their bodies they would like to change, or alter.

14 I could sit around and blame my mother for feeding me the wrong types of food. I could blame society for stigmatizing fat people. I could blame the fact that I broke my leg when I was eight years old and had to be laid up for about six months. In fact, I used to blame it on all three. Then it happened.

15 I realized that it wasn't about blame, or anger, or that scared little 10-year-old anymore. It was about me being happy. That's all. I also realized that no matter how much I worked out, I was still going to be big. Not necessarily overweight, but I will probably always weigh over two hundred pounds and have a 36-inch waist.

16 My personal revelation was enough for me, but my friends and family wouldn't buy it. When I tried to explain to them that there was so much more in life to worry about and happiness is paramount, they disagreed.

17 So, as you can see, I can't change society. I will try to change whatever I can.

Source: Dennis M. Kalup, "Body Image, Positive or Negative, Shapes People's Lives," *The Digital Collegian*. Reprinted by permission of the author.

18 I get so excited whenever I see someone on television that is not the epitome of svelte and isn't the object of derision. Too often in the media, people who are overweight or not the ideal body of fitness are the butt of jokes.

19 There is my mother's favorite saying, "She (or he) has such a pretty face . . . it is a shame she (or he) is so big . . ." and then a lecture about their horrid eating habits.

20 I am sure this person doesn't go around thinking, "Gee, I am so glad I am pretty, it is a shame I ruined it with all of this weight."

21 Which brings me to another point. When you make fun of someone's weight, those insults can be the most damaging.

22 I am proud to be gay, I am proud to be a feminist, as the result of a community of people and support. There really aren't too many people rallying around to support people who are being made fun of because of their physical appearance.

23 Think about it.

24 So I tell you, I am proud of my body. It might not be the "physical ideal" but to be cliché for a moment, it is all I got. So, I make the most of it.

25 A friend of mine—the archetypal big, buxom woman—was the one that truly helped me with this issue. Her nonchalance in the face of people who would ridicule her was amazing, and she reeked of self-confidence. One of her favorite phrases is, "I take up a lot of space in this world." This has been my motto ever since.

26 This is not to say it doesn't get to her sometimes. I would be lying if I said it didn't. But her resolve is amazing, and it never gets to her long. Why? She takes up space in the world, and no one is going to take that away from her.

27 So, to those of you who might consider yourselves fat, ugly, or unappealing, this is my charge to you: Take up some space. Be proud of your space. It isn't easy, but it is the first step out the door to the rest of the world.

Questions 1–8 work well as a homework assignment.

Analyze the Reading

1. Kalup makes two assertions: one about his own body image and one about the topic of body image in general. See if you can find these assertions and highlight them in green. (*Hint:* They aren't in the usual places of the beginning or the end of the selection.)

2. In general, what is Dennis Kalup's point of view about body image? What can you tell about Dennis Kalup from his essay?

3. When a writer uses the word *I*, as Kalup does in this article, we say he or she is writing in the *first person*. The writing term that means that you can hear the *person* behind the words is *voice*. Do you sense a strong voice or individual identity coming through the words in this article? Explain your answer.

_____

_____

_____

_____

_____

4. In this essay, Kalup expresses a definite point of view toward his own body. State that point of view:

_____

_____

_____

_____

_____

_____

5. What is Kalup's point of view toward society's attitude about body image?

_____

_____

_____

_____

_____

_____

6. Notice all the quotations. What is the purpose of the quotation ("/")
marks?

_____

_____

_____

_____

7. How do those marks help you read the text?

_____

_____

_____

_____

_____

8. Generate a rule for quotation marks.

_____

_____

_____

_____

_____

Explore Point of View

00:45

You may want to do these activities in small groups or as a class. You will probably want to begin the discussion with homework questions 1–8 and then do these.

1. From the opinions Kalup expresses in his article, what do you think his
point of view toward the following would probably be? (You are making
an *inference*—an assumption based on what is presented.)

    a. A woman who can't go into the water at the beach because she won't
wear a swimsuit because of her figure

_____

_____

_____

_____

b. A man who communicates in a chat room regularly with a woman he finds interesting and then asks for a picture of her

_____

_____

_____

c. Swimsuit competitions in beauty pageants and beauty pageants in general

_____

_____

_____

_____

d. Large-sized models

_____

_____

_____

_____

e. Photography businesses, usually in malls, that make a woman look very glamorous

_____

_____

_____

_____

f. Men who get calf implants

_____

_____

_____

_____

2. Here are some statements on the subject of beauty. Try to match the quotations to the person who said or wrote them. After each quotation, describe what you can *infer* about the speaker's point of view toward beauty. Do you think her occupation influenced her point of view, or do you think her point of view influenced her choice of career?

- Helena Rubinstein, developer of a successful line of cosmetics
- Jean Kerr, humorist and playwright
- Gloria Steinem, ardent feminist and political activist

Kerr

a. "I'm tired of all this nonsense about beauty being only skin-deep. That's deep enough. What do you want—an adorable pancreas?"

_____

_____

_____

_____

Rubenstein

b. "There are no ugly women, only lazy ones."

_____

_____

_____

_____

Steinem

c. "In my own mind, I am still that fat brunette from Toledo, and I always will be."

Reminder: Students will need to have read the article "Controlling How Others See You Is Good Business" and have completed the questions following it (pages 165–176) msp. 7–15) as homework if you want to discuss the article in class.

_____

_____

_____

_____

Determining the Audience's Point of View

Just as the person writing has a point of view that is reflected in what he or she writes, the person reading the text, the *audience,* also has a point of view. You worked with audience in Chapter 6 and you learned that a writer usually writes with an audience in mind. As a *reader* you want to determine who that intended audience is because the writer is anticipating that the audience will have a certain point of view toward the topic.

As you read the following article, "Controlling How Others See You Is Good Business," determine who the intended audience is. Also, notice that an abstract precedes the main text. Think about what an abstract appears to be. What is the purpose of it? You will learn more about this in later chapters.

We designed this activity so that students could discover what an abstract is, since the joy of learning comes from figuring things out. They can arrive at a general idea and then they will have the opportunity to refine it later. If you want to use a different approach, you may define it for them as follows: An *abstract* is a kind of summary used in professional journals that presents the article's most important ideas so that readers can determine whether they want to read the entire article.

Controlling How Others See You Is Good Business

Sandra A. Miller

Abstract

Accountants should remember that every social encounter represents an opportunity for marketing their professional skills. They should also keep in mind that face-to-face encounters are perhaps the most opportune times for demonstrating professional expertise. To ensure that such encounters do not go to waste, accountants should hone their communication skills and take the time to study themselves and know what kind of impression they make on other people. Techniques for projecting positive impressions are given to assist accountants in their self-marketing campaigns. These techniques include preparing what to say beforehand, using eye contact, smiling sincerely, pausing regularly, and allowing body language to emphasize points that need to be stressed.

1   When you communicate with others, you are sending out verbal and non-verbal messages about yourself that people use to develop a feeling about the kind of person they think you are. With that feeling, they will either connect emotionally to you or tune you out. It takes only seconds of watching and listening to you for others to size you up in their minds. In less than 10 seconds, your audience of one or hundreds is deciding if you are confident, trustworthy, and whether they would be comfortable doing business with you. If the perceived impression is one of disinterest, arrogance, or insincerity, the talent and competence behind that impression may never have a chance to come out.

2   With some self-observation, honest self-appraisal, and conscious practice of new skills, you can make those first impressions positive ones. It is much easier to make a good first impression than to try and change it afterwards. With such high stakes coming from such quick judgments, the successful professional makes it his or her responsibility

Source: Sandra A. Miller, "Controlling How Others See You Is Good Business," *The CPA Journal* (October 1994). Reprinted by permission.

to be aware of how he or she is coming across at all times. Taking control of how others see you is not only smart, it is good business.

3 For those of you who aren't yet comfortable marketing yourself, for those who have not yet seen the rewards of their personal marketing efforts, and for those whose communications skills can stand some polishing, take heart. The skills and techniques to give you more control over the impressions you make on others, and the responses that follow, can be learned. It begins with raising your awareness of how you send out messages about yourself and the almost instantaneous impressions that are formed. To do that, you will need to observe yourself on videotape when you are speaking. As you watch and listen, decide what you are doing or saying that is contributing to your effectiveness and what is getting in the way. Then, focusing on one skill at a time, consciously begin to modify those less-than-effective skills and techniques until you are pleased with the impressions that are projected and the responses you get.

4 To start building an awareness of how others see us and in turn make judgments about us, think about and visualize some well-known speakers, in particular the ones who have made favorable impressions on you. What about them impressed you and how quickly were you impressed? Was it their energy? The way they used their voice? How they organized what they had to say? How about the people you choose to do business with? What did they say or do that made you agree to do business with them? You probably formed a favorable impression and an emotional connection with them almost immediately.

5 The following people are all considered good communicators. In their own way, each projects strong and favorable impressions about the kind of people they are. The verbal and non-verbal messages they send out are clear and convincing and help them get the responses they want from their listeners.

6 When Lee Iacocca speaks, he comes across as sincere, approachable, and caring. His highly effective communication style helped him win over banks, the government and unhappy employees, to turn Chrysler around.

7 Oprah Winfrey talks openly and naturally about herself and sends out messages to her listeners that she is no different than they are. The trust and comfort she establishes in her guests has gotten them to confide their deepest secrets on national television.

8 Norman Schwarzkopf's direct, clear and often humorous way of speaking helped him gain recognition as a spokesperson for the Persian Gulf War and made him a wealthy man on the speakers' circuit afterwards.

9 You can change and control the way others see you and respond to you. The next time you are scheduled to speak, whether formally behind a podium or informally around the table, have yourself videotaped. Afterwards, watch and listen to yourself as if you were a member of the audience. What messages are you sending out about yourself by how you speak, how you move, and how you act? Do you come across as confident, trustworthy, caring and someone you would be comfortable with doing business?

10 When you watch yourself on tape, look out for the following communication styles and techniques that can send out messages of insincerity, lack of interest or lack of credibility.

Is your speech punctuated with lots of filler words, "uhms," "ahs," "wells"?

Are you stretched out in your seat, leaning back in your chair or standing on one hip?

Are you holding your head down or tilting it to the side?

Do you look up for inspiration or glance sideways rather than make eye contact with your listener?

Do you get to the point or tend to ramble on?

Is how you move, sound and act in sync with the point you are trying to make?

Is your physical appearance appropriate for your audience?

Does what you say and do help your listeners to feel comfortable with you?

11   Study your image and focus on those skills and techniques that help you create the appropriate impression for that situation and that audience and what is distracting. Ask your colleagues for their impressions of you when you speak with clients and other professionals on a daily basis. What do your listeners notice and respond to? What turns them off? Then decide what verbal and non-verbal skills and techniques you will consciously take control of, and the specific modifications you need to make, in order to change the way others see you and respond to you.

12   The following techniques, if practiced and used to their full advantage, work together to project favorable impressions of you when you are speaking with people and marketing your skills and services:

1. Think about and, whenever possible, prepare what you are going to say. Speakers that shoot from the hip often shoot themselves in the foot. Even in impromptu situations, you can have a pretty good idea of what you may be asked to speak about and can plan your words ahead of time.

2. When you begin to speak, make sure your listeners know right away what they will be getting from this particular communication. Don't leave your listeners guessing as to the point you are trying to get across.

3. Use eye contact to connect with your listeners and make this communication a personal experience. People are more likely to trust you and be willing to do business with you if they feel you are real and unafraid to look them in the eyes.

4. Smile. It energizes you and helps you to look self-confident.

5. Stand or sit naturally straight so you look energetic and interested.

6. Gesture occasionally to strengthen your voice, relax your body and help emphasize the point you are trying to get across.

7. Pause. It makes your words seem more important and gives others a chance to respond.

8. Speak using a variety of speech patterns. Vary the tone and volume of your voice to keep your listeners awake and interested.

9. Practice out loud. It helps fix the words in your memory. Hearing them also tells you if you are on the right track.

13   Be sure to work on only one new skill at a time until you can use it without consciously thinking about it beforehand. Do it even if it feels uncomfortable at first. Your mind will soon catch up with what the rest of you is doing.

14 The skills and techniques to control how others see you are meant to be used every day. The more consciously you use the skills, the more comfortable you will be with them. The more comfortable you are, the more confident you will be that the messages you are sending out and the impressions that are projected, no matter where you may be or who you are speaking with, are the right ones, the ones more likely to get and grow your business.

Analyze the Reading

1. Highlight the author's assertion in green. Highlight the main ideas in blue. Highlight examples in yellow and facts in pink. State the author's thesis.

   _____

   _____

   _____

2. Who is the author's intended audience?

   _____

   _____

   _____

3. Are you a member of that intended audience? Explain.

   _____

   _____

   _____

4. From what point of view is this article written?

   _____

   _____

   _____

5. The author writes about the image a person presents to an audience. What is she saying about that image?

   _____

   _____

   _____

6. Do you agree with that assertion?

_____

_____

_____

7. Notice that the article begins with an *abstract.* Read the abstract carefully and then describe as best you can what an abstract is.

_____

_____

_____

You will learn more about abstracts in Chapter 9.

Determining Your Own Point of View

You have identified a writer's point of view and an audience's point of view. However, it is also important to be aware of your own point of view. A statement of your point of view consists of two parts: the topic and your assertion about the topic. This complete sentence is also called a *thesis statement.*

1. Practice making statements that reflect a clearly stated point of view by writing an assertion for each of the following topics. Write a complete sentence—a thesis statement—containing the topic and the assertion. The first one is done for you. The topic is underlined once and the assertion is underlined twice.

a. Body piercing

Body piercing is a form of self-expression.

_____

_____

_____

b. Tattoos

_____

_____

_____

c. Designer clothing

_____

_____

_____

We suggest that this activity is best done in class. Students enjoy reading the assertions aloud, and they are able to see how many different assertions—points of view—are possible on a given subject. Hearing other students' facts and examples helps them see that there are many ways to develop an idea.

d. Plastic surgery on sixteen-year-olds

_____

_____

_____

e. Expensive sneakers for ten-year-olds

_____

_____

_____

2. Pick one of the assertions that you wrote above and support it with a fact.

_____

_____

_____

_____

_____

_____

_____

_____

_____

_____

3. For each of the remaining assertions, write an example.

_____

_____

_____

_____

_____

_____

Go To ▶ Go to the *Writing Now* web site. There you will find specific sites that will lead you to different chat rooms. What do chatters' screen names tell you about how they see themselves? What is your screen name and why? Are you different from your usual self, somehow, when you are the person you identify with your screen name?

OPTIONS ▶ Customize

1. Write a paragraph for one or more of the assertions you wrote in activity 1 of the preceding exercise. As you did with the assertion, write from a clear point of view.

2. Read your paragraph aloud to the class.

3. Listen to other students' treatment of the same topics to see the variety of ways in which a topic can be developed from different points of view.

You may find this a good place to begin the second homework assignment. Students should read the two essays debating how women should dress at work and be prepared to discuss them. You may want them to write out the answers to the questions as well.

You can see that you already have some experience with point of view, and you are gaining experience in how it relates to writing. Often the most interesting writing has a strong, clear point of view. When your assignment is to write a response to a reading selection, the stronger the point of view in the reading selection, the easier it may be for you to respond, either positively or negatively.

Did you notice that the thesis statement usually reflects the writer's point of view? When a writer makes an assertion, that assertion is based on his or her point of view. Your response will also be an assertion, based on your point of view toward the subject.

To get a better understanding of the impact of point of view on writing, read the following two essays. Each essay gives the author's point of view toward the image women project in the workplace by the way they dress. As you read, determine whether or not these two authors share the same point of view. Try to analyze what led you to that conclusion. (*Note:* These authors are British and use some words differently than we do as Americans. For example, they write: "businesswomen have a different agenda *to* women in general" where we might expect to see *from* or *than; internalised* instead of *internalized;* and *naff* for *unfashionable* or *out of style.*)

Debate: Does It Matter What Women Wear to Work?

Peter York

Yes

1   When I was on the panel judging the best-dressed business people for *Management Today* magazine last week, it soon became apparent that women haven't quite worked out a grammar for dressing at work. This is not to say that British women per se don't have any dress sense, which is blatantly untrue, but businesswomen have a different agenda to women in general and need to develop a proper code for office dressing. This means not simply choosing clothes for practicality but also choosing flattering clothes with panache.

2   Part of the problem is that there are imagined internalised constraints on working women in Britain who concentrate on trying not to

Columnist Peter York is MD of management consultants SRU Ltd.

Source: Peter York, "Debate: Does It Matter What Women Wear to Work?", *Independent on Sunday,* August 22, 1999. Reprinted by permission of Cape & Land, London, as agent for the author.

look too "sexy" when they're at work, and making sure they are taken seriously by men, a reaction in part to the fact that there are not enough women at senior management levels.

3 Particularly when women get to a senior level at work, there's an urge to shut it all away—not to be mannish exactly, but to de-sex herself so as not to be the object of attention. In France and Italy, by comparison, you can be businesslike and feminine and glamorous all at the same time. I'm not suggesting that businesswomen should start behaving like Sharon Stone during her "leg-crossing" phase—too much skin or tightness of clothes is wrong with either gender—but women need to relax about the relationship between their clothes and their profession because this fashion reserve translates into a complete lack of style. That's why we still get the Eighties power dresser, the overly relaxed dresser, or the classic "mother of the bride" matron look.

4 I'm the first to admit that men have it easier than women with work clothes because they have an accepted uniform. That's why it was easier to judge the men's side of the competition. (Lord Saatchi won, if you're wondering.) But clothes have become a vital communication tool at work and women have to decide what they want to say and work to get their own "look."

5 This already happens in Europe, with women wearing Armani couture, while the American version is probably the Donna Karan trouser suit. We are starting to catch on in Britain; but there's not enough sense of quality at the moment. This is why British women can veer from looking absolutely amazing to looking deeply naff, while Parisian women may look slightly boring in their approach to work clothes, but will always have an idea in their head about what is "good" dressing. Still, I know we'll get there eventually.

Susannah Frankel

No

1 So women should take more care over their appearance at work, should they? Well, according to a survey by Britain's "leading business magazine"—and fashion bible?—*Management Today,* they should. While men—this survey said—can more than hold their own in the workplace sartorially speaking, British women lag woefully behind their French and Italian counterparts and "need to learn how to use clothes as part of their individual marketing strategy." Stern words indeed. Apparently, however, women in this country are personally fearful of provoking criticism—of being labelled frivolous—should they pay too much attention to the way they look at the workplace. (Who are these women?) Our designers, meanwhile, are failing to produce the kind of garments a working woman needs to achieve elegance (and/or respect?) in the office. Have a word with yourself, Alexander McQueen.

2 All of this makes me wonder what planet exactly—and what century, for that matter—the brains behind such a thoroughly archaic initiative

Susannah Frankel is fashion editor of the *Independent on Sunday.*

Source: Susannah Frankel, "The No reply to the fashion debate." *Independent on Sunday,* August 22, 1999, p. 5. Reprinted by permission of The Independent, London.

hail from. It's hardly news that the single unifying factor of fashion in the Nineties is that rigid dress codes are finally, thankfully, eroding. There is no need, for example, for a woman to wear a dress so over-blown it would hardly fit through the door to a gala dinner and dance. Conversely, should she wish to wear sequins and sparkle to brighten up a wintry morning at the office, then so be it: such fashion frippery is no longer the preserve of Saturday nights at the Hippodrome, thank you.

3   More good news comes with the fact that those natty little skirt and trouser suit combos—the sort we all swore by in the label-obsessed, power-driven Eighties—are no longer the only workwear to see and be seen in. If women do want to dress like that, then so be it—they will be spoilt for choice—but anyone who expects them to do so needs their head examined. Get real, *Management Today!* Get modern! The last thing any self-respecting woman needs to worry about while she's feed-ing her children their breakfast and doing last night's washing up is her image: that prescribed lick of mascara and dash of red lipstick that will ensure she is respected at the office once she finally gets there.

4   To judge any person purely on the way they look is offensive, what-ever his or her environment. The way we all dress may, to some extent, be a reliable indication of the sort of person we are and, even more so, the particular image we choose to project. However, to suggest it has even the slightest significance where our ability to do our jobs properly is concerned is to lose the plot—fashion or otherwise. Tidy tailoring does not a tidy desk (or tidy mind) make.

5   Anyone mad enough to set store in such outmoded and proscriptive garbage should spare a moment to think on this (a minor practicality but one worthy of the *working* woman's consideration nonetheless): what exactly is the point of our spending time and money over what we wear to the office when the only people we are likely to impress by so doing are a load of boring old farts in suits?

These activities may be best done as homework, but, if possible, the an-swers should be discussed in class because they will help students for-mulate ideas for the central assign-ment.

Analyze the Reading

1. Highlight the assertions in green and the main ideas in blue. Highlight ex-amples in yellow and facts in pink.

2. State Peter York's point of view toward the debate question, "Does it mat-ter what women wear to work?":

_____

_____

_____

_____

3. State Susannah Frankel's point of view toward the same question.

_____

_____

_____

_____

4. Describe how you were able to determine the authors' points of view.

_____

_____

_____

_____

_____

_____

_____

_____

_____

5. How does the tone differ in the two essays? Discuss both authors' tone.

_____

_____

_____

6. What is York's occupation?

_____

7. What is Frankel's occupation?

_____

8. Do you think their occupations have anything to do with their differing points of view on this subject? Explain.

_____

_____

_____

_____

_____

9. State your point of view on appropriate dress for work. Make your statement general enough so that you can support it with specific examples if you wrote a paragraph about your point of view.

_____

_____

_____

_____

OPTIONS ▶ Customize

1. Discuss or debate the issue of casual Fridays in the workplace. On the board, list or cluster the points that are made for both sides of the debate. Plan in groups and select a representative to debate a representative from another group.

2. Using the appropriate points from those listed on the board from number 1 of this exercise, write an essay to support your argument of casual Fridays. Be sure to express your point of view in your essay.

3. Make a poster of appropriate dress for the workplace in the career you aspire to. Compare this with the posters of classmates who may have selected other occupations.

4. If you did the dress code activity in Chapter 3 (question 3 in the C:\Prompts for Writing section on page 73), use what you wrote as a basis for creating a dress code for your chosen occupation. If this occupation requires you to wear a uniform, write about the advantages and disadvantages of having to wear a uniform to work.

5. Begin designing a personal web page. Design your web page on paper for now; you will learn how to create and post a web page online in Chapter 9. Refer to the notes you began taking on page 158. What digital artifacts (images, text, links) would you put on your web site to present yourself as you would like others to see you?

6. Do the same as exercise 5, but instead of creating a personal web site, create a web site designed for your potential employers to see. Begin with a good resume. Go to the Web to find help on writing resumes if you don't have a good one on file. Academic sites such as the Purdue OWL (**http://owl.english.purdue.edu/—search for resume**) offer handouts on writing good resumes. Commercial sites such as Monster.com (**http://resume.monster.com**) or the I-Jive site at <**http://www.ijive.com/resume**> often sell resume writing services, but they also offer tips and sometimes discussion forums on creating your own resume. Finally, you can do your own search on "resume help" using your favorite search engine (such as **http://www.lycos.com** or Yahoo! Health—your guide to health and wellness).

7. Bring a photograph of yourself to class that shows how you would like to represent yourself on the Web. What does your choice of image say about you?

FILE ▶ Create

`00:20`

In the remaining time, you may want to allow students to plan during class time or individually in small groups. If not, you may want to use the time to read the conflict paragraphs aloud that they started at the beginning of the chapter.

Exercise 1 makes for a lively class or small-group discussion and gives students ideas for supporting their assertion.

If you are using an alternative assignment, students would begin their writing plan at this point.

You may want to spend some class time discussing writing these plans.

Writing an Essay with a Strong Point of View

1. Brainstorm on the topic *the effect of clothing choices in the workplace.* You may want to consider the following:

   dress codes

   casual Fridays

   uniforms

   fads

   freedom issues

   type of employment

   customer relations

   modesty

2. Using your answer to question 9 on page 176, formulate a thesis statement in response to either York's or Frankel's essay: (*Note:* If you find it easier to agree, then respond to the essay you agree with. If you find it more interesting to disagree, then respond to the essay you disagree with. You may disagree with both essays. In that case, you could choose either one or respond to both.)

3. Cluster your topic for 5 minutes. Jot down ideas relating to work clothing and connect them to each other and to the central circle in a way that makes sense to you.

4. Using your blue highlighter, organize your cluster.

5. Determine your audience. From now on, you will have a specified audience for all writing.

6. Determine your purpose in writing. It will be affected by your assertion and your audience.

7. Determine your tone. What would be the most effective tone to get across your individual point of view?

Some ideas for an audience for the topic *the effect of clothing choices in the workplace* might be

- The author of one of the essays reading the student's e-mailed response to the essay
- Coworkers reading the essay in a corporate newsletter
- Employees reading the views of a boss who is setting a new office dress policy
- A boss needing to be persuaded to change office dress policy
- Classmates being informed of peers' views
- An employer wanting to get an idea of an applicant's attitude toward dress policy

Tie purpose in with audience suggestions above.

If you wish to teach this as an argument, or as a response in preparation for summary/response work later, then you might want to make the purpose "to argue" and select one of the first four audience options.

Name: _____   Date: _____

Write an outline for your essay.

Topic: _____

_____

Assertion: _____

_____

_____

Audience: _____

_____

Purpose: _____

Tone: _____

I. First key point: _____

_____

_____

II. Second key point: _____

_____

_____

III. Third key point: _____

_____

_____

Add additional key points as needed.

FILE ▶ Save As

Write an essay based on your outline. Consider carefully the author's point of view in the essay to which you are responding. Make sure your point of view is clearly stated in your thesis and that each point supports that point of view.

Save your essay as a draft. In the next chapter you will learn some ways to improve your essay. Before you can do that, however, you need some clearly thought-out ideas written in a well-organized manner. Therefore, make sure this draft is complete and well developed. You will need it in order to complete the work in the next chapter.

Go To ▶ Go to the *Writing Now* web site for more information on role playing in MOOs (if you participate in them), or on creating a character in an online soap opera.

C:\Prompts for Writing ▶

You may want to assign one of these essays as a substitute for the **File: Create** assignment on page 177.

1. Reread the essay "Body Image, Positive or Negative, Shapes People's Lives" on page 159 and respond to it. You may want to describe how you have experienced or witnessed the influence of positive or negative body images on your own life or on other people's lives.

2. Pick one of the topic/assertion sentences you wrote on pages 169–170 and turn it into an essay.

3. Turn the three viewpoint paragraphs you wrote about a conflict in the **File: Open** section on page 157 into an essay.

CHAPTER 8
Different Visions, Different Versions

One sees great things from the valley, only small things from the peak.

—G. K. Chesterton

Chapter Contents

181

Log On ▶ **Reflection**

Write whatever comes to mind when you read the chapter title and opening quotation.

_____

_____

_____

_____

_____

_____

_____

_____

_____

_____

_____

_____

_____

_____

_____

_____

_____

_____

_____

_____

_____

_____

_____

FILE ▶ Open

00:10

File Open is suitable for individual activities at the beginning of a class period or for class discussion.

Review of Point of View

In the last chapter you worked with the concept of point of view. You drafted an essay in which you consciously adopted a specific point of view, stated it clearly, and supported it. In this chapter you will work again with point of view, focusing on how to stay open to another person's point of view and how what you write might affect another person.

Connecting with Experience

▶ Why did society change the words *mankind* to *humanity*, *fireman* to *firefighter*, and *stewardess* to *flight attendant*?

▶ What do you think about referring to *waitresses* as *waitpersons*?

▶ What impact do you think what you call people has on their image of themselves—their personal identity? For example, would an advertisement for a *cocktail waitress* bring in women with a different self-image than an ad for a *server*?

Connecting with Previous Learning

▶ How would you define *point of view*? (*Hint:* You may want to go back to Chapter 7, page 157, and add to your cluster, then use what you have discovered as the basis for your definition.)

▶ As a result of the work you did in Chapter 7, what did you learn about seeing something from multiple points of view?

▶ Why do we use the word *you* instead of a person's name (for example: "I will hand *you* the ball first")? Why do we use the word *she* instead of a name (for example: "I called Tranise, and *she* said *she* would bring the cake")?

FILE ▶ New

00:35

Sexist Language

The concept that speakers or writers should be careful about the pronouns they use is based on the idea that a person's self-image can be affected by language. One kind of language that some find demeaning or offensive is known as *sexist* or gender-specific language. Sexist language is the use of a pronoun that includes an assumption of the gender of the person to whom the pronoun refers. For example, a *waitress* is assumed to be a woman and a *waiter* to be a man. What sex is a *mailman* assumed to be? If a company decides to appoint someone as *chairman*, it might give the impression that only men are eligible for the position and thus the term would be considered sexist. A more appropriate term would be *chair* of the committee or board.

Before exploring sexist language in more detail, read the following paragraph and circle any words you suspect might be considered sexist.

Question 2 is an enjoyable way for students to become familiar with what might be considered sexist language. You may want students to rewrite the paragraphs in class, either individually or in small groups. Alternatively, if you have students do this as homework, you may want to allow time for them to take turns reading sentences aloud when they return to class. If the class overlooks some words that you know might be considered sexist, do not point those words out at this time. Students will be going over this paragraph again in a follow-up activity later in the chapter and will then be able to see how their understanding of sexist language has increased as a result of the readings, activities, and discussions in the chapter.

The Fire

We had a terrible disaster in our office building yesterday. A fire broke out on the seventh floor in the beauty parlor. When the alarm went off, everyone starting running for his nearest stairway. It was every man for himself as people were pushing and shoving to get out. A waitress in the restaurant on the second floor got knocked down. The mailman was shoved and envelopes went everywhere. The salesmen ran from the cellular phone store. The girls in the office were screaming. The chairman of the corporation on the ninth floor tried to organize everyone but he just wasn't man enough to handle the crowd. It was dark on the stairs and difficult for anyone to see his way. When the firemen arrived, only about half of the businessmen were out of the building. The TV station sent so many reporters that they even had the weather girl out there reporting. The police chief said to put the best man on the job to organize the escape. He told every policeman available to man the stairs to help evacuate. It seems that all the manmade materials in the building were creating a good deal of smoke that made it harder to evacuate. It took nine manhours to get the fire out. It was a tribute to mankind's achievements that no one was killed. I intend to write my congressman about what a good job the firemen and policemen did.

Analyze the Paragraph

1. How many words did you circle?

_____

2. On a separate sheet of paper, rewrite the paragraph, omitting sexist language.

3. What is your point of view toward using the words you circled in the original passage?

_____

_____

4. Does your rewritten paragraph sound better to you than the original? Why or why not?

_____

_____

This is a good place to begin a homework assignment. You may want students to read, highlight, and answer questions on pages 185–192.

Some people believe that using different words for men and women in occupations emphasizes gender difference and may lead to possible gender discrimination. For example, for many years waitresses made less than waiters. Finer restaurants placed ads for male waiters only. Now the term *server* is used, and federal law forbids gender discrimination in hiring.

Language geared to men—such as *manmade, man-hours, mankind*—can make women feel invisible. And many of our gender-specific expressions—such as *the right man for the job*—imply that one gender is more or less capable than the other.

Another objection to sexist language is that the use of gender-specific names for certain professions—such as *mailman, metermaid,* and *policeman*—implies that members of the other gender are not engaged in that profession, thereby defining and limiting the ambitions of young children. A young man, for example, would not be likely to apply for the position of "metermaid," even though he might enjoy that work.

Not everyone has the same point of view on this subject. Read "Non-Sexist Language Can Be Ridiculous" and determine the author's point of view toward changing the language to make it gender-neutral.

Non-Sexist Language Can Be Ridiculous

Emilie Muto

Grade 8, Hazel McCallion Sr. Public School, Mississauga, Ontario

1. For years and years, women have fought for their right to be treated with respect, to be treated equal to men. Slowly, they've acquired these rights. For example, women are now getting better, higher paying jobs, and have moved into positions of power such as the former Prime Minister of Canada, Kim Campbell, and the mayor of Mississauga, Hazel McCallion.

2. Yet, this isn't good enough for some. Now, feminists have to go and rewrite the dictionary, changing words that aren't to their liking. One example is changing "manhole" to "sewer access hole." Will this nonsense never end?

3. I am a strong believer in women's rights, but I know where to draw the line. What Margaret Doyle, the author of "The A–Z of Non-Sexist Language," doesn't understand is that it's not the word that you have to change, it's the attitude. A word's a word and making it politically correct isn't going to change the way the world thinks. Not only is this issue ridiculous, it's not going to do any good for women. This will be seen as another attempt by radicals to get their own way. How can women expect to be treated with respect and like intelligent people when they do such absurd things? Rewriting the dictionary is a disservice to women and it makes women look like petty fools.

4. Words like "snowman" and "mailman" were never created to be offensive to women. Things that should be important, like a woman's job and working conditions, have been changed. And if a woman holds a position such as chairman, she is called a chairwoman, or chairperson. If a person wants to make a female "snowman," he/she will call it a "snow-woman." It's that simple.

5. You don't have to go rewriting the dictionary to change how people talk. Women should start fighting for more important rights. Words don't change attitudes. The way something is said doesn't make a difference. Is an "abominable snow creature" any less abominable because you change its name?

Analyze the Reading

1. Highlight the thesis statement in green and topic sentences in blue. Highlight examples in yellow and facts in pink.

2. What is the author's point of view toward her subject?

_____

_____

_____

3. How does the author support her assertion? (facts, examples, both, other?)

_____

_____

_____

4. Write an appropriate example for the author to use to support her assertion.

_____

_____

_____

_____

_____

5. What is the point of view toward using sexist language in this essay?

_____

_____

_____

_____

6. Who is the audience?

_____

In spite of Muto's opinion, today gender-neutral language is preferable to the conventional language of the past, which tended to use primarily masculine nouns and pronouns. Instead of *chairman,* most people today prefer *chair* or *chairperson.* The typical way society has dealt with this issue has been to

CHAPTER 8 Different Visions, Different Versions | **187**

change the masculine term to a non-gender-specific term. It is simple to change *mankind* to *humanity.*

In using pronouns, most people are careful to say *his and her* instead of *his.* In writing, however, repeatedly using *his* as the neutral pronoun is no longer acceptable, but *his or her* can be awkward. Avoiding sexist language can also create problems with pronoun reference. The "How to Avoid Sexist Language" box shows you some ways to avoid sexist language in your writing.

How to Avoid Sexist Language

1. Many times you can simply change a gender-specific pronoun to *a, an,* or *the:* "Everyone needs to determine *a* point of view on this subject."

2. If *a* doesn't work, as in the sentence "Everyone should be aware of *his* point of view," you can make the subject, verb, and pronoun reference plural: "*People* should be aware of *their* point of view."

3. Sometimes you can eliminate the pronoun altogether: "Everyone should be aware of point of view."

4. When appropriate, you can use the second person: "*You* should be aware of *your* point of view."

5. Also when appropriate, you can use *one:* "*One* should be aware of *one's* point of view." However, today, *one* is used mostly in very formal writing. Be sure that you have not created additional awkwardness by using *one* in a more casually written piece.

6. Sometimes, instead of modifying the original term, you may want to search for another term altogether. Instead of *policeman,* use *police officer;* instead of *mailman,* use *mail carrier.* Nouns ending with the suffix *-ess* (or *-ette*), indicating the feminine form of the word, are considered unacceptable. Instead of *waiter, waitress,* or the awkward *waiterperson,* many establishments now have employees say, "Hi, I'm Bob, and I'll be your *server.*"

In deciding which option to use in avoiding sexist language, you must consider your audience and the sentences surrounding the sentence in question. Reading your paper aloud will give you an idea of whether you have made a choice that fits smoothly as well as grammatically. For example, if you changed the sentence, "Everyone should correct his paper," to "Everyone should correct *a* paper," that might change the meaning to include the option of checking another student's paper. Similarly, if you change the sentence, "A person should consider his budget," to "A person should consider *their* budget," to avoid the sexist *his,* then you have made a subject-verb agreement error. "Person" is singular, but "their" is plural. A better choice would be "his or her" in this case. Making an appropriate choice is not as easy as you may think, so be careful.

Read the following essay by Jennifer Griffith on eliminating generic-male language. Griffith offers ways to avoid using sexist language. She also lists four ways in which using gender-inclusive language can improve your writing. **Highlight these four ways in blue as you find them.**

Eliminating Generic-Male Language: Political Statement or Just Good Writing?

Jennifer Griffith

1 "Do I really have to use 'he or she'?" the student asked me. "Is this one of those teachers who will get upset about just saying 'he' to refer to an undefined person?" You could tell by the student's tone that "those teachers" were either screaming liberals or grammar heretics. The student may have been influenced by previous teachers who thought that purposefully changing the rules of English grammar was akin to burning the flag. There are plenty of strong opinions about inclusive language, and the concern about motives often obscures the concern we all have for effective communication. Eliminating generic-male language may have political and social implications. For people concerned about effective communication, however, eliminating generic-male language can help produce more clear, concise, and accurate writing.

2 Traditional rules of writing, those that most of us learned in school, say that "he" stands for both "he" and "she" and that "man" stands for both men and women. Generic-male language, however, is confusing to read. Many studies have shown that when people read "man" and "he" they assume that the writer means a male person. Researchers in these studies gave participants writing samples and asked them to match the subjects with pictures; a majority of the participants matched the writing which included generic-male language with pictures of men rather than with pictures of women or men and women.

3 If we follow traditional generic-male rules in our writing, we will construct sentences which do not fully express what we mean to say. For example, "If an opthamologist suspects glaucoma, he should administer the proper tests," suggests that any person in the group of opthamologists will be male.

4 Some people suggest that changing generic-male language only results in wordy, ungraceful sentences. Indeed, writing "he or she" or "his or her" in every sentence becomes just as monotonous as the exclusive use of "he." However, using a generic "he" to represent any member of a group which could contain women forces the reader to stop and examine the meaning behind the writer's words: Does the writer mean a specific man, or is this one of those cases in which "he" is supposed to represent any man in the group, or does "he" mean any man or any woman?

5 There are several relatively easy ways to write accurately and leave out generic-male references. The subjects can be made plural: "A doctor must use his own judgment in prescribing medication" becomes "Doctors must use their own judgment. . . ." Using words such as "one," "someone," "anyone," "the one," and so on is also helpful. For example, instead of writing "He who loses the battle sometimes wins the war," try "One who loses the battle sometimes wins the war."

6 Eliminating the pronoun altogether is also an option. A sentence such as "When he arrives at the scene, the officer should assess the

---

Source: Jennifer Griffith, "Eliminating Generic-Male Language: Political Statement or Just Good Writing? WORD WRAP, September 1994. Originally published on the RSCC Online Writing Lab, **http://www2.rscc.cc.tn.us/~jordan_jj/OWL/Articles.html**.

scope of the emergency" can be changed to "Upon arriving at the scene, the officer . . . ." Recasting the sentence in second person is another solution. "Man never understands his strengths until he has been tested" can be changed to "You never understand your strengths until you have been tested."

7   What will all of these changes do for your writing? First, changing the generic-male pronouns and nouns to some of the alternatives discussed here will make your writing more interesting because you will be making an effort to use a variety of forms and structures in your sentences. You will not be using writing off the top of your head, which is often full of clichés. Instead of writing a boring sentence such as, "Stone-age man found ways to tame his environment," you can write a sentence such as, "Stone-age agriculturists and hunters used their survival skills to tame their environment."

8   Using gender inclusive language will also help you write more specifically, which always improves writing. Instead of writing about "workmen," you can instead write about "carpenters," or "plumbers," or "construction workers," or "janitors," or "architects," whatever it is that you actually meant by workmen.

9   Gender inclusive language will help your reader follow your argument without being distracted by wondering what you mean by generic-male use of "man" or "he." Although traditional grammar rules tell us that "man" stands for both men and women, "man" is used far more often to refer to men only. When these words are used to refer to women as well the reader has to stop and process this meaning before continuing with the reading. Distractions like this may mean that the reader never finishes what you have written.

10   Finally, using gender inclusive language will make your writing more accurate. Using generic-male "man" and "he" to represent all human beings is not an accurate reflection of reality, and your readers will react to this discrepancy. Writing inaccurately will discredit the message in your writing.

11   While the argument over eliminating generic-male language rages on, both in and out of the classroom, as writers we must always concern ourselves with accuracy and clarity. We must, in fact, offer up the best possible writing if we are to win the arguments ourselves. Using inclusive language is not about championing a cause so much as it is about producing prose which has the power to grip and to shape readers' thinking.

Analyze the Reading

1. Highlight the thesis statement in green and the main supporting ideas in blue. Highlight examples in yellow and facts in pink.

2. What methods does Griffith offer for avoiding the use of sexist language?

_____

_____

_____

_____

_____

_____

_____

_____

_____

3. According to Griffith, in what four ways can avoiding sexist language improve your writing?

a. _____

_____

b. _____

_____

c. _____

_____

d. _____

_____

4. How does Griffith's attitude toward sexist language differ from Muto's?

_____

_____

_____

_____

5. Can you make any guesses about why Griffith's and Muto's points of view may differ? What information do we have about the authors that gives us some insights into their points of view?

_____

_____

_____

_____

6. Analyze the effectiveness of Griffith's writing. How does Griffith support the topic sentence in each of the following paragraphs?

Students will learn more about these patterns of development later. The purpose is to begin to create an awareness now.

Paragraph 3:

_____

_____

_____

_____

Paragraph 4:

_____

_____

_____

_____

Paragraph 5:

_____

_____

_____

_____

Paragraph 7:

_____

_____

_____

_____

What is the transition word that continues the listing in paragraph 8?

_____

What is the transition word that continues the listing in paragraph 10?

_____

What does Griffith do to make an effective conclusion?

_____

Now that you have had some experience with sexist language, take another look at the following paragraph, which you originally worked with on page 184. Circle all the words you now consider sexist.

hair salon; All were on their own
server
mail carrier
sales staff/women
chair
he couldn't handle
see the way/firefighters
employees, business
people, or professionals
weather reporter
best person
police officer
work the stairs
synthetic materials
person-hours or work-hours
humanity's
congressperson
firefighters/police officers

The Fire

We had a terrible disaster in our office building yesterday. A fire broke out on the seventh floor in the beauty parlor. When the alarm went off, everyone starting running for his nearest stairway. It was every man for himself as people were pushing and shoving to get out. A waitress in the restaurant on the second floor got knocked down. The mailman was shoved and envelopes went everywhere. The salesmen ran from the cellular phone store. The girls in the office were screaming. The chairman of the corporation on the ninth floor tried to organize everyone but he just wasn't man enough to handle the crowd. It was dark on the stairs and difficult for anyone to see his way. When the firemen arrived, only about half of the businessmen were out of the building. The TV station sent so many reporters that they even had the weather girl out there reporting. The police chief said to put the best man on the job to organize the escape. He told every policeman available to man the stairs to help evacuate. It seems that all the man-made materials in the building were creating a good deal of smoke that made it harder to evacuate. It took nine man-hours to get the fire out. It was a tribute to mankind's achievement that no one was killed. I intend to write my congressman about what a good job the firemen and policemen did.

Analyze the Paragraph

1. Compare the words you just circled in this paragraph with the earlier rewrite of this paragraph you did on page 184. How many did you circle the first time? _____ How many did you circle this time? _____

2. How has your understanding of sexist language changed as a result of your work in this chapter?

_____

_____

_____

_____

_____

_____

_____

_____

_____

_____

_____

_____

_____

_____

TOOLS ▶ Language

00:45

Before you begin this class session, you may want to take time to review student responses to the homework questions.

The first rewriting activity is good for individual, small-group, or class activity. Students will enjoy reading their versions aloud (which also gives them some good reading practice in a safe setting with familiar material).

If you have time, consider including items 1 and/or 2 in **Options: Customize** on page 198.

Pronouns

Pronouns, as you may recall, are words we use in place of nouns. Some common pronouns are *I, me, he, she, it, you, they,* and *their.* Instead of repeating a person's name over and over, we use *he* and *his* or *she* and *hers.* You can find detailed information on pronouns in any English usage handbook, or the Internet, or on the *Writing Now* web site links. We cover only the most common considerations here. Before we begin, however, try experimenting with pronoun usage to see what you already know.

The following essay reminds us of how special we all are. As you read it, circle the pronouns.

My Declaration of Self-Esteem

Virginia Satir

What I am is good enough if I would only be it openly.

Carl Rogers

The following was written in answer to a 15-year-old girl's question, "How can I prepare myself for a fulfilling life?"

I am me.

In all the world, there is no one else exactly like me. There are people who have some parts like me but no one adds up exactly like me. Therefore, everything that comes out of me is authentically mine because I alone choose it.

I own everything about me—my body, including everything it does; my mind, including all my thoughts and ideas; my eyes, including the images of all they behold; my feelings, whatever they might be—anger,

1

2

3

4

Source: Virginia Satir, "My Declaration of Self-Esteem" is used with permission of AVANTA, The Virginia Satir Network, 2104 SW 152nd Street #2, Burien, WA 98166. All rights reserved.

joy, frustration, love, disappointment, excitement; my mouth and all the words that come out of it—polite, sweet and rough, correct or incorrect; my voice, loud and soft; all my actions, whether they be to others or myself.

5 I own my fantasies, my dreams, my hopes, my fears.

6 I own all my triumphs and successes, all my failures and mistakes.

7 Because I own all of me, I can become intimately acquainted with me. By so doing, I can love me and be friendly with me in all my parts. I can then make it possible for all of me to work in my best interests.

8 I know there are aspects about myself that puzzle me, and other aspects that I do not know. But as long as I am friendly and loving to myself, I can courageously and hopefully look for the solutions to the puzzles and for ways to find out more about me.

9 However I look and sound, whatever I say and do, and whatever I think and feel at a given moment in time is me. This is authentic and represents where I am at that moment in time.

10 When I review later how I looked and sounded, what I said and did, and how I thought and felt, some parts may turn out to be unfitting. I can discard that which is unfitting and keep that which proved fitting, and invent something new for that which I discarded.

11 I can see, hear, feel, think, say and do. I have the tools to survive, to be close to others, to be productive, to make sense and order out of the world of people and things outside of me.

12 I own me and therefore I can engineer me.

13 I am me and I am okay.

The purpose of this exercise is to simulate realworld writing tasks. Students must examine the use of pronouns in context, which promotes an understanding of how pronouns work. In addition, as students copy the texts of professional writers, they focus on spelling, word choice, and sentence structure to a greater degree than when they are simply reading. If you have time, we recommend item 2 in **Options: Customize** page 198 as an additional class activity to follow the rewrite of the declaration in the second person.

You may want to ask students to read "Using Pronouns" (page 195) as a homework assignment to be discussed in the next class.

Experiment with Pronouns

On a sheet of notebook paper, carefully copy Satir's "Declaration of Self-Esteem," beginning with "I am me," but changing all the first-person pronouns (*I, me, mine*) to second-person pronouns (*you, your*). The first sentence will now read, "You are you." Make any other necessary changes in wording. If you like, give the declaration to a friend as a reminder of how special you think he or she is.

 Go To ▶

1. Go to the *Writing Now* web site to compare our version of the essay written in the second person with yours.

2. Go to the web and do a search for "sexist language." You will find sites such as Purdue University Online Writing Lab's "Non-Sexist Language" at **<http://owl.english.purdue.edu/handouts/general/gl_nonsex.html>**, and "Non-Sexist Language: Some Notes on Gender-Neutral Language" by Carolyn Jacobson, graduate assistant, English Department, University of Pennsylvania, at **<http://www.stetson.edu/departments/history/ nongenderlang.html>**. Find a site that you think is helpful, and write a brief recommendation to your classmates about it, including the URL where you found it.

3. Go the the National Archives site at **<http://www.nara.gov/exhall/ charters/declaration/decmain.html>** to find a copy of the Declaration of Independence. Consider the wording ". . . all *men* are created equal" [our italics]. Do you think it was intended to refer to men and women *both*, or even *all* men? How would you write this phrase to reflect what we would want it to mean today?

You may want to assign pages 195–198 as a homework assignment to be discussed in class during the next session.

Now that you have some experience with pronouns, take a closer look at how they are used.

Using Pronouns

Check your pronoun usage against the following common conventions:

▶ *Make sure the pronoun matches the noun in number.*

If the noun is singular, the pronoun must be singular.

Example: *Each of the men must have <u>his</u> uniform on by noon.*

(Each one of the men would have <u>his</u> uniform. All of them would have <u>theirs</u> on.)

▶ *Avoid indefinite pronoun references.* Always check whether what your pronoun refers to is clear.

Example: *Latoya and Monica will be there and <u>Latoya</u> will bring the drinks.*

(We cannot use <u>she would bring the drinks,</u> or we would not know which woman was bringing them.)

▶ *Keep pronouns consistent.* If you start out saying <u>you</u>, then don't switch to <u>one</u>.

Example: <u>One</u> *must always be sure to save <u>one's</u> file before one exits.*

OR <u>You</u> *must be sure to save your file before <u>you</u> exit.*

▶ *Remember that collective nouns are singular. Group, club, crowd,* and others take a singular pronoun and singular verb.

Example: *The group is going to have <u>its</u> annual meeting in Tahiti.*

(Not <u>their annual meeting.</u>)

▶ *Avoid the indefinite "they."* Make sure your pronoun has a clear referent. If it does not, you must repeat the noun.

Example: *I want to go to Florida for spring break, but <u>my parents</u> won't let me.*

(Not *but they won't let me.*)

▶ Test compound pronouns for the right case. If you are unsure, for example, whether to use *Jim and I* or *Mike and me,* test the sentence using just the pronoun to determine the appropriate choice.

> Example: *Jim and I/Jim and me will meet you there:*
>
> Test: *I will meet you there./ Me will meet you there.*
>
> Correct: *Jim and I will meet you there.*
>
> Example: *Give it to Jim and I/Jim and me:*
>
> Test: *Give it to I. Give it to me.*
>
> Correct: *Give it to Jim and me.*

▶ *Use "you" to address your audience only when your intent is to put the reader into a role.* Do not use *you* if it would put your audience into a role they cannot identify with.

> Example: *When you get to class, you have to have your homework on your desk right away, or you will get an F for the day.*
>
> (If your audience isn't that class, *you* is inappropriate. Use *we* or *the students/they* instead.)

Using your draft of the central assignment, which you wrote in Chapter 7, circle all the pronouns. Go through the "Using Pronouns" guidelines and check off each item as you examine your draft for conventional usage. Draw an arrow from every pronoun to the word it refers to. Make any necessary corrections in different-colored ink.

The Find and Replace function in your word processor can help you find specific words.

Help Screen

Word Processing Skills:

Find and Replace

The Find and Replace function in your word processing program makes checking pronoun use in your writing easy. For example, if you know you have a tendency to use *you* inappropriately, you can use Find and Replace to highlight each instance of *you,* and then if needed, replace it with a better word choice.

In your word processing program, go to the Edit menu on the Menu bar at the top of your screen. On the Edit pull-down menu, choose Replace or Find and Replace. Then, in the Find What window, type the word you want to find—in this case, *you.*

If you are certain of what word(s) you want to replace *you,* you can type your replacement into the Replace With window. Or, you can decide on replacements individually, at each occurrence of *you.* It is best, especially if you are not yet familiar with this tool, to proceed with caution and check them one at a time.

At this point, you have the opportunity to replace all occurrences of your Find word with one click on the Replace All command. However, this kind of *global replacement* can cause unanticipated problems, so it's best to avoid this choice until you are an extremely practiced user. For example, watch what happens in the following sentence when you use the Replace All command to replace *you* with *a child:*

> Original sentence: *If you had grown up on the bayou, you would have been expected to take care of your younger siblings.*

> With Replace All: *If a child had grown up on the baa child, a child would have been expected to take care of a childr a childnger siblings.*

What happened? Every time the three letters *y, o,* and *u* appeared in a row, the Replace All command converted them into *a child,* even in unrelated words such as *bayou, your,* and *younger.*

Including a space before and after your Find word *and* your Replace word can help, but this precaution would still result in the Find function missing words related to *you,* such as *your,* that you might also want to change:

> Original sentence: *If you had grown up on the bayou, you would have been expected to take care of your younger siblings.*

> With Replace All: *If a child had grown up on the bayou, a child would have been expected to take care of your younger siblings.*

The best way to get help from the Find and Replace function is to take your time and replace words one by one. As you make replacements, be careful to look for other words that also need to be changed, to be sure that the sentence will still make sense. For example, in our bayou sentence, if you replaced *you* with *a child,* you would then have to replace *your* with either a matching singular pronoun, which would lead you into sexist language (*he, she*) or into using the more cumbersome *he or she.*

To avoid sexist language, you could rewrite the sentence as follows:

> Original sentence: *If you had grown up on the bayou, you would have been expected to take care of your younger siblings.*

> Gender-neutral rewrite: *Children growing up on the bayou were expected to take care of their younger siblings.*

Power User

The Find and Replace tool has other functions you may find useful.

Revising   Sometimes you latch on to a favorite word or expression, then catch yourself and wonder if you may have overdone it. Use the Find command to point out each time the expression appears in your writing. If you see you've used the expression too often, go through your document again and replace the element with another word or phrase that means the same thing—or better, that says the same thing in more specific detail.

Formatting   If you cut and paste (see Chapter 4) a selection into your word-processed document from an e-mail message, the Web, or another program, you may find that the text you bring into the document has forced carriage returns, meaning that lines will be forced to end before they reach the right-hand margin on the screen. Most word processors will let you show nonprinting characters such as tab, space, and carriage return markers. Selecting one paragraph at a time and replacing carriage returns (¶s) with spaces will automatically format the text to wrap at the end of a line in a document, instead of where it happened to wrap in the document you've taken the selection from. Be sure to give credit to the author if you copy and paste a selection that you didn't write. Use whatever source citation format your instructor recommends, or use an Internet search engine (see Chapter 11) to find MLA or APA guidelines for citing sources.

Typing Shortcut   If you are using a long phrase several times in your paper and you don't want to keep typing it out in full, you can create an abbreviation for the phrase and then use Find and Replace to replace it later. To avoid the problems that can occur with global replacements, be sure to use a combination of letters and/or symbols for your abbreviation that do not normally occur together in a word—for example, *hsc* or *h.s.* for *high school* or *dcc* for *Delgado Community College*. When you are ready to replace your abbreviation, choose Edit/Replace and enter the abbreviation in the Find window. Write your replacement in the Replace window, click on Replace All, and your work is done.

OPTIONS ▶ Customize

Pronoun Choice

1. Using a fresh sheet of notebook paper, rewrite Virginia Satir's "Declaration of Self-Esteem," on pages 193–194, beginning with "In all the world," this time changing all the first-person pronouns (*I, me, mine*) to either a friend's name or the appropriate third-person pronoun (*he, him, his, himself; she, her, hers, herself*)—whatever makes sense in context. Make any other necessary changes in wording (being careful with the verbs). If you like, give the declaration to your friend to say how special you think he or she is. For example, you can begin with the sentence "Byron is special," using whatever name you choose instead of Byron. *Hint:* Your first two sentences might read, "In all the world, there is no one else exactly like Byron. There are people who have some parts like him, but no one adds up exactly like him."

2. Instead of using one person's name as in activity 1, rewrite the declaration using the names of two friends and make the pronouns plural. For example, instead of *Byron*, you would write *Byron and Yolanda*. Notice what happens when you change the pronouns. You will need to make changes in other wording as well.

3. Find a short article in a magazine or newspaper that describes something a specific person has done. Imagine that the same thing had been done by a person of the opposite sex. Rewrite the article to reflect the change in gender.

4. Find a similar article on the Web. Copy and paste it into your word processor, and try using the Find and Replace tool to change the gender of the person described.

Peer Revision Worksheet

Reviewed by: **Date:**

Focus of review: pronouns and sexist language

Reviewing paper written by:

Peer Revision Questionnaire

Ask yourself the following questions about your draft. Then, if possible, ask a friend or classmate to read your draft and answer the same questions about it. If your answers do not match, you haven't succeeded in communicating what you think you did. Where answers don't match well, discuss them together and try to think of ways to make your essay clearer.

- What is this essay about? (topic)

- What is the event or situation that prompted the essay? (prompt)

- What do you have to say about your topic? (thesis or main idea)

- Who is your intended audience?

- What is your purpose in writing about this topic?

- What personal experience (life, reading, TV, stories you've heard, and so forth) have you had with this topic?

- What purpose does each paragraph serve? How does each support the thesis?

- Are the assertions well supported?

- Is the language gender neutral?

- Are the pronoun references clear?

- Is there anything else the reader should know? Are there any questions in the reader's mind left unanswered by the essay?

FILE ▶ Edit

00:45

You may wish to have students do some revising in class so they can engage in peer revision, get help, use the computer, and so on. This material is suitable for a class session right before the final version of the essay is due.

Revision for Pronoun Usage

You are now ready to revise the essay you drafted in Chapter 7. Reread your draft, circling all pronouns and any words that might be considered sexist. Change the sexist words. You may find the Find and Replace word processing tool helpful in this edit.

Name: _____

Date: _____

Topic: _____

FILE ▶ Save

You may want students to turn this checklist in with their essay. You can use it for evaluative feedback.

Essay with a Strong Point of View

After carefully examining your usage of pronouns and gender-neutral language, you are ready to do a final edit of the paper you began in Chapter 7. Perform all the revision and proofreading techniques you have learned so far.

Revision Checklist

☐ I have a strong, clear, and consistent point of view.

☐ I have used gender-neutral language.

☐ My pronoun references are clear.

☐ My pronoun use is appropriate.

☐ I have clearly stated assertions about my topic.

☐ I have a defined audience.

☐ I have kept my subjects and verbs consistent—either both singular or both plural.

☐ I have kept any items in a series parallel.

☐ I have arranged my ideas in an order appropriate to the topic.

☐ I had someone read and annotate my essay.

☐ I have an appropriate title.

☐ I have a clearly stated topic.

☐ I have developed a topic that is appropriate, neither too broad nor too specific.

☐ All paragraphs support my overall topic.

☐ Each paragraph has a different focus relating to my topic.

☐ Each paragraph has well-developed supporting examples and/or facts.

❑ I revised my word choice to use descriptive and appropriate words.

❑ My tone is clear and consistent throughout the essay.

Proofreading Checklist

❑ I have read each sentence aloud, starting with the last sentence and working backward, making sure that each sentence is clear and uses appropriate language conventions.

❑ I have used my proofreading frame to check for spelling.

❑ I have had a classmate read my draft and complete the Peer Revision Worksheet.

 Go To ▶

1. Go to the National Council of Teachers of English (NCTE) web site **<http://www.ncte.org>** and do a search on nonsexist language. In your search results you will find a link to the council's *Guidelines for Nonsexist Use of Language in NCTE Publications*. In addition to offering alternatives to problem words, this document provides historical background on the council's work to change American language habits, and the reasons for this effort. Do you agree with the council's recommendations? Make a list of sexist words that you want to remind yourself to avoid.

2. Go to the *Health Promotion on the Internet* web site at **<http://www.monash.edu.au/health/pamphlets/BodyImage/>** to find more information on body image and to take a self-quiz to see how your perception of your body image stacks up.

3. Go to the *Writing Now* web site for links to additional readings on the subject of image.

C:\Prompts for Writing ▶

1. Do you stop to look in every mirror that you pass? Do you look at your reflection in store windows? Do you look at yourself first in a pack of photos and wish you could tear many of them up? Write an essay discussing the importance of appearance in our society.

2. Write an essay discussing whether commercials and print and Web advertising sell products based on quality or promote lifestyle images, implying that buying the product will give you access to these lifestyles.

Log Off: ▶ **Review and Reflect**

Take some time to reflect on what you have learned about writing in Chapters 7 and 8. How has your writing changed as a result of the discussions, readings, and activities in these two chapters?

_____

_____

_____

_____

_____

_____

_____

_____

_____

Refer to the two paragraphs you wrote on page 157 in Chapter 7 describing a conflict from two points of view. How well do you think you were able to see the other person's point of view?

_____

_____

_____

_____

_____

In what person did you tell the other side of the story: first person (*I*), second person (*you*), or third person (*he or she*)?

_____

How has your ability to see another point of view changed as a result of the work you have done in Chapters 7 and 8?

_____

_____

_____

_____

_____

_____

_____

_____

_____

CHAPTER 9
Live to Work, Work to Live

Income seldom exceeds personal development.
—Jim Rohn

Chapter Contents

Log On ▶ **Reflection**

Write whatever comes to mind when you read the chapter title and opening quotation.

_____

_____

_____

_____

_____

_____

_____

_____

_____

_____

_____

_____

_____

_____

_____

_____

_____

_____

_____

_____

_____

_____

FILE ▶ Open

00:45

The first three activities can be used as (1) freewriting activity; (2) an e-mail activity for writing practice; or, if time is short, (3) class or small-group discussion.

Connecting with Experience

▶ How would you introduce yourself to a new classmate? What would you say to give your classmate some idea of who you are?

▶ Would that differ from the way you would introduce yourself to a new neighbor? If so, how?

▶ What would you take out or leave in to introduce yourself to a new coworker?

▶ Name a special interest of yours and describe how you would *introduce* a friend to your hobby.

▶ How were these introductions different?

▶ *Why* were these introductions different?

Connecting with Writing

▶ What is an introduction in a piece of writing?

▶ What seems to be the *purpose* of an introduction in a piece of writing?

▶ How is an introduction to a person similar to an introduction to a piece of writing?

▶ What would make an introduction effective?

Connecting with the Topic

▶ Describe the job you are currently holding or, if you are not currently employed, the last job you held. *Introduce* it to your classmates in writing.

▶ What career do you hope to pursue? Describe the career to someone who may not know what it involves. *Introduce* it to them.

Connecting to New Material

▶ Cluster the term *introduction*, including as much information as you can.

▶ List what you already know about how to write an effective introduction.

▶ In small groups, share what you know and write a master list to put on the board or on an overhead projector.

▶ In small groups, discuss what the class has put on the board and write a draft of "How to Write an Introduction."

▶ As a class, make a list of what you want to know about introductions.

Go To ▶
1. Go to Google <http://www.google.com> and do a search on a career that interests you. Be as specific as possible in naming your career, and include the word "career" in your search. For example, you might search for <career + book editor> or <career + nurse>, or <career + truck driver> (omitting the angle brackets). Scan the list Google gives you, then pick the three sites that look most interesting and quickly scan *them*. Add any new ideas you find to your cluster.

FILE ▶ New

This section works well as a home-work assignment.

Writing an Introduction

An introduction creates a *first impression.* One way to understand the importance and function of an introduction is to think about other kinds of first impressions. For example, your first job is an introduction to the world of work. According to Mary Conroy in the following reading selection, a first job creates a lasting impression. As you read, pay careful attention to the introduction as it relates to the rest of the article.

Our First Jobs Leave Us with Lasting Impressions

Mary Conroy

1 They can teach us values. They can steer us toward careers. And they can make us run from jobs that don't suit us. They are our *first* jobs, and their impression lasts.

2 Joyce Post was a tour guide at a cave when she was just 14. Now an electronic pre-press operator, she remembers the job as being fun. She also remembers what she learned: "How to deal with people and keep a sense of humor. Some of them were rude and impatient, while others were real nice," she says.

3 Duane Wood learned a similar lesson in his first job, which he's kept for 30 years now. Working in the stock room at the University Hospitals and now in the state lab, "You get to know the doctors, the nurses, and even some of the patients," he says.

4 While Duane stuck with his first job, Dora Pierce was the original job-hopper. At 18, she was stripping tobacco in a warehouse on Bedford Street. Pierce learned just how much the place stunk—"Especially if you sat right next to the room where they kept it damp. A lot of people got sick from that."

5 After a year, she worked at Madison General Hospital making beds and washing dishes. Pierce didn't think much of that, either, so she moved on to Red Dot Potato Chips, where she sorted the bad chips from the good ones.

Source: Mary Conroy, "Our First Jobs Leave Us with Lasting Impressions," *Capital Times,* Madison, WI, April 2, 1997. Reprinted by permission of the author.

6 Of those early jobs, she says, "They weren't easy. We made 50 cents an hour if we got that. But I was the oldest child, and I had to have a job or my mother would have shot me," she says. Most important, she learned not to stick with a job she didn't like.

Analyze the Reading

1. Highlight the assertion in green.

2. Examine the introduction. Explain why it did or did not effectively introduce the article.

_____

_____

_____

_____

3. How is Conroy's first job an introduction to the world of work?

_____

_____

_____

_____

 Go To ▶ Go to the _Writing Now_ web site if you would like to read the rest of this article.

When you apply for a job, you participate in a job interview. This interview is a way to introduce yourself to a prospective employer in such a way that he or she would like to hire you. What might some of the consequences be of the first impression a person makes during a job interview?

_____

_____

_____

_____

_____

The following reading selection offers a viewpoint on the importance of first impressions. As you read the article, notice how the subject—the importance of a good impression—is handled and think about how this may relate to the concept of introductions in writing.

You Look Somebody Over and Size 'Em Up in 3 Seconds

Lisa Faye Kaplan

1   Nobody gets a second chance to make a first impression.

2   In fact, we don't even get a whole minute to make impressions that may last forever, says Camille Lavington, author of *You've Only Got Three Seconds: How to make the Right Impression in Your Business and Social Life* (Doubleday).

3   "It's totally subconscious," says Lavington about the snap judgments people make all the time. "Whether it's a decent thing to do or not, it's done all over the world."

4   What's worse, once the conclusion has been drawn, it's nearly impossible to change.

5   "It's difficult because you've already hit an emotional button," says Lavington, a New York City communications consultant who teaches businesspeople how to promote themselves. "People respond emotionally before thedo intellectually. If they're comfortable, the interaction will continue. If they're uncomfortable, they'll never get to the substance, the intellectual side of it."

6   *You've Only Got Three Seconds* teaches readers how to talk, walk, dress, and act to make a good first impression, a useful skill on job interviews or first dates.

7   "Our idealized world is a meritocracy in which hard work is the key to rising to the top of an organization," Lavington writes. "In the real world, however, it's the combination of connections, charm, and finesse that makes the cream rise."

8   First impressions are constructed from countless personal details—your smile, handshake, voice, even the shoes you wear or the pen you carry.

9   "It's not totally superficial," Lavington says. "Cats, dogs, and kids instantly know danger or comfort. It's mostly instantly drawn from past experiences."

Source: From Lisa Faye Kaplan, "Workplace: On Job Interview, Make Your First Few Seconds Count," *Detroit News*, February 28, 1997. Copyright 1997, Gannett Co., Inc. Reprinted with permission.

Analyze the Reading

1. Highlight the assertion in green.

2. Consider the first two paragraphs as the introduction. How does the introduction relate to the rest of the text?

_____

_____

_____

3. Did this article support or contradict the thesis of Mary Conroy's article? Support your answer.

_____

_____

_____

_____

_____

_____

Go To ▶ Go to the Web to look at a few web pages on a subject that interests you. We've all heard the cliché, "You can't judge a book by its cover," but the preceding two articles suggest that many of us do just that when we first meet people. Is that also true when you are surfing the Web? What characteristics of a web page make you want to stop and read the page? What makes you hit the Back button to get away as soon as you can?

_____

_____

_____

The following excerpt from an article in the *Equal Employment Opportunity Career Journal* gives some good pointers on handling the job interview. Note your expectations from reading the introduction, and then reflect at the end on whether the author met those expectations.

Back to Basics: Mastering the Interview

From *EEO BiMonthly: Equal Employment Opportunity Career Journal*, December 31, 1998.

1 In the realm of the job hunt, a resume, references, and experience are all very important, but it is the interview that's king.

2 Whether you have ambitions to move up within a company, to leave your present job, to return to the work world after an absence or to secure your very first job, it is that face-to-face meeting that can make or break your candidacy.

Source: "Back to Basics: Mastering the Interview, *EEO BiMonthly Equal Employment Opportunity Career Journal*, 12/31/98. Reprinted by permission of Cass Recruitment Media.

3   It's no wonder that a slew of interviewing advice books now crowd the how-to market. Mastering good interviewing techniques can make the difference between being employed and unemployed, being poorly paid and well paid.

4   Most people arrive at job interviews unprepared, maintains William C. Byham, author of *Landing the Job You Want* and CEO of Development Dimensions International, Inc. (DDI), a human resource consulting company in Bridgeville, Pennsylvania.

5   A recent study conducted by DDI found that four out of five people believe preparing for an interview isn't as important as having a positive attitude.

6   This is not the case, according to James Welkins, a career planning consultant and founder of Career Planning Services based in Scarborough, Maine. "The key to a successful interview is being well prepared," he emphasizes.

Analyze the Reading

1. Highlight the assertion in green. Where is the assertion located?

_____

_____

_____

2. Examine the introduction. What does it tell you about what might be contained in this article? The author's point of view? The thesis?

_____

_____

_____

_____

3. Highlight the facts in pink and examples in yellow.

4. How did the author develop the material presented in the introduction?

_____

_____

_____

5. Do you consider this to be a good introduction to the article? Why or why not?

_____

_____

_____

Go To ▶ Go to the *Writing Now* web site to read the rest of this article. It has sections entitled "Preparation," "The Interview," and "The Bad Interview." Put together a checklist of ideas from the article to use when you interview for a job.

You can see that you already have a general idea of what an introduction is. The next step is to acquire enough additional information and practice to write an effective introduction. We will provide you with some general guidelines and direct you to further information. As you read this section, highlight any new information and add it to your project, "How to Write an Introduction," from page 207.

Just as the first impression you make on people causes them to make certain decisions and assumptions about you and creates a lasting impression, so the first paragraph of your writing gives readers an idea of the interest of the topic and the quality of your writing. Often readers use the introduction to decide whether to continue reading the text. If they do continue reading, your introduction gives readers a way to begin relating to what you will present. It should be one of your strongest paragraphs.

Think of this first paragraph as meeting your audience. Make them feel interested and comfortable and guide them into your ideas. Just as you would in meeting someone at a party, give readers enough information to begin a discussion with you—in this case, a mental discussion. Focus their attention on the subject by considering your audience and their point of view.

Imagine you had to introduce two people at a party. You couldn't do so without having some idea of who the people were. Similarly, in a piece of writing, you may want to write most of your introduction after you have a clear idea of your topic and how you want to present it. Once you know what you want to say, it is easier to introduce it. Furthermore, the hardest part of writing is beginning. If you have too much anxiety over how to begin, you may postpone writing the paper and run into problems meeting your deadline. Therefore, it is a good idea to write a rough draft of an introduction first, based on what you intend to write. Then, after you have drafted the whole paper, return to the introduction and revise it.

In Chapter 5 you worked with topic and assertion. Now that you are writing longer papers with introductions, you will put the topic and assertion—that is, your *thesis statement*—in the introduction. (Did you notice that you found the assertions of the introductions in the reading selections you examined?) Next, as in a social situation, your introduction should give the reader some idea of what your paper is about. Finally, your introduction should create interest. Remember, your audience is an important factor to consider in creating interest.

You can include all these three aspects of introduction—thesis, awareness of subject, and interest—in several ways. The methods you can choose from will be somewhat limited by the subject matter and the way you intend to approach it, but the more methods you are aware of, the more choices you will have in constructing an effective introduction.

You may want to end the homework assignment here. Pages 214–218 would be ideal to do as a class or a small-group activity.

Twelve Methods of Introduction

Following are twelve ways in which you can introduce your topic.

1. Directly address your topic. Begin with your thesis and give a brief explanation or comments about it.

2. Begin with an explanation or description of what you will do in the paper. You may want to indicate why you, personally, are addressing this subject. Tell the reader if you have any experience with or expertise in this subject.

3. Start with an example, story, or anecdote illustrating the argument you will present or the situation you will describe.

4. Use a quotation that introduces the subject and gets the reader's attention.

5. Refer to a current issue or an idea being discussed by others that prompted you to write a response.

6. Give an explanation of the issue you wish to address. Provide background information that will help readers understand your text.

7. State the opposing side of a controversy before arguing your point.

8. Raise a question and then present your answer in your paper.

9. Place the subject in a more general perspective.

10. Explain the importance of your subject.

11. Begin with a fact and then discuss its importance in the paper.

12. Surprise the reader by presenting a view that is contrary to general opinion or by making a bold, provocative, or contradictory statement.

By analyzing introductions and discussing how they relate to the rest of the article, students see that there are many effective ways of writing an introduction.

Sample Introductions Using the Twelve Methods of Introduction

Following are some examples of how the preceding twelve methods can be used to introduce an essay. The following introductions are presented in random order. As you read each introduction, determine which method is being used and write the method number in the margin. Only a fine line separates some of these methods, so you may find that one introduction could logically fit into more than one category. However, since there is one *best* choice for each method, you may want to get together in small groups after making your list and debate the best choices where there is disagreement. In the end, however, how you label the method matters less than your ability to recognize that there are many effective ways to begin your papers and to adapt these methods to your own writing.

Method 2: Iwashita states why his topic is important to him personally and tells the reader what he will do in his text.

Why I Quit the Company

Tomoyuki Iwashita

When I tell people that I quit working for the company after only a year, most of them think I'm crazy. They can't understand why I would want to give up a prestigious and secure job. But I think I'd have been crazy to stay, and I'll try to explain why.

Source: From Tomoyuki Iwashita, "Why I Quit the Company," *New Internationalist*, May 1992. Used by permission of the Guardian/Observer News Service.

Method 7: Knowdell tells the reader the previous attitude toward his subject and then lets the reader know that he is going to present a new way of looking at the subject.

The 10 New Rules for Strategizing Your Career

Richard L. Knowdell

The traditional contract between employer and employee has fundamentally changed. No longer are people expected to work for one company their whole career. The loyalty that employer and employee once expected from each other has slipped away.

Replacing it is a new and still-developing set of expectations that has broad implications for the way we plan our careers, our lives, and even our workweek. Learning what these "new rules" are and how to play by them—whether you agree with them or not—will give you a head start in the workplace of tomorrow.

Source: From Richard Knowdell, "The 10 New Rules for Strategizing Your Career," *Futurist,* June 1, 1998.

Method 12: Jarman startles the reader by relating his topic of work to a topic we don't normally associate with work—soul. The reader is curious to discover what he means.

Put Some Soul into Your Work

Max Jarman

If you feel unmotivated and disinterested in work, it might not be because you're burned out or lazy. It may be because you and your company lack soul. Not the kind Aretha Franklin has, but the kind that creates committed, empowered employees who are rewarded and challenged by their work. In their recently published book, *Awakening Corporate Soul,* Eric Klein and John B. Izzo identify four paths to creating a more soulful work experience.

Source: From Max Jarman, "Put Some Soul into Your Work," *Arizona Republic,* June 12, 1998, p. D11.

Method 10: Reynolds emphasizes the importance of his topic by mentioning that the president thinks it is important.

Accommodating Religion in the Workplace

Larry Reynolds

Inside word is that legislation is intended to assure all employees the freedom to discuss and practice their religion at work—and it's working its way onto the short list of next year's hot political issues. President Clinton put the topic on the national agenda when he issued an executive order last August reasserting the right of every federal employee to express his or her religious beliefs in the government workplace.

Source: From Larry Reynolds, "Accommodating Religion in the Workplace," *Human Resources Forum,* January 1, 1998.

Method 5: Goodman refers to a current idea being discussed by others. In fact, that is part of the assertion—that the topic is widely discussed.

Not All Sex in the Office Is Harassment

Ellen Goodman

This is not a sexy story. Which is, after all, the whole point. For the last many weeks and months, we've been awash in so many tales about sex in the workplace that it's been nearly impossible to get any work done.

Source: From Ellen Goodman, "Not All Sex in the Office Is Harassment," *Newsday,* March 1, 1998, p. B8.

Method 4: Berg quotes from a law professor to introduce the topic. Quoting an authority can be an easy and effective method of introducing a topic.

The Workplace: Employers Struggling with Office Romances— From Friendship to Intimacy to Retaliation in the Courts

Steve Berg

Boss-underling office romances pose tough, complicated questions for employers and the legal system. One law professor thinks the nation is "entering a new phase in our understanding of sexual harassment."

Source: From Steve Berg, "The Workplace, Employers Struggling with Office Romances," *Minneapolis Star Tribune,* February 24, 1998, p. 1D.

Method 3: Brand begins his article with a story that makes the point that he will then explain. This method can be a little tricky for beginning writers, who may be better off restricting examples to the body of the paper. However, it is good for students to be aware that sometimes an author will put an example first. The author's assertion is thereby *implied* by the example. This is a valuable hint for later, when students are attempting to summarize authors' writing.

Sexes: When Women Vie with Women: The Sisterhood Finds Rivalry and Envy Can Be the Price of Success

David Brand

Reported by Andrea Sachs

Laurie Bernstein well remembers starting at a small Southern law firm and getting distinctly icy treatment from the only other woman lawyer on the staff. When Bernstein was given one of her female colleague's cases to handle, resentment turned to spite; Bernstein discovered that she was not getting the court documents, letters and other important papers she needed to handle the case. Late one evening she and a senior partner found the missing material hidden in the woman's mailbox. Ms. Sabotage was severely reprimanded. "I felt terrible," recalls Bernstein, 30. "I had expected a camaraderie to emerge between the two of us as the only female lawyers at the firm. But quite the opposite occurred."

Source: From David Brand, "Sexes: When Women Vie with Women," *Time*, February 1, 1998, p. 67.

Method 11: Leinwand gives a fact and then states that the fact is complex. We can anticipate that she is going to elaborate on that fact.

Women's Salaries: Difference of Pay or Difference of Opinion?

Donna Leinwand

The Labor Department statistics seem to lay it out in black and white: For every dollar a man earns, a woman gets about 76 cents. But many employers say it's not that simple.

Source: From Donna Leinwand, "Women's Salaries," Gannett News Services, September 7, 1999.

Method 6: Steinem is giving some background information relevant to her discussion. Method 11 would also be a correct choice, because Steinem is going to elaborate on the fact that she starts with. Again, what is important is that students discuss and analyze. It is the *process*, not the label that counts.

The Importance of Work

Gloria Steinem

Toward the end of the 1970's, *The Wall Street Journal* devoted an eight-part, front page series to "the working woman"—that is, the influx of women into the paid-labor force—as the greatest change in American life since the Industrial Revolution.

Source: From Gloria Steinem, "The Importance of Work," *Outrageous Acts and Everyday Rebellions* (New York: Holt, 1983).

Method 8: Kreitner begins with a question. You might remind students that this is often an easy strategy for beginning writers.

Nagging Inequalities in the Workplace

Robert Kreitner

Can America achieve full and lasting international competitiveness if a large proportion of its workforce suffers nagging inequalities? Probably not. Unfortunately, women, minorities, and part-timers often encounter barriers in the workplace. Let us open our discussion by focusing on women, because their plight is shared by all minorities in varying degrees.

Source: From Robert Kreitner, "Nagging Inequalities in the Workplace," Boston: Houghton Mifflin.

Method 9: Stanat is going to show readers how to look at a situation from a larger perspective. The interviewer represents the corporate world.

How to Take a Job Interview

Kirby Stanat

To succeed in campus job interviews, you have to know where the recruiter is coming from. The simple answer is that he is coming from corporate headquarters.

Source: From Kirby W. Stanat with Patrick Reardon, "How to Take a Job Interview," *Job Hunting Secrets and Tactics* (Raintree Publishers, Westwind Press, 1997).

Method 1: Carlson states his thesis immediately.

Let Go of the Idea That Gentle, Relaxed People Can't Be Superachievers

Richard Carlson

One of the major reasons so many of us remain hurried, frightened, and competitive, and continue to live life as if it were one giant emergency, is our fear that if we were to become more peaceful and loving, we would suddenly stop achieving our goals. We would become lazy and apathetic.

Source: From Richard Carlson, *Don't Sweat the Small Stuff—And It's All Small Stuff* (New York: Hyperion, 1997), p. 11.

Help Screen

Finding Quotations

The Internet makes it easy to find an appropriate quotation for almost any subject. Sometimes, looking at what others have said can spark ideas for your own writing. To find quotations, first check out your school library web site. Check for links to books of quotations. If you don't see anything there or if you want more, do a web search for quotations. You might refine your search by adding the subject area you are working with, such as "work" or "career." Find a quotation you think would be an appropriate introduction for this chapter or for an essay you might want to write related to career, and copy it below. Make sure that you copy every word exactly as it appears in the quotation, and include the name of the person you are quoting.

_____

_____

_____

_____

_____

_____

 **Go To** ▶

There is no suggested homework here. You may want students to write an introduction to a previous essay and bring it to class.

1. Go to the web and search on write +introduction. The search engine Metacrawler turned up **<http://www.researchpaper.com/13.html>**. This site gives specific information on writing introductions. What information did your search turn up? Compare what you find with what you have written. Incorporate any new information into your draft of "How to Write an Introduction."

2. Go to a site such as **<http://www.collegegrad.com/resumes/>**, for sample business writing templates. In business, your cover letter and resume serve as your introduction to a company you hope will hire you. Increasingly, the web contains sites offering templates or sample letters you can copy and personalize, sometimes for free but usually at some cost. Since these sites are so widespread, it is likely that you will be tempted to use them. Discuss in class how these sites can help and what precautions you should take before using a template for your cover letter or resume.

OPTIONS ▶ Customize

If you have three class sessions to do this chapter, you may wish to end here and do the rest of the chapter during the third session. For classes that meet once or twice weekly, you may wish to have students participate in this next activity during the same session in which they analyze the introductions. In any case, it would be helpful to have students participate in this class/group activity before you give the central assignment.

1. Individually, or in your small groups, revise your draft of "How to Write an Introduction," incorporating any new information gleaned from your web site search. How much of the information in the guidelines did your group already know?

   _____

   _____

   _____

2. Some of the questions you may have about this material will be answered as we continue to work with it. Write your questions here and look for the answers as you continue with this chapter.

   _____

   _____

   _____

3. Write an introduction to your central assignment from Chapter 4.

   _____

   _____

   _____

4. In small groups, design a class presentation on how to write an introduction. It may be in the form of

   a. A handout

   b. A poster

   c. A slide show (such as PowerPoint) presentation

   d. A web page

FILE: ▶ Create

00:45

If you have time, the next steps can be very helpful for students to do in class. The more students get a chance to hear and read others' writing, the more options they absorb for their own papers.

Writing an Essay with an Introduction

1. Write an introduction on one of the following topics relating to the workplace:

   ▶ Female bosses   ▶ Sexual harassment

   ▶ Appropriate workplace appearance ▶ Dating coworkers

   ▶ Religion in the workplace   ▶ Successful job interviews

2. Get in groups by topic. Compare your introductions to those of your class-mates. How did you see the issue differently from them? Determine which method of introduction each person in your group used. What points would you discuss if you wrote the whole essay? Discuss how each of you could develop your topic. Would each introduction produce a different development?

3. Now that you have seen how your classmates handled the subject, you may see how you could make improvements in writing an introduction. Pick another topic from the list and write an introduction for it.

4. Get in groups, again by topic, and share the introductions. This time you will be in groups with different students according to your new topic, and you will get additional ideas about how to handle a topic.

5. Read the introductions aloud in class, perhaps with each student reading the best of the two he or she has written. Notice how many different ways a subject can be introduced.

If you have time, you may want students to do this part of the assignment in class. Some instructors like to have students turn in this page before they begin writing.

You are now ready to write an essay with an effective introduction. Write your topic in the center of a sheet of paper, circle it and then cluster the topic. Using your highlighter, organize your cluster.

Name: _____   **Date:** _____

Write an outline for your essay.

Topic: _____

Assertion: _____

Audience: _____

Purpose: _____

Tone: _____

You may instruct students to omit III or add a IV, depending on the length of essay you want to assign. Some instructors prefer to leave the length open ended.

I. First key point:

_____

_____

_____

If you want students to jot down supporting details, remind them to do so.

If you want to assign an audience, some possibilities are one of the authors of the sample introductions; their classmates; their coworkers (as in an article for a corporate newsletter).

II. Second key point:

_____

_____

_____

III. Third key point:

_____

_____

_____

IV. Fourth key point:

_____

_____

_____

Help Screen

Web Search

If you need help generating ideas, do a web search and scan, don't read, the summaries for the top ten hits, then scan a couple of the pages listed.

FILE ▶ Save As

Essay with an Introduction

Write an essay based on one of the topics for which you wrote a practice introduction. Give careful attention to the introduction, but realize that after you have written your paper, you will go back, reevaluate, and perhaps revise your original introduction.

Save your essay as a draft. In the next chapter, you will learn some ways to improve your essay. Before you can do that, however, you will need some content to work with. Make sure that this draft is complete and well developed, and bring it to class.

> ## Help Screen
>
> ### Creating a Web Page
>
> Creating a web page is not difficult. You can tell that just by looking at the millions of pages available on the Web right now. However, creating a good, useful web page requires some thought, just as writing a good paper does. In fact, there are many similarities between the two tasks, especially in the early stages.
>
> As you create a web page, remember to keep in mind the difficulties involved in one-way communication—again, just as when you write an essay—and work extra hard to make sure that you are clear. As always, we encourage collaboration; have your friends and classmates look over your web page before publishing it.
>
> Now, go to the *Writing Now* web site to get started on creating your own web page.

Go To ▶ Go to the *Writing Now* web site for an article entitled "How to Brag About Yourself to Win and Hold a New Job."

C:\Prompts for Writing ▶

You may wish to substitute one of these activities for the central assignment, use one as an additional assignment, or return to one later in the semester as an assignment. If a student needs makeup work or extra credit, one of these activities may be an option.

1. Select one of the other readings in this chapter and write a response in the form of an introduction and supporting paragraphs.

2. Select one of the other topics listed and write another essay.

3. Write an essay in which you "brag" about your accomplishments to convince someone to hire you. (The activity in the Go To above can help.)

CHAPTER 10
A Work in Progress

"The better work men do is always done under stress and at great personal cost."
—William Carlos Williams

Chapter Contents

Log On ▶ **Reflection**

Write whatever comes to mind when you read the chapter title and opening quotation.

Reminder: Have students write the reflection while you are taking roll. It's a great way to get everyone busy immediately, and it "gets the juices flowing."

_____

_____

_____

_____

_____

_____

_____

_____

_____

_____

_____

_____

_____

_____

_____

_____

_____

_____

_____

_____

_____

_____

_____

FILE ▶ Open

Connecting with Experience

In the last chapter, you thought about how you would introduce yourself differently to a friend, a coworker, or a neighbor. You realized you had a great deal of information you could use to introduce yourself, but you selected certain kinds of information for each type of introduction. Even if you included certain information in most of your introductions, you may have presented the same information in a different order or in a different way. Why is this so?

Connecting with New Material

This sentence can be read two different ways: (1) The red on a tea kettle often chips, or (2) There, Don ate a kettle of ten chips.

▶ Look at the following sentence: *theredonateakettleoftenchips*

▶ Why is this sentence difficult to read?

▶ Write the sentence, creating the appropriate amount of space between the letters to break them into real words.

▶ By changing where you put the spaces, can you divide the letters into different groups to make different words and a new sentence?

▶ How would capital letters and punctuation have indicated what the author meant?

▶ What statements can you make about punctuation as a result of this activity?

▶ Complete the following sentence: *Punctuation is important because* ———

FILE ▶ New

The activities in **File: New** could be accomplished as a class activity in one class period.

Patterns of Development

The subject matter, audience, and purpose for writing a paper should affect the way in which you present the material in any writing. This manner of presentation is called the *pattern of development.* An introduction often reflects the pattern of development to follow. Depending on whether you write the introduction first or last, the introduction can determine, or be determined by, the pattern of development of your paper.

Each paragraph in a text has a general pattern of development (or occasionally a combination of patterns). The complete text may have a single overall pattern of development or a combination of patterns. At this point in your writing, it is often simpler to have one overall pattern of development for an essay, but it is not necessary to keep to this guideline. For the purpose of this chapter, you will focus on paragraph-level patterns of development.

Some of the most common patterns of development are listed here.

Patterns of Development

1. *Cause and effect/problem and solution.* You can provide a cause in the introduction and explain its effects in the paper, or you can provide an effect and discuss the causes. Sometimes you will find it effective to state a problem in the introduction and propose a solution in your paper.

2. *Classification.* You can break an idea into categories. You might list ways, types, rules, theories, styles, kinds, or reasons. You will find many ways to use this pattern, which is a typical one for textbooks and essay exam answers.

3. *Example.* You can make an assertion and then provide examples to illustrate or support your assertion.

4. *Argument.* You can introduce a position and then argue for or against it. You will need to develop each paragraph by supporting your argument with facts, research, or examples.

5. *Description/narration.* You can make an assertion in your introduction and then develop or support that idea by describing the situation in detail or telling a story that illustrates it.

6. *Analysis/explanation.* You can raise an issue in your introduction that you wish to analyze in detail or to explain to your reader. You will be giving your views or understanding of the subject in your paper.

7. *Process.* You can explain how to perform a task or the steps that readers might want to take to accomplish a goal that you have introduced.

8. *Definition.* You can present a concept in your introduction that you will define in your paper. Unlike a dictionary definition, your definition will need an explanation, examples, and/or facts. Your opinion will be evident because you will be defining the way you see an issue or concept.

9. *Comparison/contrast.* You can present a topic in your introduction, then show how it is like or different from something else in your paper. Sometimes writers contrast and/or compare methods, styles, behaviors, attitudes, or many other things. You will find many ways to use this technique. It is often a helpful pattern to use in answering essay questions.

Students will benefit from engaging in this activity as a puzzle rather than an assignment with a specified outcome. Getting students to analyze texts and talk about them is of utmost importance. If a student gives an answer other than the ones provided here, you may want to ask, "Why did you select that pattern?" Continue by asking if anyone else selected something different. (Because there is overlap, more than one appropriate answer is given here. If you look at the first appropriate answer for each paragraph in the key below, you will come out with one paragraph for each type of pattern.) However, it is the awareness of options and the experience of working with text that is more important than arriving at one best answer.

Following are some paragraphs using the nine patterns of development just described. Match the pattern to the paragraph by labeling each paragraph in the margin with the pattern. Be sure to consider the title for clues. Some patterns are quite similar to others, so pick the pattern that seems closest to the description.

example or description/ narration

1. The 10 New Rules

Richard Knowdell

The late Congressman Sonny Bono is a good example of someone who was able to recognize new circumstances in different stages of his life and be successful in all of them. He was a long-haired musician and a "straight man" in 1970, then moved into managing a restaurant, later became a mayor, and finally a congressman. He is an interesting case because his core person didn't change, but the path he followed did. He navigated his various careers carefully and was successful in whatever he did. We may have joked about him, and he didn't take himself too seriously, but he was successful in how he took on new positions in life and adapted to change internally as well as externally.

Source: From Richard Knowdell, "The 10 New Rules for Strategizing Your Career," *Futurist,* June 1, 1998.

definition, comparison and/or contrast, or analysis

2. Nagging Inequalities in the Workplace

Robert Kreitner

Driven largely by economic necessity, an estimated 25 percent of the U.S. labor force is now made up of *contingent workers.* This "flexible workforce" includes a diverse array of part-timers, temporary workers, and self-employed persons. It is growing at a much faster rate than the overall workforce. "Their common denominator is that they do not have a long-term implicit contract with their ultimate employers, the purchasers of the labor and services they provide." Employers are relying more on part-timers for two basic reasons. First, because they are paid at lower rates and do not receive benefits, part-timers are much less costly to employ than full-time employees. Second, as a flexible workforce, they can be let go when times are bad, without the usual repercussions of a general workforce.

Source: From Robert Kreitner, "Nagging Inequalities in the Workplace," Boston: Houghton Mifflin.

cause/effect, classification, or analysis/explanation

3. The Economy: Workers Who Fight Firing with Fire

Anastasia Toufexis

A TIME/CNN poll this month reports that 37 percent of Americans see workplace violence as a growing problem. Some 18 percent have witnessed assaults at work; another 18 percent worry about becoming victims themselves. Those fears help explain why two-thirds of emergency-room nurses turn their name tags upside down to deter patients from learning their identities, why some supervisors have taken to wearing bulletproof vests, and why the owner of a McDonald's in central St. Louis forbids his 120 employees to wear red or blue, the colors of the local Crips and Bloods gangs.

Source: From Anastasia Toufexis, "The Economy: Workers Who Fight Firing with Fire," *Time,* April 25, 1994.

analysis/explanation or comparison/contrast

4. The Importance of Work

Gloria Steinem

Like most truisms, this one is easy to prove with statistics. Economic need is the most consistent work motive—for women as well as men. In 1976, for instance, 43 percent of all women in the paid-labor force were single, widowed, separated, or divorced, and working to support themselves and their dependents. An additional 21 percent were married to men who had earned less than ten thousand dollars in the previous year, the minimum then required to support a family of four. In fact, if you take men's pensions, stocks, real estate, and various forms of accumulated wealth into account, a good statistical case can be made that there are more women who "have" to work (that is, who have neither the accumulated wealth, nor husbands whose work or wealth can support them for the rest of their lives) than there are men with the same need. If we were going to ask one group "Do you really need this job?" we should ask men.

Source: From Gloria Steinem, "The Importance of Work," *Outrageous Acts and Everyday Rebellions* (New York: Holt, 1983).

process

5. Back to the Basics: Mastering the Interview

EEO Bimonthly Equal Employment Opportunity Career Journal

Step two involves focusing on yourself, your goals and qualifications for the particular position. "Ask yourself what it is [you] have to offer this employer and then put it in writing [for yourself]," Elkin advises. Bring the notes to the interview. While you should not read directly from them, you'll feel reassured that you can quickly refer to them when necessary. "Having the points you want to make in writing reinforces them," Elkin explains.

Source: From *EEO Bimonthly Equal Employment Opportunity Career Journal,* December 31, 1998.

comparison/contrast

6. Debate: Does It Matter What Women Wear to Work?

Peter York

This already happens in Europe, with women wearing Armani couture, while the American version is probably the Donna Karan trouser suit. We are starting to catch on in Britain; but there's not enough sense of quality at the moment. This is why British women can veer from looking absolutely amazing to looking deeply naff [sic], while Parisian women may look slightly boring in their approach to work clothes, but will always have an idea in their head about what is "good" dressing. Still, I know we'll get there eventually.

Source: From Peter York, "Debate: Does It Matter What Women Wear to Work?" *Independent on Sunday,* August 22, 1999, p. 5.

classification

7. How to Stop Sabotaging Yourself Personally, Professionally

Loraine O'Connell

Self-defeating behaviors are observable in every arena: sports (the ballyhooed athlete who gets busted for cocaine); politics (the philandering politician who dares the press to catch him in the act—can you say "Gary Hart"?); business (the Wall Street investment guru who tosses away a seven-figure income to make a fast buck on insider trading), and everyday life, in which people dash their chances for promotion and doom their personal relationships by their own actions.

Source: From Loraine O'Connell, "How to Stop Sabotaging Yourself Personally, Professionally," *The Dallas Morning News;/Orlando Sentinel.*

description/narration

8. Why I Quit the Company

Tomoyuki Iwashita

In fact, the quality of married life is often determined by the husband's work. Men who have just gotten married try to go home early for a while, but soon have to revert to the norm of late-night work. They have little time to spend with their wives and even on the weekend are expected to play golf with colleagues. Fathers cannot find time to communicate with their children and child rearing is largely left to mothers. Married men posted abroad will often leave their family behind in Japan; they fear that their children will fall behind in the fiercely competitive Japanese education system.

Source: From Tomoyuki Iwashita, "Why I Quit the Company," *New Internationalist,* May 1992. Used by permission of the Guardian/Observer News Service.

argument, analysis, or
description/narration

9. Imaginative Approach Works for Job Seekers

Diane Kunde

"We don't get jobs the way we used to," said Helen Harkness, a Dallas career counselor and author. "You don't go into an employer's office and sit there and wait until they ask you questions. You have to know what you can do for that person, and that involves strong research. Then you have to do a presentation on how you would do the job if you worked there," she said. One Dallas mother left an accounting job to be home with her son. When she tried to re-enter the job market in financial planning, she put together a presentation using cutting-edge computer software. She sold herself and her up-to-date abilities using the tools of the trade. "If I was comfortable making a presentation like this in a job interview, that would speak well for my abilities as an account manager dealing with a client," said the woman, who asked not to be identified. She's been with her new employer for about a year.

Source: Diane Kunde excerpt from "Imaginative Approach Works for Job Seekers," from *The Dallas Morning News*, 10/14/98, p. 1D. Reprinted with permission of *The Dallas Morning News*.

This class activity stimulates discussion on introductions and patterns of development and links the two. It is probably not a good homework assignment because as homework it defeats the purpose of exploration and discussion and leads to an attempt to label texts too specifically.

Answers:
Cause and effect: a, l
Classification: c
Examples: e, i
Argument: j, h
Description: h, i
Analysis: d, g, h

Now take some time to work with introductions and patterns of development.

1. Go back to the sample introductions on pages 215–218 in Chapter 9. For each of the nine patterns of development given on page 228, find at least one introduction that fits. Label the patterns on page 228 with the letter of the appropriate introduction type, making sure that you find an introduction for every pattern of development.

2. Get into small groups and compare your answers for each introduction. If your choices differ from those of other members of the group, argue in favor of your pattern of development by explaining how you would develop material to support your introduction.

Go To ▶ Go to the *Internet Public Library's* site at <**http://www.ipl.org/teen/aplus/ linksowls.htm**> to get more information on patterns of development. Jump to the link to "Links for Writing" to find handouts from many OWLs organized by category. Advanced users can come back to the main page and scan the information listed under other OWLs for further information. You can also visit the *Writing Now* web site for more information on patterns of development and OWLs.

OPTIONS ▸ Customize

Select one of the introductions on pages 215–218 and write an essay using that introduction as your first paragraph. Be prepared to discuss why you selected a particular pattern of development to develop the ideas in the introduction you chose.

FILE ▸ Edit

This may be a good place to begin the homework assignment.

Revision for Paragraph Development

Review the essay you wrote as your central assignment in Chapter 9. Identify and examine the pattern of development in each paragraph. Taking them one at a time, look at the topic sentence and examine the patterns of development. Can you think of a better pattern for developing that idea? Revise the essay using a more effective pattern of development wherever necessary. Label each paragraph with its pattern of development. You will probably have one overall pattern, but it is also possible to have paragraphs using different patterns.

TOOLS ▸ Language

Sentence Variety and Complexity; Punctuation

In Chapters 9 and 10 you have been learning how to improve your writing. So far you have expanded and developed your essay by adding an introduction and consciously selecting a pattern of development that will allow you to handle your material more effectively. A third way to expand and develop your essay is to develop your sentences by including more detail by combining two or more sentences into one more interesting one, or by changing the order of ideas in a sentence.

You can improve your sentences in several ways:

▸ *Use different sentence patterns for variety.* Using the same sentence patterns over and over, particularly the subject-verb-object pattern, can be boring to your audience. Try rewriting some sentences in a different order.

▸ *Write more complex sentences.* Too many short sentences can make your writing sound choppy. Include more details by adding phrases.

▸ *Combine short sentences for variety.* You can often eliminate fragments when you do this.

▸ *Use a variety of punctuation to create more interesting sentences.* Doing this can also help you eliminate run-on sentences.

Using all of these strategies can improve your essays by helping you create varied and more interesting sentence structures.

Examine the following sentence taken from one of the sample introductions earlier in the chapter. This is an extremely complex sentence and not one that you would be likely to imitate, but it shows a great variety of punctuation.

> Self-defeating behaviors are observable in every arena: sports (the ballyhooed athlete who gets busted for cocaine); politics (the philandering politician who dares the press to catch him in the act—can you say "Gary Hart"?); business (the Wall Street investment guru who tosses away a seven-figure income to make a fast buck on insider trading), and everyday life, in which people dash their chances for promotion and doom their personal relationships by their own actions.

Highlight the commas in the previous sentence in pink. Highlight the semicolons in yellow. Highlight the colon and the dash in blue. Number each punctuation mark to match the number of the following explanation that describes its use.

1. First, there is a **colon :,** used to introduce a complex list. Note that a complete sentence precedes a colon.

2. Next, we see **parentheses (),** used to set off a phrase that is incidental to the sentence (such as one that explains something but is not essential to the meaning of the sentence).

3. Then comes a **semicolon ;.** In this case the semicolon separates items in a list. Commas usually separate items in a list, unless, as in the example sentence, items within the list have additional punctuation.

4. Within the parentheses, we see a **dash —.** Dashes are usually created by inserting two hyphens (minus signs) right next to each other, with no spaces before or after them. Sometimes you will see a space, a hyphen, and a space, but a double hyphen is the more conventional usage. Word processors often automatically change the two hyphens to a single, longer dash. Dashes, like parentheses, set off nonessential information, sometimes to add detail and sometimes to add emphasis. Dashes are generally considered very casual, and are used by writers who are, or who want to appear to be, in a hurry. A dash can come before and after a phrase, or only on one side of it if the phrase appears at the beginning or end of a sentence, as the one in this example does.

5. The name *Gary Hart* appears in **quotation marks.** Quotation marks enclose words, phrases, or sentences that someone speaks. They show us that the writer is using the exact words the person *quoted* actually said.

6. Finally, we see a **comma,** used to set off a long phrase that adds additional detail to a sentence. This phrase is often not essential to the meaning of the sentence and could be set off in parentheses or with dashes. Commas, however, are the least intrusive form of punctuation that can do this job, and most of the time you will not want to call attention to the phrase by using less common punctuation marks such as exclamation points or dashes.

As you read either textbooks, novels, newspapers, or magazines, pay attention to the punctuation the author chose to help convey his or her meaning. On index cards write down sentences that you like or that use punctuation in a way you would like to remember. You will notice that writers or editors often use punctuation in ways that don't agree with the rules you are learning. As language changes and grows, so does the use of punctuation. It is best for beginning writers to stick to the tried-and-true methods of punctuation to make sure their writing is clear.

The following sentences use punctuation in ways you are most likely to use in your writing class. Study the sentences carefully. Try to determine the purpose of the punctuation.

00:45

You may wish to do these activities as a class.
comma before conjunction (*but*) used to separate two independent clauses

comma after introductory phrase

semicolon used to separate independent clauses

dash used to set off nonessential information
comma pair to set off nonessential phrase; commas used to separate items in a list

comma used to separate a dependent clause from an independent clause

> *He is an interesting case because his core person didn't change, but the path he followed did.*
>
> *Driven largely by economic necessity, an estimated 25 percent of the U.S. labor force is now made up of contingent workers.*
>
> *Married men posted abroad will often leave their family behind in Japan; they fear that their children will fall behind in the fiercely competitive Japanese education system.*
>
> *Economic need is the most consistent work motive—for women as well as men.*
>
> *In 1976, for instance, 43 percent of all women in the paid-labor force were single, widowed, separated, or divorced, and working to support themselves and their dependents.* (This sentence shows commas used for two different purposes.)
>
> *When she tried to re-enter the job market in financial planning, she put together a presentation using cutting-edge computer software.*

Can you tell why the writers used the punctuation they did? We'll help a bit. Below you will find a few guidelines for using punctuation inside the sentence. Copy the sentence from the above list that matches the guideline, and circle the punctuation mark. (One of the sentences will be used twice.)

You can copy the sentences on the lines below the guidelines, or make an index card for each. If you create index cards, remember to write the sentence on the front of the card and the guideline on the back.

Commas

Commas separate three or more items in a list.

_____

_____

_____

Commas separate two sentences that could stand separately, called *independent clauses*, but are joined by *coordinating conjunctions* such as *and, or, but,* or *so.*

_____

Commas separate a clause beginning with a subordinator, such as *when, if, while,* or *because* from an independent clause when the subordinator comes before the independent clause.

Commas can be used to set off an *introductory phrase*—a few words that come at the beginning of the sentence—before the subject and verb.

A pair of commas separates a nonessential phrase from the rest of the sentence.

Semicolons

A semicolon separates two independent clauses that do not have a coordinating conjunction between them.

Dashes

A dash or pair of dashes separates nonessential information from the rest of the sentence. Remember to use dashes sparingly.

Now create two new index cards for each of the guidelines, writing the guidelines on one side. Look at other papers you've written to find examples of sentences using the punctuation described here. If you can't find two sentences, write two new ones or find appropriate sentences from readings. Make sure to write the guideline on the back of each card and circle the punctuation the guideline refers to.

As you become more confident in your writing, you will want to begin using inside-the-sentence punctuation in other ways. Refer to an English handbook for more information, or see the **Go To** exercise at the end of this section for information on where to get help on the Web.

Select two or three sentences from your central assignment. Rewrite these sentences different ways by using the following punctuation marks:

1. Dash:

_____

_____

_____

2. Semicolon:

_____

_____

_____

3. Colon:

_____

_____

_____

4. Comma(s):

_____

_____

_____

Go To ▶ Go to the *Writing Now* web site for more information on sentence construction and punctuation use. You will be directed to OWLs (Online Writing Labs) and to a web site featuring Strunk and White's well-known text *The Elements of Style,* a classic guide to good punctuation and editing.

OPTIONS ▶ Customize

1. Select an essay you have previously written. Rewrite the essay, combining shorter sentences into longer sentences using semicolons, dashes, and/or commas. Read the first and the revised essay aloud to hear the difference that more interesting sentence structure can make.

2. Trade drafts of your newly written essay with a classmate. Rewrite sentences from your classmate's draft into longer, more interesting sentences and then show these sentences to your classmate.

FILE ▶ Edit

You may want to assign the rest of the chapter as homework.

Revision for Sentence Construction and Punctuation

Using the draft of the essay on which you are currently working, revise the essay, creating longer sentences out of shorter sentences you may have used. Sometimes students write sentence fragments—that is, a "fragment" of a sentence standing alone when it should actually be attached to elements that will make it a complete sentence. Be on the watch for fragments and attach them to an appropriate sentence.

Avoiding Fragments

I missed two important phone calls while I was on the Internet. If you punctuated this sentence with a period after *calls* as if the phrase were two sentences, the second portion of the sentence would be a fragment because it is dependent on the first part to complete its meaning.

Checking your sentences and combining them into longer, more interesting sentences often solves the fragment problem. Would it be appropriate anywhere to connect two sentences with a semicolon, colon, or dash? Check your comma usage. Is it appropriate?

You might want to model this for your class by having a volunteer read his or her paper aloud, and have the class answer the questions together. Ask the writer if the class had the same answers as the writer did.

Peer Revision Worksheet

Reviewed by: **Date:**

Focus of review: introduction, patterns of development, and sentence variety

Reviewing paper written by:

Peer Revision Questionnaire

Ask yourself the following questions about your draft. Then, if possible, ask a friend or classmate to read your draft and answer the same questions about it. If your answers do not match, you haven't succeeded in communicating what you think you did.

- What is this essay about? (topic)

- What is the event or situation that prompted the essay? (prompt)

- What do you have to say about your topic? (thesis or main idea)

- Who is your intended audience?

- What is your purpose in writing about this?

- What personal experience (life, reading, TV, stories you've heard, and so on) have you had with this topic?

- What purpose does each paragraph serve? How does each support the thesis?

- Is there anything else I should know? Are there any questions in the reader's mind left unanswered by the essay?

FILE ▶ Save

After carefully examining your pattern of development and revising for more effective sentence structure, you are ready to do a final edit. Perform all the revision techniques you have learned so far.

Revision Checklist

☐ I have clearly stated assertions about my topic.

☐ I have a defined audience.

☐ I have arranged my ideas in an order appropriate to the topic.

☐ I had someone read and annotate my essay.

☐ I have an appropriate title.

☐ I have a clearly stated topic.

☐ I have developed a topic that is appropriate, neither too broad nor too specific.

☐ All paragraphs support my overall topic.

☐ Each paragraph has a different focus relating to my topic.

☐ Each paragraph has well-developed supporting examples and/or facts.

☐ I revised my word choice to use descriptive and appropriate words.

☐ My tone is clear and consistent throughout the essay.

☐ My pronoun references are clear.

☐ My pronoun use is appropriate.

☐ I wrote an introduction that contained my assertion and an idea of what the essay is about.

☐ I used appropriate patterns of development for the topic, the purpose, the audience, and the introduction.

☐ I used a variety of sentence structures.

☐ I eliminated fragments and run-ons.

Proofreading Checklist

☐ I have read each sentence aloud, starting with the last one first and working backward to make sure each sentence is clear and uses appropriate language conventions.

☐ I used my proofreading frame to check for spelling.

☐ I asked a classmate to read my draft and to complete the Peer Revision Worksheet.

Now you are ready to submit your polished essay for evaluation and feedback from your instructor.

Go To ▶ Go to the *Writing Now* web site for a variety of links to information on careers. There you will also find links to newsgroups on careers, so you can engage in conversations with others about choosing careers and on career obstacles. Newsgroups were an early Internet way of communication. They predate the Web but are still going strong today. How long they will last, though, is anybody's guess. You will also find current links to sites like the ones listed here.

▶ Careers.org, **<http://www.careers.org/>**, posts job listings—and listings of those seeking jobs. *Careers.org* also offers *Job Sleuth*, which scours the Internet for you, finding and e-mailing the jobs you want; and *Company Sleuth*, which scours the Internet for free, legal, inside information on the companies you select.

▶ The Career Resource Homepage at **<http://www.careerresource.net>** offers a wealth of job-related resources: newsgroups, job listings, university resources, resume listings, and more.

▶ Career Magazine online **<http://www.careermagazine.com/>** is a great place to keep up to date on career trends and get help finding a job.

C:\Prompts for Writing ▶

1. If you know what your career will be, write an essay describing it. Write a brief narrative about how you got interested in this field as your introduction.

2. Career counselors are suggesting that the day of the lifetime career is gone. People are changing careers rapidly for many reasons. What circumstances might lead you to think about changing careers?

3. Education plays a crucial role in career preparation. Write an essay describing several changes that your institution might make to help students not just with getting a degree, but with lifelong learning.

Log Off: ▶ **Review and Reflect**

Take some time to reflect on what you have learned about writing in Chapter 10. How has your writing changed as a result of the discussions, readings, and activities in this chapter?

_____
_____
_____
_____
_____
_____
_____
_____
_____

How has your ability to write introductions changed as a result of the work you have done in this chapter?

_____
_____
_____
_____
_____
_____
_____

What did you learn about punctuation or sentence construction that you didn't know before?

_____
_____
_____
_____
_____

CHAPTER 11
Simplify, Simplify

Live simply so that others may simply live.
—Mahatma Ghandi

Chapter Contents

Log On ▶ **Reflection**

Write whatever comes to mind when you read the chapter title and opening quotation.

_____

_____

_____

_____

_____

_____

_____

_____

_____

_____

_____

_____

_____

_____

_____

_____

_____

_____

_____

_____

_____

_____

_____

_____

_____

FILE ▶ Open

`00:45`

Connecting with Experience

▶ Think of a movie you have seen recently.

▶ Describe the movie in the following ways:

1. Write a one-sentence description like those used in TV listings.

2. Write a four-to-seven-sentence description of the movie as if you were explaining it to a friend.

3. Write your opinion of the movie in two to three sentences.

4. E-mail a friend who hasn't seen the movie, using what you wrote in items 2 and 3 to advise your friend about whether to see the movie or not. Try to leave out key elements so that you don't give the plot away.

Connecting with Writing

▶ Refer to the article on page 165 in Chapter 7, "Controlling How Others See You Is Good Business." Notice that the article begins with an *abstract*. Reread the abstract and skim the article.

1. In one to two sentences, write the definition of an abstract as you understand it from studying the example on page 165.

2. Highlight the areas in the article the abstract was taken from.

3. What kinds of information were not included in the abstract? (Look at the areas that were not highlighted.) Write your answer.

4. If you were assigned to write a summary of this article, what type of information might you include to complete the assignment successfully? Was it the same information included in the abstract?

5. If you were searching the Web for information on how to make a good impression at a job interview and you got several hundred hits to your search query, how would it help your search to have abstracts for each site?

Connecting with the Topic

▶ In one to three sentences, describe the concept *simplicity* as you understand it.

▶ What would it mean to simplify your life and how would you go about doing that? (three to five sentences)

▶ Cluster *simplicity* on a separate sheet of paper.

It is helpful to discuss this question in class. You will want students to come up with a response like, "A movie review is a simplified version of the story with an opinion about it included." You are working toward the concept of summary/response.

You are looking for a response like, "A summary is a simplified version of something."

Students may not have a definition of *summary* at this point. They are trying to *guess* from what has come out of this prewriting or to remember where and in what context they may have heard this word. If you have time to do a large cluster on the board with everyone contributing, students will be surprised at how much they know *as a class.* Students realize that when they work together they have more information and that each one of them has something to contribute to the overall picture.

This is an enjoyable activity in which students can experiment with writing a summary. They will want to tell the whole story, but forcing them to pare it down helps them see what to select and what to leave out. An effective way to do this is as a class activity, with students reading their stories aloud. However, it can be done by e-mailing the stories, by sending the stories to the entire class through a connected computer program, or by a *read-around,* in which each student passes the story to the person on the right and reads the story from the person on the left until the original story returns to its writer.

Think of some way in which the concept *simplicity* and a movie review are related. Write your theory in one sentence.

Think of some way in which the concept *simplicity* and summary are related. Write your theory in one sentence.

Connecting with New Material

In this chapter you are going to learn how to write a summary. At this point you may not be very familiar with the concept.

▶ Discover how much you already know about summary by clustering. Write down anything that comes to mind as you think about the word *summary.* Cluster for at least 3 minutes to dig out almost-forgotten information.

▶ How is an introduction like a summary? Write your thoughts in two or three sentences.

▶ Have you ever let a situation get out of control by making it more complicated than it needed to be? Go over the entire event in your mind. Now condense that story into three sentences that explains the situation and how it got out of control. Yes, you only get three sentences to tell the entire story! In other words, you are going to write a summary of what happened.

 Go To ▶

1. Go to the *All reviews.com* web site at **<http://www.all-reviews.com/>**, which asks visitors to submit their reviews on a variety of things, including movies. Read several reviews to get a sense of how reviews are written and what they contain. Then write a review of one of your favorite movies based on what you've learned about reviews from this site. Submit your review, then compare it to what others have written about the same movie.

2. Go to *Amazon.com* web site **<http://www.amazon.com>**. In the search box, type in the title of a recent book you have read. Read the reader reviews of the book. Compare a reader's review to your opinion of the book.

FILE ▶ **New**

Summary

When you clustered the concept of *simplicity*, you may have discovered that simplifying life is a way of stripping it down to its most important essentials. A *summary* is a way of simplifying a piece of writing; you strip it down to its essential meaning. You did the same thing when you described the movie. You couldn't tell your friend everything that happened. You just covered the highlights. When you reread "Controlling How Others See You Is Good Business," (pages 165–167) you saw that an abstract was a simplified version of the article. An *abstract* is a kind of summary used in professional journals that presents the article's most important ideas so that readers can determine whether they want to read the entire article. Examining an abstract can give you a good idea of how a long article can be summarized.

In this chapter you are going to learn to write a summary, which you will turn into a summary/response essay in Chapter 12. You are already familiar with writing a response. So far, your readers have usually been your classmates, so they are familiar with the text to which you are responding. In many situations, however, you will be responding to a text that your readers may not have read. Therefore, before giving a response, you must first summarize the text for your readers, that is, give them an idea of the author's assertion and the major points that support it.

Most summaries you will be asked to write in college will call for a careful strategy before you start. Students are often required to summarize extensive technical material in an essay exam or summarize lengthy articles in a summary or "reflection" activity as homework. Many colleges require a summary/response essay on material that requires analysis and critical thinking. In order to summarize this material, you must understand it thoroughly and have a "plan of attack" or strategy.

Three basic strategies for analyzing a text before writing a summary are given here. You can choose the strategy that works best for you, keeping in mind that your choice may depend on the organizational pattern of the text, its length or difficulty, the specific assignment, and/or the purpose for summarizing.

These basic strategies for summarizing are:

1. The paragraph strategy

2. The list strategy

3. The problem/solution strategy

The Paragraph Strategy

In the *paragraph* strategy, you determine the main idea of each paragraph of an essay, one by one. This type of strategy takes several steps.

1. After the first reading of the essay, reread each paragraph, determine the main idea of that paragraph, and write it down *in your own words.* Continue doing that until you have a main idea for each paragraph in the order they occur. You will notice that sometimes succeeding paragraphs express the same main idea.

2. After you have written a sentence summarizing each paragraph, read over the sentences and determine the overall main idea of the essay. Write this main idea at the top of the page. It is the author's thesis.

3. Reread the essay and determine if the author draws a conclusion. If so, write the conclusion at the bottom of your paper.

4. Read over all the sentences and eliminate any repetition.

5. Next, combine sentences when ideas are similar.

6. You now have a rough summary. Use this as the basis for writing your final summary, which you will create by adding transitions between sentences.

This process may be time consuming, but it is an effective strategy, especially if the text is difficult.

In the following excerpt, entitled "How We Feel When Doing Different Things," author Mihaly Csikszentmihalyi suggests that activities create a mental/emotional response in us that we may not be aware of. As you read the passage, think about how this information could help you simplify your life. After you read it, you will practice writing a summary by summarizing this excerpt.

How We Feel When Doing Different Things

Mihaly Csikszentmihalyi

1   Despite the bad reputation of certain days of the week, on the whole people seem to experience each day more or less like the next. True, as one would expect, Friday afternoons and Saturdays are marginally better than Sunday evenings and Monday mornings, but the differences are less than one would expect. Much depends on how we plan our time: Sunday mornings can be quite depressing if one has nothing to do, but if we look forward to a scheduled activity or a familiar ritual such as going to a church service, then it can be a high point of the week.

2   One interesting finding is that people report significantly more physical symptoms, such as headaches and backaches, on weekends and at times when they are not studying or working. Even the pain of women with cancer is tolerable when they are with friends, or involved in an activity; it flares up when they are alone with nothing to do. Apparently when psychic energy is not committed to a definite task it is easier to notice what goes wrong in our bodies. This fits with what we know about the flow experience: when playing a close tournament, chess players can go for hours without noticing hunger or headache; athletes in a competition can ignore pain and fatigue until the event is over. When attention is focused, minor aches and pains have no chance to register in consciousness.

3   Again, with time of day as with the other parameters of life, it is important to find out what rhythms are most congenial to you personally.

Source: From *Finding Flow: The Psychology of Engagement with Everyday Life* by Mihaly Csikszentmihalyi. Copyright © 1997 by Mihaly Csikszentmihalyi. Reprinted by permission of Basic Books, a member of Perseus Books, L.L.C.

There is no day or hour that is best for everyone. Reflection helps to identify one's preferences, and experimentation with different alternatives—getting up earlier, taking a nap in the afternoon, eating at different times—helps to find the best set of options.

4 In all of these examples, we proceeded as if persons were passive objects whose internal states are affected by what they do, who they are with, where they are, and so forth. While this is true in part, in the last analysis it is not the external conditions that count, but what we make of them. It is perfectly possible to be happy doing housework with nobody around, to be motivated when working, to concentrate when talking to a child. In other words, the excellence of daily life finally depends not on what we do, but on how we do it.

5 Nevertheless, before looking at how one can control the quality of experience directly by transforming information in consciousness, it is important to reflect on the effects that the daily environment—the places, people, activities, and times of day—has on us. Even the most accomplished mystic, detached from all influences, will prefer to sit under one particular tree, eat a certain food, and be with one companion rather than another. Most of us are much more responsive to the situations in which we find ourselves.

6 Thus the first step in improving the quality of life is to pay close attention to what we do every day, and to notice how we feel in different activities, places, times of day, and with different companions. Although the general trends will probably apply also in your case—you'll find yourself happier at mealtimes and most often in flow when in active leisure—there might be also surprising revelations. It may turn out that you really like being alone. Or that you like working more than you thought. Or that reading makes you feel better afterwards than watching television. Or vice versa on all these counts. There is no law that says we have to experience life in the same way. What is vital is to find out what works out best in your case.

Analyze the Reading

1. Highlight the assertions in green and the main ideas in blue. Highlight the examples in yellow and the facts in pink.

2. How could this information help you simplify your life?

   _____

   _____

3. What did you learn that surprised you?

   _____

   _____

   _____

4. Write the main idea of each paragraph.

   1. _____

   _____

You will probably want to go over these main ideas as a class or have students compare and revise in small groups, then put the best main ideas on the board. Students often need extra help again with the main ideas at this point.

2. _____

_____

3. _____

_____

4. _____

_____

5. _____

_____

You may want to end the homework assignment here.

6. _____

_____

5. State the author's thesis.

_____

_____

You can use a 45-minute class session to go over the answers and make sure students understand the assignment. You may want to let students compare answers in small groups for about 25 minutes before regrouping as a class and sharing the answers. Or you may want to have students do the second reading and questions in class. Another alternative is to use the class period to write a summary of the texts they have just read or another text.

6. State the conclusion. (The author may either directly state it or expect readers to draw the conclusion themselves from reading the text.)

_____

_____

7. To turn this exercise into a summary, you would combine these sentences to make a paragraph. Condense sentences or join ideas as necessary until you have a complete summary. If you are using a word processor, the cut and paste tools will help you condense sentences quickly.

00:45

As a class or in small groups, compare your summaries to your list in activity 4. Put the best phrasing of the main ideas on the board. Then condense these sentences and eliminate repetition. Add transitions to complete the summary.

OPTIONS ▶ Customize

1. Work in small groups to turn the main ideas from the Analyze the Reading activity into a summary. "Publish" your summary by printing it from the computer. Distribute copies to the other groups and discuss the differences.

2. Find an article on the Web and write a summary of it. Then cut and paste the article into your word processor. Click on Tools: AutoSummarize. Compare the computer's summary to your own. Can you see the pattern the computer uses to create its summary? Would you want to use this tool to write summaries for you? Why or why not?

3. A summary's length is determined by its purpose. If you are writing a summary response essay based on a short article, you might want to include more details from the original article than if your were writing a summary of a chapter from a textbook or novel with the intent of reminding yourself of the main points the author is making. For practice, find an article on the Web that interests you, then copy and paste it into your word processor. Use Tools: Word Count to see how long the article is. Then write three summaries. The first summary should be one sentence only, expressing the thesis, or main idea only, of the article. The second summary should be about three to five sentences long, expressing the author's main and the most important points made to support that thesis. The final summary should be about 25 percent of the length of the original article. (Divide the word count you got by four, and try to make your summary about that long.) Unless your article is very short, this summary should include the main idea, and major supporting details, and still have space for details that give support to the major supporting details! When might each type of summary be most useful?

 Go To ▶

1. Go to an OWL, or Online Writing Lab, such as Purdue's OWL at **<http:// owl.english.purdue.edu/>** to see if your school or one nearby has an OWL. Examine how at least three OWLs offer help with writing summaries.

2. Go to a textbook publisher's site, such as Houghton Mifflin's at **<http:// college.hmco.com>**. Select "Students" and then "Developmental English." On the right-hand side of your screen, you will find a Resource Center where you can link to online tests and URLs that will help you improve your writing.

This section seems to be a good place to begin the second homework, pages 252–259.

The List Strategy

In many texts, an author will list information as *ways, theories, steps, parts, kinds,* and so on. Sometimes the author categorizes information into *types* or *kinds.* Texts that list are usually easy to summarize because the author often explicitly identifies his or her main ideas by using words such as *first, second, another,* and *finally.* Your goal in summarizing is to make sure that you include all of the steps, ways, and parts in the text but not the details that support each step.

Answering the following questions will help you prepare to summarize:

1. What is being listed or categorized?
2. What is the author's purpose in making this list?
3. What categories or items are on the list?
4. Does the author draw a conclusion about the items listed?

Read "Internal Strife: Stop the Clutter from Personal Problems" and determine what kind of a list Elaine St. James creates.

Internal Strife: Stop the Clutter from Personal Problems

Elaine St. James

Simplify Your Life

1 Whenever I write about getting rid of clutter, I receive a tremendous response. More than any other topic, this one strikes a chord. People really want to get rid of the stuff that's getting in the way of a simpler life.

2 But there's another kind of clutter that is even more debilitating than the stuff in your attic, garage and junk drawers. It's the clutter in your mind and heart—those inner messes that often prevent you from being happy and fulfilled.

3 Here's a challenge: Resolve to send these seven "boxes" of inner clutter to the trash.

4 Grudges: We often see family members carry grudges to their graves and friends who break up over insults they can't even remember years later. If you'd like to make contact with the other person so you can both put the past behind you but you're having trouble taking the first step, have a friend or family member act as a facilitator, or write a letter to break the ice and free you both.

5 Friends who hold you back: Are there people you call friends whose values and goals are incompatible with yours? Do you surround yourself with those who support your best self, or with those who reinforce your worst instincts? Take an honest look at the people in your life. Is it time to let go of some?

6 Hurt feelings: Have you ever experienced the way a casual remark can throw you off-balance? A neighbor who had a child in her late 40s was out walking with her new baby, and a stranger remarked, "Your granddaughter is so beautiful." It ruined her day. How sad, and how un-

Source: Elaine St. James, "Internal Strife: Stop the Clutter from Personal Problems." © Elaine St. James. Reprinted by permission of Jane Dystel Literary Management, Inc.

necessary, to waste an entire day on a comment that was meant as a compliment. We attain true mastery over our feelings when we can rise above negative comments.

7   Judgmental attitudes: When we judge others, we close off an opportunity to learn something new. The next time you're tempted to judge, open your mind, broaden your horizon and listen instead.

8   Addictions: Addictions aren't easy to eliminate. It may be a substance, such as coffee, alcohol or cigarettes. It may be a behavior, such as shopping or gossiping. Start small and change what you can, a little bit at a time. Every tiny victory brings much more control to your life.

9   The desire for approval: The next time you're tempted to ask another person, "How do I look?" or, "How did I do?" turn the question inside and ask it of yourself. It's nice to get approval from others, but to gain true security in our lives, we need to be the judge of our own performance.

10   The need to be right: A friend of mine has a boss who can't stand to be challenged. It's exhausting for her to work for him because she's constantly making one of two untenable choices: either keep quiet even when she disagrees, or argue and make him angry. But my friend has recently come to realize that the need to be right is actually much more exhausting for her boss than it is for her. The strain of holding yourself on that pedestal and constantly worrying that you'll be knocked off can be debilitating. Let it go. It'll greatly simplify your life if you're not afraid to be wrong once in a while.

Analyze the Reading

The easiest way to begin this summary is to briefly state the items the author listed. Then write the overall thesis that explains what the list is about. Finally, your concluding sentence should reflect the conclusion the author gives or wants readers to draw from these lists. (Sometimes the conclusion states the overall importance of the list.) Try this strategy by taking it step by step.

1. Refer back to the reading "Internal Strife" on pages 252–253. Highlight the main ideas in blue and the examples in yellow.

2. What kind of a list does this text present?

_____

3. Why is the author listing these items in particular? What is the author's purpose?

_____

4. Take each item from the author's list and make it into a complete sentence (by adding an assertion). (*Hint:* Look for the obvious clue that will help you locate the items in the author's list.)

    a. _____

_____

    b. _____

c. _____

_____

d. _____

_____

e. _____

_____

f. _____

_____

g. _____

_____

5. Write a one- or two-sentence introduction to this list that explains what it is and why the author wrote it. Include the author's thesis in this introduction.

_____

_____

_____

6. Finally, write a concluding sentence.

_____

_____

You now have the basic outline of a summary. In Chapter 12 you will learn how to polish your summary and make it read more smoothly.

7. How could the ideas in this text help you simplify your life?

_____

_____

_____

The Problem/Solution Strategy

Some essays are written in a two-part pattern in which the author presents a problem and then offers a possible solution to the problem. We can call this type of essay a *problem/solution* essay. Sometimes this type of essay is also called a *cause/effect* essay because the author describes the effects resulting from a problem or a cause identified in the first part of the essay. The cause/effect essay can be presented in reverse order, as well, in which the author discusses an observed situation, or effect, and then proceeds to discuss the possible causes. Both types of patterns, problem/solution and cause/effect, can be handled in the same manner. Since problem/solution is more common, we will use it as the example.

The basic steps involved in this strategy of analyzing text for summarizing are:

1. Identifying the problem
2. Listing the key supporting idea(s)
3. Identifying the solution
4. Listing the key supporting idea(s)
5. Examining the problem and the solution to determine the thesis

In an essay entitled "Give Up on the Idea That 'More Is Better'" from his best-selling book, *Don't Sweat the Small Stuff,* Richard Carlson challenges our materialistic attitudes. As you read, try to determine the problem he describes and his suggested solution.

Give Up on the Idea That "More Is Better"

Richard Carlson

1   We live in the most affluent culture the world has ever seen. Estimates are that although we have only 6 percent of the world's population in America, we use almost half of the natural resources. It seems to me that if more were actually better, we would live in the happiest, most satisfied culture of all time. But we don't. Not even close. In fact, we live in one of the most dissatisfied cultures on record.

2   It's not that having a lot of things is bad, wrong, or harmful in and of itself, only that the desire to have more and more and more is insatiable. As long as you think more is better, you'll never be satisfied.

3   As soon as we get something, or achieve something, most of us simply go on to the next thing—immediately. This squelches our appreciation for life and for our many blessings. I know a man, for example, who bought a beautiful home in a nice area. He was happy until the day after he moved in. Then the thrill was gone. Immediately, he wished he'd bought a bigger, nicer home. His "more is better" thinking wouldn't allow him to enjoy his new home, even for a day. Sadly, he is not unique. To varying degrees, we're all like that. It's gotten to the point that when the Dalai Lama won the Nobel Prize for Peace in 1989, one of the first questions he received from a reporter was "What's next?" It seems that whatever we do—buy a home or a car, eat a meal, find a partner, purchase some clothes, even win a prestigious honor—it's never enough.

4   The trick in overcoming this insidious tendency is to convince yourself that more isn't better and that the problem doesn't lie in what you don't have, but in the longing for more. Learning to be satisfied doesn't mean you can't, don't, or shouldn't ever want more than you have, only that your happiness isn't contingent on it. You can learn to be happy with what you have by becoming more present-moment oriented, by not

Source: From Don't Sweat the Small Stuff . . . And It's All Small Stuff by Richard Carlson, Ph.D. Copyright © 1997 by Richard Carlson, Ph.D. Reprinted by permission of Hyperion.

focusing so much on what you want. As thoughts of what would make your life better enter your mind, gently remind yourself that, even if you got what you think you want, you wouldn't be one bit more satisfied, because the same mind-set that wants more now would want more then.

5   Develop a new appreciation for the blessings you already enjoy. See your life freshly, as if for the first time. As you develop this new awareness, you'll find that as new possessions or accomplishments enter your life, your level of appreciation will be heightened.

6   An excellent measure of happiness is the differential between what you have and what you want. You can spend your lifetime wanting more, always chasing happiness—or you can simply decide to consciously want less. This latter strategy is infinitely easier and more fulfilling.

Analyze the Reading

1. Highlight the thesis in green, the main ideas in blue, the examples in yellow, and the facts in pink.

2. How does the title help you determine the thesis?

_____

_____

_____

3. Determine the problem and state it in your own words.

_____

_____

4. List the basic information Carlson provides to support his assertion that this is a problem. Don't go into great detail; just summarize the support.

_____

_____

5. Determine the solution that Carlson proposes and state it in your own words.

_____

_____

6. List the information Carlson provides to support his proposed solution. (Keep your answer brief.)

_____

_____

7. Consider the problem and the solution and state the author's thesis in your own words.

_____

_____

8. Go back to the reading and look at what you highlighted in pink and yellow. Did you include any of that information in your summary sentences in the preceding exercise? If so, you want to redo that section. Specific facts and examples that the author uses to *support* his main ideas are *not* included in a summary. Examples are asked for in item 6 simply to help you understand the main ideas. Examples are only included in a summary if the entire piece to be summarized consists of one or two long examples, and then it would be necessary to summarize the long example in a sentence or two. Remember, only the main points are included in a summary.

You now have the basic skeleton of a summary. Now that you know how to attack a text to extract the information necessary to write a summary, you are ready to review the steps we have taken so far to write a basic summary. This boxed guideline includes the finishing steps that you will need to take to write a summary. Steps 8, 9, 10, and 11 will be covered in Chapter 12, where you will learn how to polish your summary.

Steps in Writing a Summary

1. Read the text carefully.

2. Reread the text, looking for its overall organizational pattern, thesis, and key ideas.

3. Pay special attention to the title and the first and last paragraphs of the text. These are often good places to find the thesis.

4. Annotate the text. Highlight the main ideas. You may wish to mark examples in yellow. Underline assertions. Make marginal notes summarizing ideas as you go.

5. Ask yourself these questions after reading the text:

   a. What is the author's purpose for telling me this?

   b. How does the author support the statements made in the reading?

   c. What does the author want me to get from reading this?

6. Determine your strategy for writing a summary.

7. Write the basic sentences of the summary in your own words.

8. Eliminate redundant ideas and combine ideas into sentences, using transitions to show the relationship between the ideas.

9. Turn these sentences into a paragraph.

10. Read your summary aloud and ask yourself whether someone would understand what the text was about from reading your summary.

11. Proofread the final draft.

In addition to proceeding in a logical manner through these steps, you will want to keep in mind the following *general guidelines* for writing a summary.

Guidelines for Writing a Summary

1. Always name the author and the title in your first or second sentence of your summary. If you give the author and title in the second sentence, then your first sentence will be a general introduction to the topic.

2. The author's main idea, or thesis, should be stated in the sentence with the author's name and title or in the sentence immediately preceding or following that one. For example, if you were summarizing the article from Chapter 5, you might write *In the article "What Computers Can, Cannot, and Should Not Do," Timothy Trainor and Diane Krasnewich make the point that while computers can be very helpful to human beings, they will never replace people.*

3. Write the summary in your own words. Any time you use the author's words or phrases, you must put quotation marks around them. Use quotes sparingly, though. Too much quoting means your summary will be longer than it should be or needs to be. After highlighting the text, it may help to turn the essay over or close the book, and write from memory. Then go back and check your summary against the passage to make sure what you have written is accurate.

4. Refer to the author periodically in your summary to indicate that these are the author's ideas, not yours. It is customary to use the author's full name the first time you give it and use only the last name thereafter. You will want to vary this practice by using *he* or *she*, and *the author*, rather than repeating the name several times in a row.

5. The summary must be of an appropriate length, which will vary according to the length of the text being summarized, its organizational pattern, its content, your purpose in summarizing, and the specific assignment. As a general rule, however, you would not want to include more than one sentence of summary per paragraph in a longer piece. Sometimes the guideline "summary = one-fourth the original length" works. Keep in mind that your objective is to give the author's thesis and main ideas in as concise a manner as possible.

6. Do not give your opinion in the summary. Be careful to present the author's ideas objectively, as he or she would want them presented. This is not the place to evaluate them.

7. Keep ideas in the same order that the author did.

8. Keep the same balance between ideas as the author did. Give ideas the same emphasis as the author did. If you provide more explanation of one idea than another, it may appear that the author emphasized that point more.

OPTIONS ▶ Customize

00:45

You may want to spend the last 45-minute session of the unit going over the steps and guidelines on pages 257–258. An alternative would be to spend the class having students turn their skeleton of a summary into real summaries and read some of them aloud at the end of class. This could be done in small groups or individually. You may want students to begin the **File: Create** homework assignment from page 260 in class. If your class seems to have a good grasp of the material, you may want to select an activity from **Options: Customize** here.

1. Prepare an oral presentation (speech) for your class or another group on the topic of your intended career. Make notes to glance at rather than to read word for word. Use one note card for each main point you want to make, and fill in the details from memory while doing the presentation. The main points that will be included on each card will pertain to aspects of your intended career, such as educational requirements, salary information, skills required, job description, and opportunities for advancement. You can use your notecards to write a *summary* of your presentation.

2. Write a summary of one of your classmates' presentations. Then see if your summary matched the speaker's note cards. They should!

3. If you have a web site, create a section for your favorite links instead of doing an oral presentation. Don't put in just the links, though; include the web page title, the URL, then a *summary* of what the viewer will find on the linked site.

4. Teach one of the readings in this chapter or a related reading of your choice to your classmates by doing a slide show presentation, using software such as PowerPoint. In presenting a slide show, you want to put only the main ideas on the screen, one idea per slide, using as few words as possible to help focus your audience's attention on what you are saying. Visual learners who have trouble writing a summary may find it helpful to design a slide show (on paper) to *summarize* the article, then use the ideas from the planned slides as an outline for the summary.

Help Screen

Giving an Oral Presentation

Do you have trouble making an oral presentation or speech? Instead of reading word for word what you want to say, you will be a more natural and interesting presenter if you glance at notes and expand on them. You can use props to enhance your delivery and make it easier for your audience to see and remember your main points.

Posters, handouts, and overheads are props that might help your audience connect with your presentation. Increasingly, however, presenters are using their computers and projectors to present slide shows to stress the points they want their audience to focus on.

A *slide presentation* is a visual summary of what you want to say. Your audience can both see and hear your main ideas; color, graphics, and even sound add interest to keep them focused. Slide presentation software packages such as PowerPoint are relatively easy to use. Most important, of course, is your content. Before you even begin to use the software, you should identify your main idea, and the most important supporting details you want to use to illustrate your main idea. Identify your target audience, the purpose of your presentation, and the tone you want to set.

You can find more information about how to prepare a PowerPoint presentation online at: PowerPoint in the Classroom **http://www.actden.com/pp/**; Indiana University/Purdue University at Indianapolis PowerPoint tutorial at **http://www.science.iupui.edu/SAC98/ppt.htm**; or do a web search for PowerPoint tutorial if you find that better suits your needs.

FILE ▶ **Create**

Summary/Response Essay

In this chapter you will write the summary section of a summary/response essay. In Chapter 12 you will add the response section to this paper. So far, you have worked on analyzing a text and getting the basic outline of a summary down on paper. You have written the author's thesis and main ideas in your own words. Now you want to take this information and put it into a paragraph. This piece of writing does not involve the usual brainstorming steps that you did in earlier writing. That is because you are not *generating your ideas* here. You are *analyzing the author's ideas*. There is no place for your opinion in a summary. That will come later in the response, as you will see in Chapter 12.

Pick one of the texts you analyzed earlier in this chapter. Using the answers you wrote down to help you, complete the following plan:

You may want to discuss *tone* in relation to writing a summary.

Title of article to be summarized:

_____

Author's Name: _____

Audience: _____

Purpose: To summarize the text and to respond to the author's thesis.

Tone: _____

Author's Thesis:

_____

_____

_____

Author's Key Points: (please label them A., B., etc.)

A. _____

_____

_____

B. _____

_____

_____

C. _____

_____

_____

(add more as needed)

FILE ▶ Save As

1. Reread the Guidelines for Writing a Summary on page 258.

2. Following the steps given in Steps for Writing a Summary on page 257, write a draft of a summary of the text you chose in **File: Create**. The summary will be the first paragraph of the essay you write in Chapter 12. As you complete each step, put a checkmark next to the step in pencil. You have already done most of the planning work by answering the questions in the chapter.

3. Save your essay as a draft. In the next chapter you will learn some ways to polish your summary and you will learn how to write the rest of the essay, the response to the text. But before you can do that, you need some good content to work with. Therefore, make sure that this draft has a thorough summary and bring it to class.

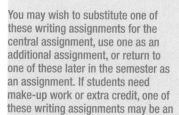

You may wish to substitute one of these writing assignments for the central assignment, use one as an additional assignment, or return to one of these later in the semester as an assignment. If students need make-up work or extra credit, one of these writing assignments may be an option.

1. Write a summary for all the texts included in this chapter instead of just one. Read your summaries to classmates and pick the best one to use in the next chapter.

2. Get in groups and have each group pick a different text in this chapter to summarize. Read the summaries aloud.

3. Get in groups and have each group write a summary of the same text. Compare the summaries and discuss how they differ.

4. Pick a reading from an earlier chapter that interested you and write a summary. Do not include the author and title of the article. Have classmates see if they can recognize the reading you are summarizing.

5. Pick a magazine article that you particularly enjoyed and that made you aware of something you didn't realize before. Summarize that article in five to eight sentences for your classmates.

Go To ▶

1. Go to the *Writing Now* web site for additional articles on simplifying your life. If you enjoyed this subject, you can find other suggestions for additional reading at the web site.

2. Go to a search engine on the Web and search on *summary*. Compare what you find to what has been given here.

Help Screen

Web-Savvy Searching

You are probably already familiar with web searches, but if you often find the results that you get more frustrating than enlightening, you may be interested in learning some tricks to searching the Web that will bring back more exact and useful results.

Hundreds of search engines are available to help you find information on the Web. Many search engines exist inside *web portals* and *indexed sites*, sites that may offer free e-mail, chat rooms, and forums as well as search capabilities. Yahoo, at **<http://www.yahoo.com>**, is probably the best known search engine, but it is far from your only choice. Since it is likely that the best search engine includes no more than about 15 percent of the sites available on any given subject and there is much overlap among sites covered, you will have to use several engines to get comprehensive, but not complete, coverage for your topic.

First, go to your favorite search engine and search for the word "summary". How many hits did you get? Are the hits on the first few pages the kinds of sites you are looking for? Why or why not? Does your initial search tell you anything about the importance of good summaries? In other words, would so many different kinds of sites have shown up with *summary* as a keyword unless many people use summaries for many different reasons?

Now design an advanced search to focus on what you are looking for. Since search engines have different ways to perform advanced searches, the best way to learn how to do one is to go to your favorite search engines and check out their *Help* or *Advanced Search* links.

The easiest kind of search engine allows for *natural language* searches: you key in a question, and the search engine translates it into a limited search for you. These kinds of search engines are great, as long as you realize computer programs don't really speak English—not yet, anyway—and sometimes you will get a lot of answers that look weird to you but that the computer judged were related to your question. Try it out. Write a natural language question at **<http://www.ask.com>** or **<http://www.altavista. com>**. You might want to try, "Where can I get help writing a summary?" or "How can I write a good summary?"

Advanced searches use special symbols to help the search engine narrow your search. Many use what are called *Boolean delimiters,* such as a plus sign before a term to show it must be included and quotation marks around a phrase to show that the whole phrase must appear exactly as typed. Capital letters mean the word must be capitalized; lower case includes both. Suffixes on words, even an *s* to show that a word is plural, may limit the number of hits on the word. Use the root form of the word when you want the most possible interpretations. Try three searches in Yahoo, using the following keywords: rock and roll (not limited), +rock +roll (all words), and "rock and roll" (exact phrase). Which search gave you the most useful information most quickly? Remember, a good search isn't the one that produces more hits than you can deal with, it is the one that lists useful sites in the first several hits.

Limited advanced searches can make your searches more efficient, but each engine has its own way of performing these searches. It is worth your time to practice and read the advanced search guides in your favorite search engines.

Some sites will do a combined search for you. Metacrawler, at **<http://www.metacrawler.com/>**, searches about a dozen of the most popular search engines and combines the results so you don't get duplicated sites. Another feature that you might find helpful is an engine that categorizes results for you, such as NorthernLight, at **<http://www.northernlight.com/>**.

You can find links to more complete tutorials on searching the Web on the *Writing Now* web site. One such site is *Sink or Swim: Internet Search Tools & Techniques*, at **<http://www.ouc.bc.ca/libr/connect96/search.htm>**. You will also find a link to *About.com*, which has a great list of resources for people at all levels of expertise who want to hone their Internet searching skills.

Another way of maximizing the efficiency of your search is to go to the kind of site that is likely to have the information you want. When you want help on learning to write a good summary, you might consider checking out some OWLs or go to a web site of English textbook publishers, since many of them now offer such information online. Check the *Writing Now* web site for current links to some of these sites.

CHAPTER 12
Making Transitions

> If only we'd stop trying to be happy
> we'd have a pretty good time.
>
> —Edith Wharton

Log On ▶ **Reflection**

Write whatever comes to mind when you read the chapter title and opening quotation.

_____

_____

_____

_____

_____

_____

_____

_____

_____

_____

_____

_____

_____

_____

_____

_____

_____

_____

_____

_____

_____

_____

FILE ▶ Open

00:45

As usual, the **Connecting** exercises are best done in class the first day of a new unit. In this case, the Connecting exercises or schema will not take the entire class period allowing you to review the summaries that students wrote as homework in preparation for this chapter. You may want students to get into small groups and do a readaround of the groups' summaries or have a few students read their summaries aloud. If you have a student who consistently performs well, you may want to put that student's summary on the overhead for the class to discuss. Whatever method you use, your goal is to reinforce the concept of summary before moving on to summary/response.

Even though the concept of transitions has not been formally introduced, students did read one text on making transitions earlier in this book. Now you want students to see what they already know and to attempt to make some connections. Students should simply make their best attempts here; they realize by now that this section is nonthreatening and not graded.

Connecting with Experience

Before you answer the following questions, turn to page 45 in Chapter 2 and review "Making the Transition to College."

▶ During your first few weeks in college, you were expected to make a transition from high school behaviors to college behaviors. What does that mean? Describe some of those behaviors and changes that you made.

▶ A honeymoon was originally considered to be a period of transition from the single life to married life. How would that transitional period be different from the period before, when one was a single person, and the period after, when one was adjusted to married life?

▶ Can you think of any other transitional periods during a person's lifetime?

▶ Can you think of small transitional periods during your day?

▶ Do transitional periods serve a purpose? Describe that purpose as best you can.

Connecting with Writing

▶ Usually writers add a *transition* between two paragraphs in order to link them together or to make a smooth change between two different ideas. On the basis of your answers to "Connecting with Experience," how would you describe a transition as used in writing?

▶ If you are familiar with the term *transition,* can you think of any *transitional words* or *phrases?* List as many as you can think of.

▶ In Chapter 11, you learned to write a summary. In earlier chapters, you learned to write a response. In this chapter, you will put the two types of writing together into a summary/response. How does that relate to the concept of *transition?* Brainstorm on this question.

▶ What do you already know about writing a summary/response? How will it be similar to, or different from, earlier essays?

Connecting with the Topic

▶ Even though you have not yet learned about the specific nature of writing transitions so far in this course, you may have some ideas about the nature of transitions generally. Spend at least 3 minutes clustering *transition* with anything that comes to mind.

Go To ▶

1. Go to more than one online thesaurus to see what words are similar to *transition*. A good place to start is with a visual thesaurus, such as the one at Plumb Design **<http://www.plumbdesign.com/thesaurus/>**. Read the instructions on how to use the site, then click away. You can click on any of the words displayed as synonyms, and that word will move to the center of the screen. Do you see a smooth *transition* from one meaning to another?

2. Search the Internet to find descriptions of how to write a summary/response from other college courses across the country. Practice using advanced searches to find material as you did in Chapter 11. Print out any helpful guidelines you find. Do any of the descriptions or guidelines differ from what you have been taught in this class? Prepare to discuss those in class.

FILE ▶ New

After you have spent class time re-viewing students' summaries, you may want to begin the homework assignment. Have students cover pages 269–275.

Sometimes it's helpful to let students realize that there is something they don't know so that they will acknowledge the gap and be more attentive to the new information when it is presented.

Summary/Response Essay

Since you have already written both a summary and responses, the type of essay known as a summary/response or reader response should be easy to learn. In this chapter, you will focus on perfecting your skills as well as on refining content, using conventional language, and getting your writing to flow. You will also improve your revision skills.

A summary/response is a type of writing widely used in freshman composition courses throughout the country. In many schools, an exit exam in the form of a summary/response essay is required to pass a first-year composition course. In addition, this format is used extensively in many academic courses, from the freshman through the doctoral level, to measure students' understanding of assigned material and to help them think critically about a subject. For example, a student studying to be a social worker might be asked to read three journal articles a week on topics covered in the course and to write a *summary/response* for each one. A doctoral student might be asked to read a book a week and write a *reflection*, an informal summary/response, on each book.

Another version of this format is common in the work environment. For example, an employee might be asked to evaluate several types of copy machines and suggest which one the company should buy. This employee would have to *summarize* the description of each copy machine and *respond* with arguments in favor of the one he or she deemed best for the company's needs.

Clearly, this is a skill that will benefit you in many situations in your academic and professional career. As you can see, there are quite a few purposes for writing a summary/response and many versions of this format. In this chapter, you will write a traditional academic summary/response as used in composition classes. Because the format is widely used, it has become somewhat standardized and can follow a general formula, though there are some minor differences from school to school or from instructor to instructor. Be prepared to adapt this formula, now and in the future, to the requirements of your instructor or purpose.

As you have already learned, it is helpful to study the writing of others carefully in order to model your writing after theirs and incorporate new techniques into your own writing. The following is an article about making a transition to fatherhood. Thinking about this article will help you learn the concept of *transition*. In addition, the sample response that follows contains transition words in its topic sentences. See if you can recognize them now and circle them if you can. If not, you will have a chance to come back and look at them later in this chapter.

Transition to Fatherhood

David Knox

1 The fatherhood role begins with the woman's pregnancy and the husband relating to his wife as a mother-to-be. This means sharing her excitement about the pregnancy with parents and close friends. "It was like telling people that we were getting married," said one father. "We delighted in breaking the news to people who were as excited as we were."

2 Beyond this, husbands do very little to prepare for fatherhood. In a study of 102 first-time fathers (Knox & Gilman, 1974), only one-third attended parenthood classes offered by a local university, whereas one-fourth attended Lamaze classes. It would be inaccurate to assume that the fathers-to-be already knew what to expect from the fatherhood role. In fact, only 25 percent of them had discussed fatherhood with another male on several occasions, and more than 40 percent had never fed a baby or changed a baby's diapers. In another study (Price-Bonham & Skeen, 1979), 160 fathers reported that "trial and error" was their first source of help with fatherhood.

3 When 30 husbands whose wives were in their last month of pregnancy were asked about their impending new role (Fein, 1976), most were concerned about what labor and delivery would be like and worried about how to actually take care of a baby. Others said their fathers had been emotionally distant with them when they were growing up, and they did not want to repeat this pattern when they became fathers.

Source: David Knox, *Choices in Relationships*, pp. 477–478.

Now study the following example of a summary/response addressing the article "Transition to Fatherhood." As you read, prepare to formulate some guidelines for yourself about how a summary/response is written.

Fathers Need Training, Too

1 In "Transition to Fatherhood," David Knox argues that, while fathers-to-be may be very excited about their first baby, they don't do much to prepare themselves to be fathers. He cites a study by Knox & Gilman (1974) that found that no more than a third of first-time fathers attended classes. A second study (Price-Bonaham & Skeen, 1979) showed that most fathers used the "trial and error" method of parenting. Knox concludes with a third study by Fein (1976) that showed that fathers whose baby was due within a month still had concerns about how to take care of the baby. I agree that fathers know little about how to care for a child because our society has built-in training for mothers that it doesn't provide for fathers.

2 From the time a girl is little, she is preparing for motherhood, but little boys aren't. A little girl begins playing with dolls. She learns to care for her "baby." The child can even feed and diaper some baby dolls. If she is lucky, a girl has younger siblings she can play "mommy" with. In fact, many girls are expected to help take care of their younger siblings. This gives the young girl the expectation that she will be a caretaker of children later in life. Boys seldom play with dolls or play house with

younger siblings and are not expected to take care of their younger siblings to the degree that girls are.

3   Second, a teenage girl is also "trained" to take care of children, but teenage boys aren't. Often the first source of income for a girl too young to work is babysitting. Her experience with her younger siblings can prepare a girl for this job. Schools and churches often provide babysitting courses for young teens. In addition, the girl's mother and the baby's mother offer instruction on babysitting. Sometimes, on her first babysitting job, the mother may supervise the babysitting and instruct the daughter. Teenage boys generally have much less experience in this area. They seldom attend babysitting courses and are not usually a parent's first choice as a babysitter. Therefore, they don't acquire the experience in taking care of children during their teenage years.

4   Finally, a young married woman without children frequently socializes with friends and their children but a young married man doesn't. As women visit with each other socially, the young woman observes her friends' style of parenting. She gains information and experience in this way. If she is thinking of having a child herself, she will actively seek information from her friends and pay special attention to the skills necessary to care for the baby. When young men socialize, they tend to do it out of the house, at sporting events, parties, or other occasions. It is less common to find two men socializing while caring for a young baby. So again they are not gaining as much experience as women in caring for a baby.

5   Therefore, fathers-to-be come to the experience without the gradual accumulation of knowledge that women have. Because men are not accustomed to participating in these child-caring activities, they may be more reluctant to attend parenting classes. For fathers to be more prepared as parents, I think our society's attitude toward men and women's roles in childcare will have to change. Therefore, given the fact that our society now includes more single-father homes than ever before, it is important that we begin to give our young men more experience with childcare.

Analyze the Reading

1. What is the topic of the essay, "Transition to Fatherhood"?

2. What is the assertion of the essay, "Transition to Fatherhood"?

3. What is the topic of the summary/response essay, "Fathers Need Training, Too"?

4. What is the assertion of the summary/response essay, "Fathers Need Training, Too"?

5. Note that the summary/response addresses the issue of the lack of preparedness of fathers-to-be by responding with what the writer believes to

be the causes. Another writer might have responded by arguing that fathers don't need classes, giving reasons and support for that assertion. A third writer might have responded by stating that fathers are better prepared than the study would indicate, giving support to show that fathers know a great idea about how to care for their children. An additional option is that a writer may have agreed with the author and supported his or her statement by illustrating how poorly prepared fathers are. Many assertions are possible with the topic "Transition to Fatherhood." In writing your own summary/response, you would brainstorm to accumulate as much information as you could to determine your individual thesis.

Write two different thesis statements that could have been used for the response.

a.

_____

_____

b.

_____

_____

6. Look at the summary part of the summary/response on page 270. Compare the summary paragraph to the text of "Transition to Fatherhood." Highlight in "Transition to Fatherhood" the sources of the information in the summary.

7. Highlight both Knox's thesis and the summary/response writer's thesis in green. Highlight the main idea of every paragraph in blue. Do the paragraphs all stick to the subject of "Transition to Fatherhood" and the fact that fathers are underprepared for their new role? Please comment.

Notice that the author is citing his own study (Knox & Gilman, 1974) as support for his argument. Do you think this enhances or detracts from his credibility? Explain.

_____

_____

_____

CHAPTER 12 Making Transitions | **273**

Here are some guidelines for writing a summary/response. Remember, these guidelines can vary somewhat as required by the institution or purpose.

Summary/Response Guidelines

- The summary portion of a summary/response essay follows the basic format of summaries described in Chapter 11. This means that the first or second sentence of the essay will include the author, title, and author's thesis. You will then write several sentences summarizing the text to which you will respond. The last sentence in the first paragraph will be your response thesis. In a summary/response, *the response thesis must clearly respond to the author's thesis* as you have stated it in your first or second sentence.

- The second paragraph states your first assertion in support of your response thesis. This assertion will be *in response to* what was stated as the author's thesis and to the author's assertions. It will be in your own words.

- The following paragraphs will continue to support your response thesis in response to the author's text.

Help Screen

Positioning Your Thesis Statement

In writing a simple response essay, you have been making your thesis the last sentence of the first paragraph of your response. Some schools suggest or require that your thesis statement be the last sentence; others make it the first sentence of the second paragraph. Your instructor can guide you with the preferred method at your institution. If there is no preference, you may wish to position your thesis as the last sentence of the summary paragraph.

Copyright © Houghton Mifflin Company. All rights reserved.

In the summary response essay you are putting together the two kinds of essays you have already written. However, you should keep the following special points in mind.

Help Screen

Tips for Summary/Response

1. Read the article several times carefully, highlighting key ideas.

2. Check to make sure you have stated the author's thesis correctly. Otherwise, your entire response will be off base.

3. Read the author's thesis, then your thesis, to make sure they relate logically to each other. Are you truly *responding* to the author's thesis?

4. Reread your summary.

5. Did you clearly show how the author supported his or her thesis in your summary?

6. Did you include the major assertions?

7. Did you summarize rather than restate? Is the summary in your own words?

8. Is the topic you address in your response actually addressed in your summary?

9. Reread the author's thesis, then your major assertions in your response. Are you responding to the author's thesis?

10. Reread your thesis, then your assertions. Are you supporting your thesis?

11. Refer to the author and his or her ideas. You may say, "As Gray suggests, men and women do have a different way of communicating." It is very important that you make clear which ideas are yours and which are the author's.

12. Add transitions that help readers distinguish between your ideas and the author's and allow them to follow your train of thought. Example: "*While* the author believes that [his point], I think [your point]."

13. Keep the big picture in mind. Be very careful that your response does indeed *respond* to the material you presented in the summary.

14. Is your response balanced? Did you discuss the points equally in approximately the same amount of detail?

15. Does your response indicate that you have given the subject careful thought? Does it reflect critical thinking? Have you checked the details of the article you are responding to?

16. Reread your summary/response as a whole. Does it flow? Does it sound smooth when you read it aloud?

You are now ready to write your first draft of a summary/response. The following steps will guide you through the process. (If your instructor has you use the summary you wrote in Chapter 11, then you will have already accomplished some of these steps.)

1. Read the essay again, highlighting the key ideas.

2. Outline the key ideas.

3. Write a statement of the author's thesis.

4. Circle the topic and underline the assertion in the author's thesis.

5. Brainstorm on the topic (not the assertion).

6. Gather similar ideas from your brainstorm map and group them.

7. Formulate your assertion about the topic.

8. Brainstorm again on that assertion.

9. Gather similar ideas and group again.

10. List additional facts or examples.

11. Outline your response.

12. Write the summary/response.

13. Turn to the checklist on page 274 and check your summary/response.

Be sure to keep a good copy of this draft to use later in this chapter. It will become the central assignment that you will turn in to your instructor. Bring it to class.

OPTIONS ▶ Customize

1. Pick a topic that you feel strongly about, and find an article on that topic in a newspaper, magazine, or web site. Keeping that in mind, practice writing a summary/response essay. Bring in a copy of the article, summarize it, and write a response.

2. On the *Writing Now* web site, you will find links to articles that discuss transitions in people's lives. Choose one of the articles, and write a summary and response to it.

TOOLS ▶ Language

00:45

This next activity is designed to be experiential—giving students some experience in noticing transitions before a definition and specific transitions are provided. It is a discovery process that will provide a mental structure for students to relate the new information to. It may be done in class either individually, in small groups, or as an entire class. You may want to have students do this activity twice—once before they learn about transitions and once after, using different-colored ink. In this way they can see how much they learned.

Transitions

Before you study the specifics of transitions, experiment here with what you already know. As someone with many years' experience in language, you have an inner understanding of how transitions work even if you don't yet have a name for what you know. In the following text, Pam Hayes-Bohanan has written down some ideas for simplifying your life on the job. She has put these ideas in the form of a list. Read the article and think about the ways that a list is different from a paragraph.

Simplify Your Life at Work

Pam Hayes-Bohanan

- Telecommute if possible. You will save on travel time, gasoline, and auto maintenance costs. And you'll spend less time with annoying co-workers (if you have any).

- Live near where you work. Cut commuting time, get to know your community, and get a good work-out twice each day.

- When thinking about accepting a promotion, consider whether the extra income is worth the extra hassles. If you do take a promotion, consider negotiating time off in lieu of some of the extra pay.

- Don't always answer your phone, especially if you have voice mail or other messaging service.

- Make difficult phone calls (or do other difficult tasks) early in the day, so that they are not worrying you the rest of the day.

Analyze the Reading

Changing a List to a Paragraph

We recommend that you do the following activities as a class or in small groups with time allowed for sharing small-group answers with the entire class. Because this is a discovery process for students, it requires thoughtful discussion and progress toward some understanding.

1. Using dark ink, cross out the bullets. Reread "Simplify Your Life."

2. Did you notice that the article still sounds like a list? Try to figure out why. Write your best answer.

_____

_____

_____

_____

In small groups or as a class, have students read some paragraphs aloud. Individually, in groups, or as a class discuss what students noticed about the differences between the list and the paragraphs. As a class, examine the words that were used in different paragraphs to link the items in the list together. You may want to make a list of the words on the board.

3. Individually or as a class, brainstorm on the ways a list is different from a paragraph. Put your final answer here.

_____

_____

_____

_____

4. Individually or as a group, turn the list into a smooth paragraph by adding whatever words or phrases you need in order to connect the ideas. Write these words directly onto the printed text. Reread the text and comment on how these words changed the text.

5. Turn to "Ten Joys of Journaling" in Chapter 1, page 10. Using four of the items from the list in that text, write a paragraph. Use additional (transitions) to make it flow. Read your paragraph to your classmates.

Help Screen

Transitions

Words or sentences that link one idea to another are called *transitions*. They help readers *follow the ideas* in a text *and* let readers know when a *change in ideas* is occurring. A writer adds transitions to achieve coherence and make the writing flow more smoothly. *Coherence* within a paragraph means that a paragraph makes sense. The sentences relate, or connect, to each other in a meaningful way. This connection between sentences can be forged with *transitional words and phrases*.

An essay is *coherent* if all of its paragraphs relate to the overall thesis and there is a logical movement from one paragraph to the next, showing how they relate. *Transitional sentences* between paragraphs can provide that overall coherence between paragraphs.

Both between sentences and between paragraphs, transitions show relationships. Your awareness of transitions will enable you to write a smoother, more coherent text.

Students can find and write in an example of each type of transition from earlier readings (see pp. 229–232). This probably should be a scaffolded activity either led by the instructor or accomplished in small groups with the instructor's approval of sentences before they are written into the guidelines. These guidelines will be more meaningful to students because they have found the examples themselves.

Transitional Words and Phrases

Transitional words can be organized into several categories, depending on the organizational flow the writer wants to achieve. Some transitions, you will notice, can be used with more than one organizational pattern. Some of the possible categories are given here. Several possible relationships can be made clear by the use of transitions. Using the readings on pages 229–232, find examples of each type of transition. Quote a 2–4 word phrase that includes the transition. In order to do this activity, you will have to identify the relationship pattern in the paragraph.

He was a long-haired . . ., then moved into . . ., later became . . ., and finally, a congressman.

Relationship in time: *after, at the same time, at last, before, during, eventually, finally, first (second, third), following, gradually, in the beginning, later, meanwhile, next, now, previously, suddenly, then*

_____

_____

_____

No example given. Have students write their own.

Relationship in space: *above, alongside, behind, below, beneath, beside, in front of, inside, near, nearby, next to, on the other side, outside, to the left (right, front, back, rear, north, south),* with (No example is given in the readings. Make up four phrases in your own words.)

_____

_____

_____

Some 18 percent have . . .; another 18 percent . . .

Relationship of additional information: *also, a final, and, another, first (second, third*—but don't use these for every item), *in addition, finally, furthermore, lastly, moreover, still another.* Sometimes an author will repeat key words to show the continuation of a list rather than using these transitional words.

_____

_____

_____

In 1976, for instance, 43 percent . . .

Relationship of example to assertion or topic sentence: *as an illustration, for example, for instance, specifically, thus, to illustrate*

_____

_____

_____

Not shown here. Have students write their own example.

Relationship of least important to most important: *above all, best of all, especially, even more, in addition, moreover, most important, not only . . . but also, particularly important* (No example is given in the readings. Make up four phrases of your own.)

_____

_____

_____

Step 2 involves . . .

Relationship of steps in a process: *after, at last, at the same time, before, during, finally, first (second, third), following, in the beginning, later, next, now, then*

_____

_____

_____

First, because they are . . .

Relationship of cause and effect: *another cause (effect) is, as a result, because, consequently, due to, first (second, third), hence, one cause (result) is, since, therefore, thus*

_____

_____

_____

This already happens . . ., while the American . . .

Relationship of contrast or comparison: *also, although, and, but, even though, however, in comparison, in contrast, in the same way, in spite of, just as, likewise, nevertheless, nonetheless, notwithstanding, on the contrary, on the other hand, similarly, too, unlike, whereas, while, yet*

_____

_____

_____

Transitional sentences help you to achieve coherence within an entire essay by showing the relationship of one paragraph (or one topic sentence) to another. A transitional sentence can be written in two ways. In the last sentence of a paragraph, you can mention the topic of that paragraph and introduce the topic of the next paragraph: *While these ideas may be easily used to rid your bedroom of clutter, it is somewhat more complicated to rid a kitchen of clutter.* Alternatively, you may want to begin a paragraph with a reference to the previous one while also introducing that paragraph: *Now that you have rid your bedroom of clutter, you are ready to tackle a bigger project—your kitchen.* You would use one or the other, but not both types of transition to link two adjoining paragraphs. These transitional sentences alert the reader that you are moving from the bedroom to the kitchen for the next group of steps in the process of uncluttering your life.

1. Refer to the sample summary/response on pages 270–271. Highlight the transitional words and phrases.

2. Refer to pages 229–232 in Chapter 10. In that chapter you worked with different patterns of organization. As you have seen in this chapter, transitions help a reader follow the author's pattern of organization.

   Circle the transitions in each paragraph. Notice how knowing the pattern of organization can help you find the transitions. On the other hand, finding the transitions can help you understand the pattern of organization, which in turn helps you follow the author's main points.

Go To ▶ 1. Go to the Web to find more information on transitions. You can find information in several places, such as those listed here. If you need a reminder, turn to the Help Screen on page 263 of Chapter 11.

▶ Visit an Online Writing Lab (OWL), such as Purdue's OWL at **<http://owl.english.purdue.edu/>**.

▶ Find a search engine that allows a natural language search, and ask where to find help on using transitions in writing. One such search turned up this web site: **<http://webster.commnet.edu>**. When you get to the Webster site, be sure to select the "search engines" button on the home page. Once you get to that page, you can choose from a variety of search engines. You can also do an advanced search on transitions by keying in "using transitions in writing" + transition + writing.

▶ While visiting the sites suggested in bulleted items 1 and 2, print out a list of various types of transitions and place it in your binder.

▶ You may have noticed that some transitions are more appropriate for certain organizational patterns. We have been looking at writing organized by lists or categories. List all transitions you found on the Web that are appropriate for organizing by list or categories.

_____

_____

_____

_____

_____

OPTIONS ▶ Customize

1. As in writing, you should consciously use *transitions* to advance your argument when you create a slide show. Slide show programs usually offer a variety of *transitions* between slides to help the presenter move the audience from one point to another. Transitions should be in keeping with the general tone of the presentation, conservative or flashy, depending on audience and purpose. Look back at the slide presentation you created on page 259. Did you incorporate *transitions* originally? Would your decisions about *transitions* be different for a future slide show, based on what you have learned? Redo the slide show, or create one now, in which you add some transitions.

2. Write an e-mail to the author of "Simplify Your Life at Work" with your ideas about how you simplify your life. Be sure to identify yourself as a student doing a class assignment. Your instructor will indicate whether the e-mails should be sent.

3. Search any other readings in *Writing Now* for transitional words, phrases, or sentences. Write them in a list, giving the phrase, the page number where you found it, and the relationship it expresses. Compare these with what your classmates found.

FILE ▶ Edit

The second homework assignment for this chapter could be to revise the summary/response draft as described here.

Revision for Continuity

You are ready to revise your essay in light of what you have learned in this chapter. If you typed your essay on a word processor, print it out and make annotations on the hard copy in brightly colored ink. If you wrote your essay by hand, use a different color of bright ink to make your annotations.

Your next-to-last revision is for content. (As always, the final one is for proofreading.) The revision for content in a summary/response essay consists primarily of making sure that you have an appropriate response to an author's text. You can have a good summary and a good response, but if your thesis is not actually responding to the author's thesis, you haven't completed the assignment by actually writing a *response*. Furthermore, the support you use must not only support your thesis, it should also support or refute the author's thesis, depending upon whether you are agreeing or disagreeing with the author.

In this chapter you also learned about the importance of transitions. Carefully read over your essay to check your transitions. First, read each paragraph one at a time. After you read the individual paragraph, check to see if you used any transitional words or phrases to link the ideas in one sentence to another. If not, think about the pattern of organization you used in the paragraph and write in appropriate transitions where necessary. Don't overdo it. If you have trouble thinking of appropriate transitional words or phrases, refer to the list of transitional words and phrases on pages 278–279.

After you have revised each paragraph in the manner just described, you are ready to see if you used transitional sentences to make a smooth flow from the main idea of one paragraph to the main idea in the following paragraph. Reread the last sentence of one paragraph and the first sentence of the following one. Is there a smooth transition? If not, rewrite either of those sentences in the margin in brightly colored ink. Be sure to check this last/first combination for every paragraph.

Now reread your essay (aloud, if possible). Does it sound better to you? Make any necessary additional revisions in brightly colored ink in the margin.

Peer Revision Worksheet

Reviewed by: _____ **Date:** _____

Focus of review: response thesis and support and use of transitions

Reviewing paper written by: _____

Peer Revision Questionnaire

Ask yourself the following questions about your draft. Then, if possible, ask a friend or classmate to read your draft and answer the same questions about it. Also have your reader mark any nonconventional sentence constructions or punctuation. If your answers do not match your reader's, you haven't succeeded in communicating what you think you did. Where answers don't match well, discuss them together and try to think of ways to make your essay clearer.

- What is this essay about? (topic)

- What is the event or situation that prompted the essay? (prompt)

- What do you have to say about your topic? (thesis or main idea)

- Who is your intended audience?

- What is your purpose in writing about this?

- What personal experience (life, reading, TV, stories you've heard, and so forth) have you had with this topic?

- What purpose does each paragraph serve? How does each paragraph support the thesis?

- What methods of development did you use in each paragraph to support your thesis?

- Is there anything else I should know? Are there any questions in the reader's mind left unanswered by the essay?

FILE ▶ Save

00:45

The third 45-minute session of this unit can be used to give students computer time for writing the final revision of their paper, for peer group revision, for reviewing or spending more time on material in this pair of chapters, or for getting back on schedule if necessary by joining this activity to the previous homework assignment.

You may want students to turn the revision checklist in with their essay.

Summary/Response Essay

You are now ready to proofread your final revised draft before turning it in to your instructor. Perform all the proofreading and revision techniques you have learned so far.

Revision Checklist

☐ I have arranged my ideas in an order appropriate to the topic.

☐ I had someone read and annotate my essay.

☐ I have an appropriate title.

☐ I have a clearly stated topic.

☐ I have developed a topic that is appropriate, neither too broad nor too specific.

☐ All paragraphs support my overall topic.

☐ Each paragraph has a different focus relating to my topic.

☐ Each paragraph has well-developed supporting examples and/or facts.

☐ I revised my word choice to use descriptive and appropriate words.

☐ My tone is clear and consistent throughout the essay.

☐ I wrote an introduction or a summary that contained my assertion and gave an idea of what my essay is about.

☐ I used gender-neutral language.

☐ My pronoun references are clear.

☐ My pronoun use is appropriate.

☐ I used appropriate patterns of development for the topic, the purpose, the audience, and the introduction.

☐ I used a variety of sentence structures.

☐ I eliminated fragments and run-ons.

☐ My major points in response to the author's text are clearly stated.

☐ I keep my subjects and verbs consistent—either both singular or both plural.

☐ I keep any items in a series parallel.

☐ I checked for appropriate subject-verb agreement.

☐ I checked for appropriate and consistent verb tense.

☐ I checked for consistent pronoun usage.

☐ I stated the name of the author and the title of the text in the first or second sentence of the summary.

☐ I clearly and accurately stated the author's thesis in the first or second sentence.

❑ I selected an appropriate technique to examine the text and include the major points the author made.

❑ I presented the author's points as presented in the text.

❑ The summary is accurate, complete, concise, and balanced.

❑ The summary is written in my own words.

❑ The summary is of appropriate length for the text and the assignment.

❑ My thesis is clearly stated and clearly responds to the author's thesis.

❑ I included appropriate transitional words and phrases within paragraphs.

❑ I included appropriate transitional sentences between paragraphs.

Proofreading Checklist

❑ I have read each sentence aloud, starting with the last one first and working backward to make sure each sentence is clear and uses appropriate language conventions.

❑ I used my proofreading frame to check for spelling.

❑ I asked a classmate to read my draft and to complete the peer revision form.

 Go To ▶

1. Go to the *Writing Now* web site for information on newsgroups. Joining a newsgroup offers you the opportunity to read and respond to messages on subjects that interest you. You can also go to *Lizst, The Mailing List Directory* at **<http://www.liszt.com/>** for information on newsgroups as well as on mailing lists and IRC chats, or Google groups at **<http://groups.google.com/usenet>** to search for a newsgroup on a topic that might interest you.

C:\Prompts for Writing ▶

While these activities are intended as alternatives to the central assignment, they could be used as extra assignments if time allows.

1. Select one of the readings in Chapter 7 or 8 to substitute for the central assignment or to serve as extra work. Write a summary/response essay.

2. Read an editorial on the editorial page of a newspaper and write a summary/response. E-mail your response to the Letters to the Editor column of the newspaper.

3. Write an essay about your transition from high school (or the business world) to college.

4. Write an essay about an important transitional period in your life (perhaps adjusting to parenthood, loss of a parent, moving to another city, getting your own apartment, and so forth).

Log Off: ▶ Review and Reflect

Take some time to reflect on what you have learned about writing in this chapter.

How has your writing changed as a result of the discussions, readings, and activities in this chapter?

_____

_____

_____

_____

_____

_____

_____

Refer to the essay you wrote in Chapter 10. Examine your use of transitions. How has your writing improved since that essay?

_____

_____

_____

_____

_____

What transitions did you use in that essay?

_____

How has your knowledge of the writing process changed as a result of the work you have done in this chapter?

_____

_____

_____

_____

_____

CHAPTER 13
Music: The Universal Language

> Music is a universal language. Where speech fails, then music begins. It is the natural medium for the expression of our emotions—the art that expresses in tones our feelings which are too strong and deep to be expressed in words.
>
> —Charles W. Landon, *The Study of Music in Public Schools* (1886)

Log On ▶ **Reflection**

Write whatever comes to mind when you read the chapter title and opening quotation.

_____

_____

_____

_____

_____

_____

_____

_____

_____

_____

_____

_____

_____

_____

_____

_____

_____

_____

_____

_____

_____

_____

FILE ▶ Open

00:45

You may want to allow most of the time for students to search on the Internet or go to the library.

Connecting with Experience

▶ Who is your favorite musician or group? Why?

▶ How does music make you feel? How does it affect your life?

▶ Would your life be different if you had no music in it?

▶ When you and your friends discuss music, what kinds of things do you say about it? What words do you use to explain the qualities of the music, rather than what you think of the musician and the lifestyle he or she represents? Do you talk more about the videos than the music itself?

▶ Are some kinds of music bad for people? Explain.

▶ Are some kinds of music better for people than other kinds of music? Explain.

▶ Can music change a person in any way?

▶ Do you think music affects your brain? Explain.

▶ Do you think music can affect your emotions? Explain.

▶ Should schools require students to study music or learn to play an instrument?

▶ How is music like a language?

Connecting with Writing

▶ What is a report?

▶ Why do people write reports?

▶ Describe any experience you have had writing a report.

▶ What was the most challenging part of writing a report?

▶ Brainstorm and list as many circumstances as you can when you have to write a report in your future.

Connecting with Previous Learning

▶ Examine the response you wrote for the concluding assignment in Chapter 5. Where did you get the information you put into your paragraphs?

▶ What kinds of information did you put in your paragraphs?

▶ How could you have made those paragraphs longer or more developed?

▶ If you rewrote that essay, what kinds of things could you do to make it better?

Connecting with Concepts: Music

▶ Music means many different things to different people. What does music mean to you?

◗ Cluster the word *music* for 10 minutes to discover many of the things it means to you.

Connecting with Concepts: Research

◗ Give an example of research that you have done in the past.

◗ What does it take to do effective research on a topic?

◗ Why do researchers repeat their experiments?

◗ Cluster the word *research* for 3 minutes.

FILE ▶ New

Writing Reports

Throughout this text you have worked on supporting your assertions with facts and examples. You have learned that when you make an assertion you must provide support to convince readers that your point of view has merit. For the most part, you have probably used examples as support. These may have come from your life experiences, television, readings, or the newspaper. Using personal experience to support your assertions is the easiest method for most students, and that is the method you have primarily been using up to this point. Now you are ready to explore ways to develop more substantial support in your writing.

In this course you have searched the Internet to find additional facts and examples pertaining to the lessons in this text. When you did that, you were conducting *research* on a topic. You may have included facts from this research in your support.

In this chapter you will learn more about including research in your writing. This skill is important in writing compositions, because in order to develop a topic you must have something interesting to say. For example, when you are writing an effective response to another author's text, you should have something informative to say. In order to make major points in support of or against the author's thesis, you will have to support, defend, explain, illustrate, or elaborate on those major points with your supporting details or examples. This means that you need to know enough about the subject to make points and to support them. The more advanced your college courses are, the more substantial your support must be in your writing. Often you may not know enough about the subject to respond adequately. When that happens you will need to do research on the subject.

The ability to study a topic and include facts about it in your writing (that is, writing reports) is a skill that will serve you well throughout the rest of your college career in most subjects. Furthermore, as you learn this skill to write your papers, you will find that it becomes valuable to you in many other ways as you begin to manage your money, make travel plans, deal with health issues, and handle other aspects of your personal life. In addition, you will find researching to be a valuable tool on the job. Therefore, you will want to spend as much time as you can on this chapter, perfecting this skill.

In small groups, list all the ways you know to research a topic. Pick an "expert" in the group for each method. If someone knows how to use Infotrac (a common resource method used at libraries), then that person can be the Infotrac expert. Someone else may know how to use *The Reader's Guide.* Share your information and pool your resources. Your instructor may allow you to research as a small group and then write your papers individually. Even if you do your research individually, it will be helpful to know whom to ask for help in learning how to use research tools.

Go To ▶ In preparation for your central assignment in this chapter, you will need to begin your research. Your instructor may want to take you to the library to show you how to conduct a library search or allow you to use the Internet to do all the research. Research the following aspects of music:

Music and diet

Music and health

Music and learning

Music and spatial performance (geometry, design)

Music and emotion

This is a preliminary research activity. Once students have read more about their subject and have the research topic "Mind and Body and Music" (a response to an essay), they can pursue the research in specific detail.

As you conduct your research, keep in mind that you are looking for information for your central assignment.

Bookmark the sites you find that are useful or copy down the URLs. Once you have completed an overview and have a better idea of which articles will be most helpful, you can return to these sites and print out the ones you will use in your paper. (*Hint:* Always check the length of an article before printing or you may find yourself printing sixty pages or more.)

Help Screen

How Many Pages Am I Printing?

To see how many pages it would take to print out a web site in Netscape, go to File, then Print Preview. Use the magnifying glass cursor to magnify the page number on the bottom left corner of the page you are viewing. If you are looking at the first page of the document you want to print, you will see "1 of *X*" pages, with *X* being the total number of pages it will take the document to print.

Internet Explorer does not offer this feature at this writing.

If you want to print only a portion of the page or site, you can usually select the portion you want to print. Press File, then Print. Under Printer Options, choose to print only the selection.

You could also select, copy, and paste the selection into a word processor document and print from there.

Go To ▶ Go to the Web to see what kinds of music files are available. AltaVista at <http://www.altavista.com> allows you to search for music files. Look under the Web Directory box on the left-hand side of the page to access links to music files on the Web.

OPTIONS ▶ **Customize**

1. Most college libraries now have an online catalog and online database resources. Visit your college library online to see what research material you can get directly from your computer.

2. See if your public library has a web site. You may be able to renew books online and reserve books to be ordered from different branches and held for you for pickup at a convenient location.

3. Search the Web for libraries of other colleges that you can visit. Access to information is usually limited to students at a given school, but some resources may be available to the general public.

4. Visit your school or public library and see if they have a card catalog. If they do, look up your research subject and flip through the cards for ideas for your topic or assertion and for resource materials. Then look up an author you are familiar with and a book title. Compare the information provided in the card catalog with the information provided in a web site. Can you guess why many people who create web pages with lots of resources linked to them are called "cybrarians"?

5. Go to your school or public library and browse the current periodicals section. What value do you find in flipping through hard copies of magazines instead of surfing them on the Web? In what way is the Web better?

This is a good place to begin the homework assignment.

You may want to have students read, annotate, and answer pages 293–302. In addition, if the class has read "Beethoven" (p. 303) and "Take Two Sonatas" (pp. 305–306) they will also be ready to work on these readings in class. You may want to tell students that they don't need to answer the questions related to these readings. They should simply read them in preparation for doing the activities in class.

To begin to learn how to include research effectively in your writing, analyze how other writers accomplish this. Dr. Gordon Shaw and Dr. Frances Rauscher have done some groundbreaking research on the effects of music on the mind. As you read this excerpt from an article in the *Dallas Morning News,* notice how the research results are presented. Note that the author gives facts and examples to help the reader understand the research. Also examine how the examples personalize the facts and bring them to life for the reader.

The Thinking Child's Music

Olin Chism

1   Can classical music make your child smarter? Maybe—but beware those who are marketing products based on the possibility. That's the advice of a prominent researcher in the field.

2   Dr. Gordon Shaw of the University of California at Irvine and Dr. Frances Rauscher, now at the University of Wisconsin at Oshkosh, apparently kicked off the current boom by playing a recording of a Mozart two-piano sonata to a group of college students. In a test of spatial-temporal reasoning taken immediately thereafter, the students scored significantly higher than members of two other groups—one that had listened to minimalist music and another that had no music. It is Dr. Shaw who cautions against the commercialization of the music-learning link. . . .

3   Still, it's clear that Dr. Shaw does believe that music can improve some functioning of the brain. His study of Mozart and the college students was just the beginning. He, Dr. Rauscher and other scientists are continuing to look at music's effect on the mind, and finding that it seems to be real.

4   Some items from recent research:

- A two-year study of 3- and 4-year-olds in California found that children who were given piano lessons improved an average of 34 percent in tests of their reasoning skills. Other children in the study showed no improvement.

- A study at a university in Hong Kong found a 16 percent better word memory on average for adults who learned how to play a musical instrument as children. The researchers suggested that music training may be an entertaining and useful way of improving verbal memory in children.

- An experiment with 4-month-old babies found that they didn't like it when music (Mozart again) was stopped at an unnatural point, such as the middle of a phrase.

- In Chicago, a Mozart sonata was played for 29 people with epilepsy, including several in a coma. Surface electrodes measured a sharp drop in epileptic-type firings in the brains of 24 of them as the music was played.

- In Wisconsin, Dr. Rauscher exposed a group of rats to Mozart 12 hours a day for 60 days. Another group heard white noise for the same length of time, and yet another heard music of Philip Glass. Then she had the rats run through a maze three times a day for five days. The Mozart rats learned the fastest, running the maze in an average of 35 seconds on the third day. The white-noise rats averaged 44 seconds; the Philip Glass rats averaged 50 seconds.

Long-term gain

5   The California study of preschoolers will probably seem the most significant to interested parents. Dr. Shaw and his colleagues took 78 children of normal intelligence, tested their abstract reasoning ability (they were

Source: Olin Chism, "Classical: The Thinking Child's Music: Studies Suggest Link Between Exposure and Improved Brain Functioning." *The Dallas Morning News*, 1/12/99, p. 5C. Reprinted with permission of *The Dallas Morning News*.

about even), then divided them into four groups. One received private piano and group singing lessons. Another received private computer lessons, another had group singing lessons only, and the remainder had no lessons. Retested after six months, the piano group showed an amazing improvement in reasoning tests. It's significant that the improvement was long-term, whereas the effect of Mozart on the college students wore off quickly.

6   Dr. Shaw finds the results of the preschoolers study so significant that he thinks parents should consider giving their 3- and 4-year-olds piano lessons. There's no need to overdo it, however. The children in the study received simple 10-minute lessons, some once a week, some twice, and an hour a day was made available for practice. They studied pitch intervals, fine motor coordination, fingering techniques, sight reading, music notation and playing from memory.

7   Some Dallas-area parents, who are aware of the research on music and the brain and support its notions, say they may not see a connection quite as direct as the research shows.

8   Marcy England of Grand Prairie, whose 10-year-old son, Sam, takes piano lessons, sees a direct benefit in fine motor coordination and discipline. She's impressed with her son's "level of concentration, sitting there learning to do things with both hands. It humbles me to sit down and play around and try to do what he does. I realize how tough it really is." Sam excels in math, she says, but that's always been one of his strongest subjects.

9   David Figg of Dallas, whose son Eliot began taking music lessons in elementary school and is now a music student at the University of North Texas, says, "I've always believed that there is a real strong connection between mathematics and music." He says his son was strong in both subjects during his school days in Dallas.

10   Albert Quintanar of Grand Prairie has two small daughters who take piano lessons. He believes music study has given Ana Carolina, 8, and Beatriz, 7, a greater sense of responsibility and helped their concentration. That last factor is of benefit to them at school, he believes. Both have made the A honor roll at Zavala Elementary. . . .

11   Why Mozart? Dr. Shaw says he was chosen for the studies because he was such a natural genius. When he was 4, he could play pieces by ear after hearing his older sister play them at her keyboard lessons. By age 5, he was composing. "Mozart's music appears to have a structure that our brains perceive as natural," says Dr. Shaw. "He may have been directly tapping that neural structure and its language when he composed."

12   Interestingly, the piece that has become a sort of workhorse composition in several of the studies, *Mozart's Sonata in D Major for Two Pianos*, K. 448, is not included on current recordings aimed at parents of small children. Instead, they contain other Mozart pieces as well as popular short works by other composers.

"Mozart effect"

13   Research into the Mozart effect continues. Dr. Shaw and several colleagues recently concluded a study of second-graders that more directly tests the music–math link. He's reluctant to give details, because the report hasn't been published yet, but it seems clear it won't conflict with earlier research.

14   Upcoming is a much larger nationwide study that will involve schools "willing to commit for three or four years. . . . We would provide

materials and direction and testing, they would provide local re-sources." He says he hopes a Dallas school will want to take part.

15   Whether or not the Mozart effect produces the intellectual wonders the marketing departments claim, Dr. Shaw points out one sure thing: There are no bad side effects.

Analyze the Reading

1. Highlight the thesis in green, main ideas in blue, examples in yellow, and facts in pink. What differences did you notice between the facts and the examples?

2. What fact did you find most surprising or interesting?

_____

_____

_____

3. Did the author provide convincing supporting details? Explain.

_____

_____

_____

_____

_____

4. What information was most convincing to you? Why?

_____

_____

_____

_____

_____

5. What problems can you find with the research? Can you see flaws in the study? How would you improve the study?

_____

_____

_____

This is a good place to work on critical thinking skills. You may want to spend a little time talking about how to read this type of information critically.

Teachers at a school in Minneapolis believe that music actually helps their students score higher in math and reading. As you read this article, think about how you might use some of the information to help children learn better and whether or not this article is convincing.

Tuning In to Basic Skills

Kim Schneider

1 At Powderhorn Elementary School in south Minneapolis, children have been clapping and singing their way to higher scores in math and reading.

2 "Keet, keet, par-a-keet," they chant as music teacher Elizabeth Olson holds up a picture.

3 "Phant, phant, el-e-phant."

4 Just an extra half-hour per week of specialized music training has produced dramatic gains—and has given new power to the nationwide argument that music is not a cultural frill, but a key ingredient in a child's education.

5 "Some say that if you want to be better at math, do more math. We're suggesting maybe not," said Ann Kay, a music professor at the University of St. Thomas in St. Paul.

6 Kay is working with Olson and brain researcher Martin Gardiner of Brown University in Providence, R.I., on a two-year study at Powderhorn that tests the benefits of Kodàly music instruction on other academic subjects. Kodàly is a program that uses folk singing as a base for music instruction and emphasizes melodic and rhythmic elements.

7 "We're trying to find what activities most benefit brain development," said Kay, who is president of the Organization of American Kodàly Educators.

8 At least 100 teachers in the Twin Cities metropolitan area have been trained in the Kodàly method, and the Owatonna school district uses the method exclusively, Kay said.

9 General research on the link between music and academics, however, has spread to at least four Minneapolis schools searching for effective ways to get kids to master the basics. While the projects are funded by different grants and involve different research methods, the common link is the push for all teachers to work together to help kids learn reading and math, said Cheryl Paschke, the Minneapolis Public Schools fine-arts specialist.

10 The Powderhorn study, conducted by Gardiner, shows clear benefits from making music:

Source: Kim Schneider, "Tuning in to Basic Skills/New Studies at a Minneapolis Elementary School Show Promise for a Creative Method That Uses Music to Help Teach Children Math and Reading. *Minneapolis Star Tribune*, 11/29/98. Reprinted by permission.

- First-graders who received the extra half-hour a week of Kodály training doubled their scores on the math section of the Metropolitan Achievement Tests between December 1997 and June 1998.

- They scored more than 10 percent higher in some areas than a control group of first-graders who got only the standard hour of music each week.

- By June, 50 percent of the first-graders receiving the extra music scored at or above grade level, up from 25 percent in December. In the control group, 42 percent scored at or above grade level by the end of the year.

- Reading scores improved from 15 percent at or above grade level to 32 percent. That 17 percentage-point gain compares with a 9-point gain for the first-graders who got the standard music class.

- The biggest jump was in word recognition skills, with 42 percent of the Kodály group scoring at or above grade level in June, compared with 30 percent of the control group. The results support the findings of a 1996 study Gardiner conducted in Pawtucket, R.I. He concluded then that art and music skills lead to gains in math and word recognition. Key evidence of the link, Gardiner said, is the fact that students with the greatest amount of Kodály training showed the greatest learning in reading and math.

11 The Powderhorn findings may be conservative, he said, because testing was done at the end of the school year, when children weren't performing at their best—a main reason he's continuing the study a second year. He's also extending his work by studying what actually happens in the brain during the process of making music.

12 "Whether the brain figures out how to apply things learned in one area to another, or keeps the mechanisms for thinking in one place and refers to them both are possibilities," he said.

13 "Hopefully, as we study the brain and how it works, we'll get a better idea of which is happening."

International interest

14 The link between music and brain function is a hot research topic internationally. Psychologists at the Chinese University of Hong Kong recently published a study that found a 16 percent better word memory on average for adults who played musical instruments as children. The study also noted that a region of the brain behind the left ear—a section that also handles verbal memory—is larger in musicians.

15 Florida even has a law that requires state-funded day care providers to play classical music to toddlers every day, partly as a result of a 1993 University of California, Irvine, study that found college students who listened to Mozart's *Sonata for Two Pianos in D Major* scored 30 percent higher on spatial reasoning tests.

16 In Minneapolis, studies are focusing on the benefits of making, rather than listening to, music. The local efforts also stress cooperation between music teachers and other teachers.

17 At Sheridan Elementary, for example, a staff development grant allows teachers to assess students one-on-one three times a year and to share what they've learned. If a child has trouble distinguishing letter sounds, he or she is given more help in music class distinguishing between the sounds of different musical instruments, music teacher Pat Teske said.

18. At Willard Elementary—as part of a joint project with Sheridan and Seward Elementary—all first-graders sing in the hall three mornings a week to get their brains ready to learn and to introduce new vocabulary words. Songs are written on butcher paper and taped to the walls and repeated in song books stored in every desk.

19. Since few Willard students are reading when they enter first grade, it's a big step when they connect a spelling word with a song lyric, first-grade teacher Terry Abel said.

20. Whether she's teaching the kids to count by fives or to remember to brush their teeth, the former band singer puts the concepts to a melody. There's an amazing leap in comprehension, she said.

21. "Can you tell me the words to 'Do Wah Diddy Diddy'?" she asked. "We all know there are songs you can't get out of your head. By having kids sing songs over and over, they're making those connections."

"Wiring the brain"

22. At Powderhorn, teachers attend the special music classes with their students and reinforce the lessons throughout the day. In music, Olson emphasizes the letter sounds children are working on in reading class. And first-grade teacher Jean Doroff has her students hum their music songs and keep the beat with their feet as they walk to the lunchroom.

23. Students have become more fluid readers by thinking of a text as a song as they read aloud.

24. And music class has made learning fun, resulting in a huge leap in class participation, by even the most reticent students, Doroff said. In the music class on a recent day, children clamored for Olson to include their favorite activities or songs.

25. As she held up a series of cards, the children clapped out the rhythm of different musical patterns, singing a "ta" for a quarter-note and a "ti-ti" for an eighth-note. Minutes later, they moved onto "math," singing a counting song while doing complicated hand motions. When they counted backward to the melody, the hand motions reversed.

26. "We're wiring the brain," Olson said. "We're helping all these things come together."

27. While researchers continue to test the scientific links between music and learning, Powderhorn students see a clear cause and effect.

28. "It makes us smarter," declared second-grader Kiran Raghubir, who practices his songs on his baby sister.

29. "It's fun, and it's good for us," added Asia Cartlidge, 8. "When I first came here last year, I didn't know how to read. That's when I learned how to read the [song] cards, and I learned how to do math. I'm starting to like reading and math."

The Kodàly approach

30.
- Where did it come from? The method (pronounced ko-DYE) was developed by Hungarian composer Zoltàn Kodàly (1882–1967).

- How widespread? It is used in hundreds of schools across the country, including several in Minneapolis. While the basic teaching method is widely used, it often is not labeled as Kodàly.

- What is it? A singing-based, comprehensive and sequential program that starts teaching musical skills at a very young age, under the assumption that music is a language every child can speak.

- What does it do? The program develops ability to understand *music* and then transfers that understanding to reading music and composing melodies. Young children rock stuffed animals to the beat of the songs. By first and second grade, students are identifying and creating rhythmic patterns, and using hand gestures to indicate pitch. By fifth or sixth grade, children often are singing in tune, reading music and composing their own melodies. Folk music and games from around the world are the basis of the program.

- Supporters: Even before recent research studies found links between Kodàly and gains in math and reading, famous Russian violinist Isaac Stern wrote that Kodàly students see gains in memory, logic, reading ability and understanding of mathematical formulas. In its September 1998 issue, *Parents* magazine called Kodàly one of the nation's "top-notch teaching plans that dramatically boost performance." (Source: Organization of American Kodàly Educators)

Analyze the Reading

1. Highlight main ideas in blue, facts in pink, and examples in yellow.

2. Did you find the evidence convincing? Explain your reasoning.

_____

_____

_____

3. How could you adapt this information to working with your child?

_____

_____

_____

4. What is the source of the information in this article? How does that affect your interpretation of the article?

_____

_____

_____

You have been examining some recent research on music. In addition, you have read articles discussing many aspects of music in your Internet search. You have seen that the authors use facts and examples to develop and expand their articles. How can you apply what you have seen to improving your own writing?

_____

_____

_____

In researching your topic, take notes on any information that you believe you may be able to use in support of your points. Be sure to document the source you got the information from. You will learn more about documenting sources in future courses in which you write research papers. For the purposes of this course, your instructor will probably want you to use the simplest method, which is to mention the author and the source in your text and attach a photocopy of the page you found the information on. For example, you might say, "As Olin Chism describes in 'The Thinking Child's Music,' music may affect how children's brains function." If your source came from material you found on the Web, you can copy and paste the web address (URL) into your paper and set it off in angle brackets like this <>.

Help Screen

Evaluating Sources

Because there is so much information on the Web, much has been made of the need to evaluate web sources carefully before using them. Evaluation is an important step in gathering information from any source, but it is even more important when gathering information from the Web because anyone can post information on the Web. Unlike getting information from a text, you may not immediately be aware of the *source* of the information that you read on the Web. Therefore, when gathering information from the Web, evaluate it carefully by keeping the following in mind:

- What do you know about the author? Is this person an expert or merely someone offering an opinion?

- What do you know about the web site itself? Does an organization sponsor the site and, if so, does it have a personal interest in presenting certain information? For example, information about a diet pill that is presented by a site sponsored by someone trying to sell the pill could not be as trustworthy as information presented on a site sponsored by a medical organization. The notation at the end of a URL indicating *.edu, .gov,* or *.org* means that the source of the information is from an educational institution, government, or nonprofit organization. These are good sources for information.

- How responsibly and thoroughly is the information presented? Is there another side to the issue that should be addressed or is it slanted toward one viewpoint only? Is the material presented so briefly that other important facts may not be included?

- Who is the intended audience? When you write essays, you present the material according to your intended audience and so do writers on the Web. Knowing your audience can help you decide how to evaluate the information presented.

- What is the purpose of the article or information presented? You always write with a purpose and so do authors on the Web. Knowing whether the purpose is to entertain or to inform can affect how you evaluate the material.

- If it is important to you to get reliable, trustworthy information, check more than one source.

    Remember that just because the material is in print on the Web, it does not mean that it is true. Always read critically and evaluate the information thoroughly.

    Many web sites offer ideas for you to consider when you are investigating the validity of the source. A useful site is Marquette University's page at **<http://www.marquette.edu/library/search/evaluating.html>**. Using what you learned about searching the web, you can find many more sites like these. College libraries are often the best source for this kind of information. Can you think of why that would be so?

Documenting Sources

Once you have determined that a source is a good one, you need to collect documentation information. That means that you want to be able to show your readers where you got your information. We do this for many reasons, but three stand out:

- To give credit to someone whose ideas or information you are using

- To show readers who want more information where they can find it

- To lend support to what you write by showing that the idea came from an expert

    The easiest way to cite a web source is to include the URL (web address, beginning with http:// or ftp://) in your paper, usually in angle brackets<>. Include the title and author of the web page, if you can find one, in your text. Most word processors automatically turn URLs into live links, so if you submit your paper electronically, your reader, if connected to the Internet, can click on the URL and see your source immediately. If you are submitting a hard copy, or printed version, of your paper, and your word processor turns your URL into a live link when you don't want it to (the text becomes highlighted), you can hit the Undo button immediately after it changes and the URL should turn back to normal text. Alternatively, you can look under Insert Hyperlink and click on Remove Link.

    For formal research papers, you should follow the style required by your teacher. This book does not cover writing formal research papers, but information on the Modern Language Association (MLA) style, the American Psychological Association (APA) style, and other standard styles is available in varying degrees of detail on the Web.

    Because the Web is constantly changing, you might find it helpful to keep a copy of your source. Print out a web page or save it by clicking on File, Save As.

Two aspects of report writing tend to give students the most trouble. The first is researching the topic. You have already gained some experience with doing research in this chapter. However, the part that most students find so frustrating is knowing *how* to incorporate the researched material into their paper without committing plagiarism.

A report, as assigned by an instructor, must include outside information, but the information must be handled in the proper manner. You have already had some experience with documenting sources in this chapter. But even when students document the source of the information they are using, they still may commit what the academic community considers a serious offense: *plagiarism.* You cannot take long phrases or clauses from an author's work and place them word for word into your sentences. You must *completely* rephrase *in your own words* what the author said to avoid plagiarizing. For most students, putting an author's ideas into their own words is the most difficult part of writing a paper that includes research. However, if you approach this task logically and carefully, you can avoid problems.

First, if you plan to use a direct quotation, when you write the sentence in your notes, put quotation marks around it and make a note of the page number, author, and source.

For the most part, however, you should be referring to the author's ideas and comments, not quoting the author directly. This is called *paraphrasing:* you will be restating what the author said in your own words. Many times you will combine ideas from two or more of the author's sentences into one sentence of your own. You worked on this in Chapter 11 when you wrote summaries. (*Note:* You must always give the author credit for his or her ideas, even when you have expressed them in your own words.)

How do you say what the author said without using the same words? There are several approaches.

The *holistic* approach is to read a sentence or two and ask yourself, "How would I explain this to someone else? What does this mean? How else could this be stated?" Then you would state it as if you were explaining it to someone else in your own words. This works if you have a clear understanding of what the author is saying.

The *analytic* approach takes more time but is easier for most students. This method involves taking the sentence apart piece-by-piece and looking at its individual elements. You may include part or all of these suggestions in paraphrasing any sentence. First, look at the key words. These are usually nouns. Underline them. Above the key words write a synonym. Then do the same thing with the verbs. Now look at the structure of the author's sentence itself. Reverse the order of the sentence and see what happens. This may trigger another way of saying it, and you may include the synonyms. Often an author's sentence will have clauses. You may take the clause and move it to another location, which will help you in rethinking the sentence. Finally, combine two related sentences. Doing this forces you to pick out the key idea in both sentences and then add the remaining relevant material.

Regardless of which method you use, you will have to edit your paraphrasing to link the ideas and sentences together so that it sounds smooth. You may combine sentences, add words for emphasis, or add transitions. Remember that an occasional direct quotation is fine, but it should be of particular interest, not something you insert instead of putting a thought in your own words. You might use quoted material because it directly states the thesis or a key concept or because it has interest.

You may want to end the homework assignment here and have students do the next activities in class.

`00:45` Read this description of the musician Beethoven and think about which method you would use to paraphrase it.

Beethoven

Henry T. Thomas and Dana L. Thomas

(1) In keeping with his ardent temperament, Beethoven was always falling in love with some woman or other. (2) He strictly refrained, however, from poaching upon the preserves of married folk. (3) "It is one of my foremost principles," he said, "never to occupy any other relations than those of friendship with the wife of another man." (4) Perhaps it is true, as some cynics would have us believe, that chastity is largely a question of physical appearance rather than one of spiritual restraint. (5) It is easy for a homely person to remain morally pure. (6) Certainly Beethoven was not the type of man to conquer the female heart. (7) In his youth he made a proposal of marriage to the beautiful opera singer, Magdalena Willmann, but nothing came of the proposal. (8) In later years, when asked why she had refused Beethoven, she laughingly replied, "Because he was so ugly, and half crazy!"

(1) Added to his other physical defects was his deafness, which had begun to press down upon him shortly before the completion of his *First Symphony.* (2) Deafness and romance have never been on speaking terms. (3) Tender words of affection are meant to be whispered, not shouted. (4) The women of Beethoven's circle admired him, pitied him, at times even adored him; but they never loved him. (5) They showered him with invitations to give concerts at their homes. (6) So busy was he at times with these concerts that he was obliged to begin some of them as early as six o'clock in the morning. (7) And he always drew audiences to fill "the capacity of the house." (8) It was an age of musical virtuosity. (9) "In Vienna," remarked the famous pianist Hummel, "there are a hundred ladies who can play the piano better than I." (10) And these ladies were anxious to hear and to applaud Beethoven. (11) But not to flirt with him. (12) One does not flirt with a god—especially when he is homely and deaf. (13) Beethoven's deafness was almost more than he could bear. (14) For it not only isolated him from society but it removed him from the sound of his own music. (15) "This affliction," he wrote, "is more difficult for the artist than for any other man. (16) . . . it was impossible for me to say to my friends, 'Speak louder, shout, for I am deaf.' (17) Ah, was it possible for me to proclaim a deficiency in that one sense which in my case ought to have been more perfect than in all others? . . . (18) For me there can be no recreation in human society, refined conversation, mutual exchange of thoughts and feelings. . . . (19) I must live like an exile. . . . (20) A little more and I should have put an end to my life."

(1) But he soon gave up the thought of death. He had something to live for—his art. (2) "Art alone has detained me. . . . (3) I have emptied the cup of bitter suffering. . . . it shall be transformed into beauty in my soul." (4) Suffering, and patience, and work. (5) "I owe it to myself, to mankind and to the Almighty. I must write my music . . . to the eternal glory of God."

Source: From *Living Biographies of Great Composers* by Henry T. Thomas and Dana L. Thomas, copyright © 1940, 1959 by Doubleday, a division of Random House, Inc. Used by permission of Doubleday, a division of Random House, Inc.

Analyze the Reading: Examples of Paraphrasing Methods

Method 1: Holistic

Paragraph 1: Paraphrasing the Sentences

Compare the following paraphrases to the original text:

1–3   Although Beethoven was quite a womanizer, he didn't date married women.

4–5   Some people might say it is easier to be moral if you are unattractive.

6   Beethoven was not attractive to the opposite sex.

7–8   He once proposed to a beautiful opera singer, Magdalena Willmann, but she turned him down "because he was so ugly, and half crazy!"

Now look at the revised paragraph with the paraphrases rewritten into a smoothly composed paragraph:

> Although Beethoven was quite a womanizer, he didn't date married women. Some people might say it is easier to be moral if you are un-attractive, *and* Beethoven was not attractive to the opposite sex. He once proposed to a beautiful opera singer, Magdalena Willmann, but she turned him down "because he was so ugly, and half crazy!"

Method 2: Analytic

Paragraph 1: Rephrasing the Sentences

Compare the short choppy sentences with the original:

1. Because of his personality, Beethoven kept falling in love.

2. He disapproved of chasing married women.

3. He said he would only be friends with them.

4. Some people think that being moral was related more to his appearance than will power.

5. It is easy for unattractive people to avoid temptation.

6. He was not a "ladies man."

7. When he was young he proposed marriage to a beautiful opera singer, Magdalena Willmann, but was rejected.

8. Later she said she had turned him down "because he was so ugly, and half crazy!"

As you read over the eight sentences above, did they sound choppy to you? If so, it is because having several short sentences doesn't sound as smooth as using more complex sentences with dependent clauses and phrases. So if you use this method, the next step is to combine these sentences. Notice the differ-ence:

> *Although* Beethoven had the kind of personality that caused him to fall in love often, he disapproved of chasing married women *and* said he would only be friends with them. Some people think that being moral was related more to his appearance than will power *because* it is easier for unattractive people to avoid temptation *and Beethoven* was *certainly*

not a lady-killer. When he was young he proposed marriage to a beautiful opera singer, Magdalena Willmann, but was rejected. Later she said she had turned him down "because he was so ugly, and half crazy!"

Practice is essential in learning to paraphrase. There are many correct ways to restate an author's idea. However, you have to be careful that the meaning remains the same. You cannot overemphasize one aspect or distort the meaning. The following activities will be very helpful to you in gaining experience with this skill.

1. Define plagiarism:

_____

_____

2. How can you avoid committing plagiarism?

_____

_____

Paraphrase the last two paragraphs of "Beethoven." Compare your sentences in small groups. Write the best version on the board or post it on your connected computer system.

Read "Take Two Sonatas and Call Me in the Morning." Think about the meaning as you read so that you can put it into your own words.

Take Two Sonatas and Call Me in the Morning

Nancy Butcher

1 (1) Music is more than just a pleasant diversion. (2) It has long been seen as a highway to health and happiness.

2 (1) Love of music is a common denominator of humanity. (2) Since ancient times, people have valued music for its power to heal as well as its obvious recreational benefits. (3) In the myths of many cultures, it was a gift from the gods. (4) The ancient Egyptians taught that the goddess Isis brought music to earth to help human beings cleanse their souls and rein in their emotions, and the Hindus believed that the gods kept music for their own enjoyment until they were moved by pity to share it with humanity.

3 (1) The gods were the inventors of music in Greek mythology, too. (2) Apollo, the sun god, was also worshiped as the deity of music and medicine, and his son, Asclepius, was a patron of the healing arts. (3) Music was played in Asclepian temples to refresh and restore the body and soul. (4) Its great power was perhaps best exemplified by Orpheus. (5) On his voyage with Jason and the Argonauts, he played lively

Source: Nancy Butcher, "Take Two Sonatas and Call Me in the Morning," appeared in the November 1995 issue and is reprinted with permission from _The World & I,_ a publication of The Washington Times Corporation, copyright © 1995.

melodies on his lyre to energize fatigued oarsmen, and soothing tunes to calm them when they quarreled.

4   (1) The Greek philosophers frequently coupled good music with good health. (2) Pythagoras taught in the sixth century B.C. that health was a prime example of the universal harmony that was the chief subject of his studies. (3) Music and diet were the two most effective ways to purify and balance the body and soul. (4) He felt that music—along with a vegetarian diet, fresh air, massage, fasting, and other treatments—could work to bring the body into harmony with the soul and with the divine.

5   (1) Plato reveals the Pythagorean influence on his thought in the Timaeus: Music wasn't created merely as a means of giving "irrational pleasure, but as a heaven-sent ally in reducing to order and harmony any disharmony . . . within us." (2) Both Plato and Aristotle believed that music can profoundly influence not only the human body but the body politic as well, and they advocated outlawing sorrowful or raucous music considered harmful to society.

6   (1) The natives of North America held a widespread belief in music's curative powers. (2) As just two instances among many, an Aleut myth tells of a man who was resurrected from death by a singing girl, and the Lakota and Winnebago tribes believed that the spirits of wild bears imparted magic powers to healers, who could then cure others with song. (3) Later, during the dark days of slavery, songs based on African harmonies brought a measure of solace to the lives of the slaves. (4) "Field hollers" and group work songs gave pace and rhythm to hard labor; "ring shouts" enlivened leisure moments.

7   (1) Many cultures still use music today as they have throughout history. (2) Healing remains a primary purpose of music among Eskimos, North and South American natives, Australian aborigines, and sub-Saharan and Indonesian tribal peoples.

8   (1) In more advanced societies, the advent of modern medicine marked a fork in the road: (2) Medicine allied itself with science and technology, while music was relegated to the category of entertainment arts. (3) But acceptance of the idea that music can be a powerful adjunct to standard medical treatment has been on the rise within the medical community in recent decades. (4) For example, Dr. Raymond Bahr, head of the coronary-care unit at St. Agnes Hospital in Baltimore, believes that listening to classical music for thirty minutes does the same for his patients as ten milligrams of valium.

Analyze the Reading

1. Before you can put the author's text into your own words, you must make sure you understand all the words found in the reading. Use a thesaurus to do this. Find a synonym for the following words using a thesaurus. You can find a thesaurus in your word processor, on the Web, or in book form. You will see that it gives you many alternatives for each word. However, since each word has a different shade of meaning, see if you can find the choice that best fits the meaning of the sentence by mentally substituting the words in the sentences. When you feel you have made the best choice, write the synonym next to the word. Compare the choices with your classmates' choices. Then look the word up in a dictionary (found in the same forms as the thesaurus) and see if you made a good choice. If not, cross out the inferior choice and write the better choice on the line to the right.

Using a thesaurus without doublechecking in a dictionary can result in beginning writers sounding foolish because they made an inappropriate choice.

a. *diversion* _____

b. *deity* _____

c. *patron* _____

d. *exemplified (exemplify)* _____

e. *fatigued (fatigue)* _____

f. *purify* _____

g. *irrational* _____

h. *ally* _____

i. *profoundly* _____

j. *politic* _____

k. *advocated (advocate)* _____

l. *raucous* _____

m. *curative* _____

n. *resurrected (resurrect)* _____

o. *imparted (impart)* _____

p. *solace* _____

q. *enlivened (enliven)* _____

r. *leisure* _____

s. *advent* _____

t. *relegated (relegate)* _____

u. *adjunct* _____

As you can see, you would have lost much of the meaning of the article if you were not familiar with most of these words. So your first step in analyzing a text should be to circle any words you are unsure of.

2. Rewrite the following sentences in your own words:

2:1 (paragraph 2, sentence 1)

_____

_____

2:2 (paragraph 2, sentence 2)

_____

_____

5:2 (paragraph 5, sentence 2)

_____

_____

6:1 (paragraph 6, sentence 1)

_____

_____

8:1 (paragraph 8, sentence 1)

_____

_____

3. Combine the ideas in the following pairs of sentences into one sentence in your own words. Of course, when you combine you include the main idea, but not necessarily every detail.

1:1 and 1:2

_____

_____

_____

6:3 and 6:4

_____

_____

_____

7:1 and 7:2

_____

_____

_____

4. Get into groups and compare sentences that you wrote in number 3. Select the best version of each sentence to put on the board. Discuss why that sentence was the best, keeping in mind that there are many correct and effective ways to paraphrase. However, also keep in mind that a sentence that distorts the meaning of the original would not be effective.

The following article presents research on how music may affect your mind and body. As you read the essay, take note of your responses to it.

Mental Tuneup Is as Close as Your Stereo

Bill Hendrick

1 Feeling stressed? Having a hard time sleeping? Does your blood pressure rise and your temper sizzle when you're stuck in traffic or trapped in one of those inane meetings in which everybody blabs on endlessly without ever saying anything?

2 Go listen to a Mozart sonata, prescribes John A. Lennon, who has a doctorate in music, not medicine, but who's increasingly inspired these days by growing evidence that music not only can tune up our brains, but our bodies as well.

3 But not all music works the same way, adds the Emory University music professor. Beethoven, for instance, "is more emotional" than the music of Mozart or other classical composers. Beethoven might keep you up instead of lulling you to sleep. And if you need to get psyched up for a business meeting, he says, maybe try a little Fleetwood Mac, or anything else with a speedy beat, which research shows gets the heart pumping faster.

4 John Morrison, who teaches trumpet to people ranging in age from 3 to their 60s at the Georgia Academy of Music, has long used music for mental therapy "to give me a way to check out of the violence you see on the pavement" of interstates.

5 "It will work for almost anyone," says Morrison, 45. "For our students, it seems to calm them, inspire them, encourage them, and even teach them to have patience."

6 Professionals such as Morrison and Lennon also say that growing scientific research bolsters what they've known intuitively—that music has a real impact on both mind and the body.

7 In a new book, *The Mozart Effect,* musician and therapist Don Campbell presents what he says is the "tip of the iceberg" of research touting the healthful benefits of music. His book cites research by neurologists and psychologists showing that music:

- Strengthens memory and learning. The music of Mozart and Vivaldi, with mathematically precise rhythmic and tonal patterns, helps people concentrate for longer periods, so it might be good before examinations, speeches or business presentations. And listening to baroque music while studying enhances the ability to memorize spellings, poetry and foreign words. Recall is best if you listen to the same kind of music you heard when you were trying to etch things into your mind.

- Stimulates digestion. Rock music causes people to eat faster and eat more. But classical music, especially slow string music, makes people eat more slowly and consume less. So, for most people, listening to loud, thumping beats while eating isn't smart. Put on something more soothing, soft and slow.

Source: Reprinted with permission of *The Atlanta Journal and Constitution* from Bill Hendrick, "Health Watch: Mind and Body: Mental Tuneup Is as Close as Your Stereo," *The Atlanta Journal and Constitution*, 10/30/97. Permission conveyed through Copyright Clearance Center.

- Can increase the release of endorphins, opiate-like chemicals in the brain that can induce euphoria and help the body cope with pain, and enhance the body's immune system.

- Can improve concentration, memory and spatial perception (Haydn and Mozart), or evoke feelings of mysticism and enhance sympathy and compassion (Schubert, Schumann, Tchaikovsky, Chopin, Liszt).

- Stirs passions and movement. Martial music, rock, heavy metal, punk, rap, hip-hop and grunge tend to excite the nervous system and lead to dynamic behavior. Plus, says Dr. Norm Weinberger, head of the Center for the Neurobiology of Learning and Memory at the University of California at Irvine, music of African-American origin—jazz, blues, Dixieland, soul, calypso, reggae—tends to uplift, inspire and release deep emotions. And playing music or singing seems particularly beneficial, allowing expression of emotions, which reduces the secretion of dangerous stress hormones.

8   "Music exercises the whole brain and mind" and "can strengthen synapses" that allow brain cells to communicate, Weinberger says. Thus, he contends, people who appreciate almost any kind of music are likely to be healthier than those who have tin ears.

9   Campbell says it's no wonder kids like to dance to music with fast rhythms, because beat and tempo have been shown to affect blood pressure, heart rate, body temperature and respiration. Weinberger says it seems clear that people can help themselves by listening to many kinds of music, and that it can be beneficial in conditions ranging from cancer to attention deficit disorder.

10   "This is not another alternative medicine," he says. "With music, you work with your own inner psyche to know you are participating in your own wellness."

11   And you're never too old, Morrison adds, to try to develop a taste for Mozart or even to learn to play a musical instrument. "For adults, it's a tremendous outlet, a great stress reducer, a confidence builder," he says. "It makes you forget problems."

Analyze the Reading

1. Highlight the thesis in green, main ideas in blue, examples in yellow, and facts in pink.

_____

_____

2. Looking at the highlighting, did the author use more facts or examples as support?

_____

_____

3. Was the author's supporting detail convincing to you? Explain.

_____

_____

4. Write a response thesis to this article.

_____

_____

_____

FILE ▶ Create

Essay with Facts

You are ready to start the central assignment for the chapter pairs: a summary/response essay supported by your research.

Begin to formulate your thesis in response to Hendrick's thesis. As usual, you will start by clustering the topic. Do all the prewriting activities that help you get started, in whatever order works for you: brainstorm, freewrite, outline, map. Determine your thesis in response to the author's thesis as a result of the conclusion you develop in your prewriting. Next, determine your major supporting assertions. Let each paragraph be about a different effect of music on the mind or body, as suggested by the search terms given on page 291 that you searched in the first session of this chapter. Make an outline to guide your research.

Now, begin researching the subject of music's effect on the mind and body. Take careful notes. Look for material to support your assertions. In addition, think of examples that will help your reader understand the facts. Make notes about which section of the outline this material will support. Add information to your outline so that you can see how the support is accumulating in each section of your paper.

Name: _____

Date: _____

Topic: _____

Purpose: _____

Audience: _____   Tone: _____

Thesis: _____

I. First key point:

    Supporting details: _____

    _____

II. Second key point:

    Supporting details: _____

    _____

III. Third key point:

    Supporting details: _____

    _____

If your instructor requests, you will add IV, V, and so on according to how many paragraphs are assigned or what you want to include in your paper.

FILE ▶ Save As: Central Assignment

Now, draft an essay and incorporate facts that you found in your research. Be sure to document the sources of your facts. This essay will be evaluated on the basis of *content and support of assertions*. Since this is a *draft* and your primary goal is to organize your thoughts and say something meaningful and interesting, you will not be concerned with surface errors, sentence structure, spelling, and the like *at this time*. In other words, your early draft should focus on *what* you say more than *how* you say it.

 Go To ▶

1. Go to the Purdue OWL and look at the several headings under Research at: **<http://owl.english.purdue.edu/handouts/research/index.html>** for information on avoiding plagiarism.

2. Go to the Web to research song lyrics.

3. Go to the Elibrary site at: **<http://www.elibrary.com>** and examine what this site has to offer. This is a valuable source for finding recent articles or television transcripts on a given subject. You have to pay to subscribe, but your library may have a membership. At some point in your college career, you may find it worthwhile to subscribe. Does your school library subscribe to this service and allow you to use it as a student?

C:\Prompts for Writing ▶

1. Write a report on your favorite musician. Do research to find out early biographical information, such as how the band or musician got started, career history, and current status.

2. Research and write about the *type* of music you like—rock, blues, jazz, rap, classical, hip-hop, opera, country and western, or any other type. Find out about the origins of the music and how it has changed over time.

3. Should the music industry be regulated by the government or another kind of monitoring board? For instance, many adults complain that music companies market songs with inappropriate lyrics to young teenagers, so CDs now come with rating labels. In your opinion, is this enough to stop adolescents from buying music that might be deemed "inappropriate"? Alternatively, is any attempt to stop anyone from buying music too much regulation?

4. How does music affect you and others you know? Do you study while listening to music? Does it help? Do your parents complain about your music? Write an essay describing the effects of specific kinds of music on people.

5. How do you get your music? Do you buy CDs, copy CDs your friends have bought, listen to the radio, listen to music through your computer, download music from the Web, attend live concerts, attend online concerts, and/or watch music videos on television? When radio first began, music producers were frightened that free access to music would mean that people would stop buying recordings (vinyl records back then). Lately, record producers are worried that free sites will cost the recording industry money. Write an essay comparing or contrasting the effects on the music industry of broadcasting music on the radio and on the Web. Support your opinions with research.

CHAPTER 14
Music of the Self

When I heard this music I had forgotten to sing within myself. I found a way to begin my journey to find me.

—Mark Warren

Chapter Contents

315

Log On ▶ **Reflection**

Write whatever comes to mind when you read the chapter title and opening quotation.

_____

_____

_____

_____

_____

_____

_____

_____

_____

_____

_____

_____

_____

_____

_____

_____

_____

_____

_____

_____

_____

_____

_____

FILE ▶ Open

`00:45`

The words in italics are not defined here. Students can experience inferring the meanings of *infer* as a way of understanding the concept.

You may want to use this class session to check drafts of the central assignment. Students could work in groups and advise each other or could go to a computer lab or the library. You may find this a useful time to do individual consultation. If you are in a computer lab, you may want to play some Mozart to help students concentrate!

Connecting with Experience

▶ If your mother said to you, "Son [or "Daughter], get in here right this minute!" what would you *infer?*

▶ After reading this question, what can you *infer* that *infer* means?

▶ Remember a time when you broke off a relationship with someone. How did you *conclude* the relationship?

Connecting with Previous Learning

▶ Reread the information on plagiarism on page 302 of Chapter 13. What *conclusion* can you draw about what might happen if you plagiarized? What can you *infer* might be some consequences?

▶ When you are reading a text of several pages in length, how do you know when to keep turning pages or when the piece is finished?

▶ Look back at your central assignment from Chapters 11 and 12. Reread the last paragraph you wrote in that assignment. What were you doing in that paragraph? Were you introducing another assertion and supporting it? Were you ending the essay in some way? How would your readers know that it was the last paragraph?

Options: Customize

List as many types of music as you can think of on the board—for example, opera, gospel, rap, and so on. Find a student to volunteer to bring a selection of each type of music. Have any remaining students bring any music of their choice.

Your instructor will play 1 minute of various types of music and then you will write in your journal for 2 minutes about the effect that piece of music had on you. Record any mental, physical, or emotional experiences. Be sure to label each journal entry with the type of music you are responding to. After listening and responding to all the music, comment in journals or in class discussion about how the music affected you and whether you found you liked a kind of music you previously did not know you liked. Spend any remaining time discussing or journaling your conclusions about music's effects on the mind.

FILE ▶ New

This is a good place to begin the homework assignment.

Conclusions

In Chapter 9, you learned to write an introduction and you learned that its purpose was to give readers an idea of what was to come. Furthermore, it introduced your thesis. A conclusion works in pretty much the same way: It usually gives readers a recap of what came before and reemphasizes the thesis. It can also give readers a feeling of *closure*—a sense that things have been brought to an end. The conclusion may also convey the writer's conviction that he or she has achieved the purpose intended in the text.

A conclusion may achieve one or more of these effects. There are also other types of conclusions that can be more interesting than a straightforward summary. You may notice that many of the articles you read about music did not have effective conclusions. That is because newspaper articles are written in a distinct style: They move from general statements to specific details of less and less general interest. This is because only readers with a special interest in that subject will read a newspaper article all the way to the end. Also, an editor who cuts an article at the last minute because of lack of space will start at the end, where the least important information is. Even though you will not usually find conclusions in newspaper articles, academic writing requires effective conclusions.

Read "Memories Aren't Made of This" and analyze the conclusion. Consider the last paragraph *and* the last sentence together as the conclusion.

Memories Aren't Made of This

Eric Zorn

1   Something terrible has happened to popular music in this country. Over the last few years it has touched its finger to the Tar Baby of television and now finds itself unable to pull away. Consider the following depressing news:

2   ▪ There are 200 regular television programs in America that feature nothing but the combination of film clips and rock songs.

3   ▪ Warner Amex's Music Television (MTV), the cable network based solely on these music videos, hits nearly 20 million homes and is the hottest basic cable operation in history.

4   ▪ The marriage of music and television has proved to be so popular that it is credited with almost singlehandedly snapping the recording industry out of a four-year slump in 1983 and changing the face of popular music by introducing the new bands and new sounds radio wouldn't touch.

5   ▪ Today's pop-music groups find that they must produce video versions of their songs if they wish to survive. Many are making video-cassette albums that customers buy instead of records.

6   ▪ Really cool people now speak of "seeing" the latest songs as opposed to hearing them. More than a majority of MTV viewers recently sampled say they "play back" the video in their minds when they hear a song on the radio.

7   This all indicates strongly that music videos are no passing fad. They're here to stay, just like TV itself when it first came along in the late 1940s to add pictures to the old radio dramas.

8   I find this all terribly sad. The proliferation of music videos threatens to produce an entire generation of people who will all but miss out on the sublime, extremely personal element of music.

Source: Eric Zorn, "Memories Aren't Made of This," *Newsweek*, © 1984. Reprinted by permission of Eric Zorn.

9   What nobody has bothered to point out in the course of all this hoopla attendant upon rock video is that music has always had a visual element of a sort: the images, people and places that the listener sees in his mind's eye when a favorite song or symphony comes on.

10   One of the truly great but least understood components of music is the way it can tap long-forgotten emotions and unlock unconscious memories. Many feelings and old visual impressions are so deeply hidden in the recesses of the mind that sometimes only the sudden surprise of a melody can lead the way to them.

11   Special songs can act for us like the tea and madeleine cake in Marcel Proust's huge novel, *A Remembrance of Things Past,* as a simple spark that sets off a blaze of recollections.

12   "Mr. Tambourine Man" by Bob Dylan brings back the long walks my best buddy and I used to take on the beach near his mom's cottage on Cape Cod; "Mrs. Robinson" by Simon and Garfunkel conjures up the kitchen in the first house my parents ever owned; "Amie" by Pure Prairie League reminds me of springtime in the old college dormitory and my first train trip to Chicago.

13   When I hear someone fiddle "Lamplighter's Hornpipe," I think of a particular section of Altgeld Street near DePaul University where I first heard that tune on tape; and "Seasons in the Sun" by Terry Jacks, a terrible song, brings on the delightful memory of a young woman named Martine for whom I yearned so tragically in 11th grade I could scarcely move myself to speak to her.

14   For Martine, wherever she is, it is safe to say "Seasons in the Sun" has entirely different associations. That's the great thing about music. No matter how many millions of people bought that record or heard it on the radio, there will always be something about its smarmy lyrics that will be special only to me.

15   Not every song still has this power, however. I've already had a few of them ruined when, in idle moments, I have lingered too long in front of a TV set showing music videos. When, for example, I hear Michael Jackson's "Billie Jean," the first, overwhelming image I get in my mind is of the lithe little Mr. Jackson capering around and pointing his lithe little finger every which way. No good memories. No bad memories. Nothing but the exact same memories that everyone else will have of this song for decades to come.

16   Who can hear "Suicide Is Painless," the theme song from M*A*S*H," and think of anything else but helicopters? Who can hear "Yellow Submarine" by the Beatles and not be flooded with thoughts of the brightly colored Peter Max cartoons that splashed through the movie of the same name?

Antiseptic Music

17 What we're really talking about here is the wholesale substitution of common, shared memories for individual memories; a substitution that ends up robbing us of pieces of our own lives. The personal side of music is steadily being replaced by the corporate side, so that the associations and mental pictures that go along with songs for the MTV generation don't relate to *their* lives, but to the lives of the people who conceived the videos.

18   We're left with popular music that has the same distant, antiseptic feel as network television: you may enjoy it, but you must admit that it doesn't, in any meaningful way, feel as though it *belongs* to you. The combination of sight and sound not only promotes passive viewing, but serves to depersonalize the entertainment offered.

19   Young lovers today, I suspect, do not elbow each other excitedly when an old Duran Duran clip comes on the TV screen and coo, "Look, darling, they're showing our video."

20   And that's depressing news: future generations will be locked into the prefabricated memories of a false musical experience, restricted by monolithic visual interpretations of songs that preempt and defy the exercise of individual experience, motion and memory.

21   Videos will not be the death of pop music, radio or the old rock groups that never thought to film themselves moving their lips to the words. But ultimately the insidious combination of film and song will sap away some of the great power of music and change how we feel about it in a very fundamental way.

22   I wonder how many of us are really ready for that?

Analyze the Reading

1. How did the author conclude this essay?

_____

_____

_____

2. Could you tell from the conclusion that the article had ended? Explain.

_____

_____

_____

_____

3. In your opinion, was this conclusion effective? Explain your thoughts.

_____

_____

_____

_____

Read the following article, "Raised on Rock-and-Roll." In it, Anna Quindlen discusses her love for a particular type of music.

Raised on Rock-and-Roll

Anna Quindlen

1 I was born in Philadelphia, a city where if you can't dance you might as well stay home, and I was raised on rock-and-roll. My earliest television memory is of *American Bandstand,* and the central question of my childhood was: Can you dance to it?

2 When I was fifteen and a wild devotee of Mitch Rider and the Detroit Wheels, it sometimes crossed my mind that when I was thirty-four years old, decrepit, wrinkled as a prune and near death, I would have moved on to some nameless kind of dreadful show music, something akin to Muzak. I did not think about the fact that my parents were still listening to the music that had been popular when they were kids; I only thought that they played "Pennsylvania 6-5000" to torment me and keep my friends away from the house.

3 But I know now that I'm never going to stop loving rock-and-roll, all kinds of rock-and-roll: the Beatles, the Rolling Stones, Hall and Oates, Talking Heads, the Doors, the Supremes, Tina Turner, Elvis Costello, Elvis Presley. I even like really bad rock-and-roll, although I guess that's where my age shows: I don't have the tolerance for Bon Jovi that I once had for the Raspberries.

4 We have friends who, when their son was a baby, used to put a record on and say, "Drop your butt, Phillip." And Phillip did. That's what I love: drop-your-butt music. It's one of the few things left in my life that makes me feel good without even thinking about it. I can walk into any bookstore and find dozens of books about motherhood and love and human relations and so many other things that we once did through a combination of intuition and emotion. I even heard recently that some school is giving a course on kissing, which makes me wonder if I'm missing something. But rock-and-roll flows through my veins, not my brain. There's nothing also that feels the same to me as, say, the faint sound of the opening dum-doo-doo-doo-doo-doo of "My Girl" coming from a radio on a summer day. I feel the way I felt when I first heard it. I feel good, as James Brown says.

5 There are lots of people who don't feel this way about rock-and-roll. Some of them don't understand it, like the Senate wives who said that records should have rating stickers on them so that you would know whether the lyrics were dirty. The kids who hang out at Mr. Big's sub shop in my neighborhood thought this would make record shopping a lot easier, because you could choose albums by how bad the rating was. Most of the people who love rock-and-roll just thought the labeling idea was dumb. Lyrics, after all, are not the point of rock-and-roll, despite how beautifully people like Bruce Springsteen and Joni Mitchell write. Lyrics are the point only in the case of "Louis, Louis"; the words have never been deciphered, but it is widely understood that they are about sex. That's understandable, because rock-and-roll is a lot like sex: If you talk seriously about it, it takes a lot of the feeling away—and feeling is the point.

6 Some people over-analyze rock-and-roll, just as they over-analyze everything else. They say things like "Bruce Springsteen is the poet laureate of the American dream gone sour," when all I need to know about Bruce Springsteen is that the saxophone bridge on "Jungleland" makes

---

Source: Anna Quindlen, "Raised on Rock 'n Roll," from *Living Out Loud* by Anna Quindlen, copyright © 1987 by Anna Quindlen. Used by permission of Random House, Inc.

the back of my neck feel exactly the same way I felt the first time a boy kissed me, only over and over and over again. People write about Prince's "Psychodelic masturbatory fantasies," but when I think about Prince, I don't really think, I just feel—feel the moment when driving to the beach, I first heard "Kiss" on the radio and started bobbing up and down in my seat like a seventeen-year-old on a day trip.

7   I've got precious few things in my life anymore that just make me feel, that make me jump up and dance, that make me forget the schedule and the job and the mortgage payments and just let me thrash around inside my skin. I've got precious few things I haven't studied and considered and reconsidered and studied some more. I don't know a chord change from a snare drum, but I know what I like, and I like feeling this way sometimes. I love rock-and-roll because in a time of talk, talk, talk, it's about action.

8   Here's a test: Get hold of a two-year-old, a person who has never read a single word about how heavy-metal musicians should be put in jail or about Tina Turner's "throaty alto range." Put "I Heard It Through the Grapevine" on the stereo. Stand the two-year-old in front of the stereo. The two-year-old will begin to dance. The two-year-old will drop his butt. Enough said.

Analyze the Reading

1. How did the author conclude this essay?

_____

_____

_____

2. Could you tell from the conclusion that the article had ended? Explain.

_____

_____

_____

3. In your opinion, was this conclusion effective? Explain your thoughts.

_____

_____

_____

_____

Using the guidelines on the following pages, write an effective conclusion for your draft.

Types of Conclusions

1. *Restating the thesis.* This type of conclusion makes it clear that the writer has achieved his or her purpose in writing the text.

2. *Drawing a conclusion.* After presenting all the information to readers, the writer draws a conclusion. In other words, the writer injects an opinion about everything presented so far. The writer may conclude by indicating that all of this is good or bad and explain why in a sentence. For example, after presenting information on why pollution is getting worse, the author draws a conclusion about how this is a bad situation and explains why.

3. *Calling for action.* The writer presents all the facts and examples in the text, then concludes that this information means that certain action should be undertaken as a result. (For example, a writer describing types of pollution in each paragraph of the text might conclude with a statement that something specific must be done about all of this pollution.)

4. *Predicting action.* This type of conclusion is very similar to calling for action, but it predicts that as a result of the information presented, certain things *will probably happen.* (For example, the writer's conclusion might be that if this pollution continues, there are going to be health issues in the community.)

5. *Showing the importance.* The writer concludes with a statement about how the information in this text matters in some larger context. (For example, the writer states that pollution will be an important issue in the upcoming election.)

6. *Raising a question.* The writer concludes that the information presented in the text raises an important question. (The writer may question the effectiveness of current policies to deal with the pollution problem.)

7. *Solving the problem.* The writer concludes with a suggestion about what to do about the problem. (For example, the writer may suggest that the sales tax could be increased to provide revenue to deal with all the areas of pollution discussed in the text.)

Guidelines for Writing Conclusions

- Do not introduce any new topics into the conclusion. You may introduce an idea when you call for action or make a prediction, but this idea is part of the overall topic. You should not introduce anything that would be another I, II, III in your outline such as *another reason, example,* or the like.

- Do not use obvious words to introduce the conclusion such as *in summary, in conclusion,* or *I have shown that . . .*

- Do not contradict what you have already said. Sometimes beginning writers will conclude by giving the *opposing position* in a response, saying something like *but there are some reasons why . . .* (and stating the opposite of what they have argued in the paper). Do not stray from your original thesis and your assertions.

- Do not repeat what you have said. You may restate your overall thesis in a different way, or summarize what you have said in a sentence or two, but do not repeat all of your key points.

TOOLS ▶ Language

You may want to start class by reviewing the homework on conclusions and then continue with the following activities.

Making Inferences

What does it mean to "read between the lines"?

_____

_____

When we read the work of another, we often have to "read between the lines," or *infer* certain things, based on our understanding of what has been said and what has been *meant*. We speculate about what we read. We might apply what we have read to other aspects of our lives, *inferring* that there may be a connection. We draw conclusions and make *assumptions.* All of these are ways of inferring something that isn't in the text but that we assume would be true based on what *is* in the text. The better we are at making inferences, the better we will be at figuring out the author's thesis. In addition, it will be easier for us to respond to the author's ideas because we can address some of the issues based on assumptions, conclusions, or connections that we have inferred. Making inferences is an important tool for critical thinking. As you analyze the following text and make inferences, you may come up with ideas that you could research in order to make effective arguments in support of or against the author's thesis.

Turn back to page 309 in Chapter 13 and reread "Mental Tuneup Is as Close as Your Stereo." Read the article very critically. Be prepared to make some inferences.

Suggested answers:.

Playing specific kinds of music may help with studying.

Analyze the Reading:

1. Analyze the text.

2. Reread paragraph 8. What could you infer about a new study technique you might want to experiment with?

_____

_____

_____

Based on paragraph 9, one could lose weight if he or she played classical music while eating.

3. Reread paragraph 9. What could you infer from this passage about how to lose weight?

_____

_____

_____

For a family who wants to have more quality time at the dinner table, classical music may enable the family to eat more slowly and take the time to enjoy each other's company.

4. What could you infer about a family who wanted to have more quality time at the dinner table?

_____

Music might make those who wait more patient.

5. What could you infer would be helpful to a place where people have to wait?

_____

_____

_____

6. What changes could you infer a restaurant owner who read this article might make?

_____

_____

_____

_____

_____

Music that would enhance compassion might be helpful in the waiting room of a counseling practice.

7. Reread paragraph 11. What can you infer about appropriate music for the waiting room of a counseling practice?

_____

_____

_____

According to the reading, Haydn's music might help people who are studying—especially when studying math.

8. What can you infer about the music of Haydn?

_____

_____

_____

_____

People like to dance to martial music, rock, heavy metal, punk, rap, hip-hop, and grunge because it stirs movement. Individuals may like this music because it helps to express emotions.

9. What can you infer from paragraph 12?

_____

_____

_____

TOOLS ▶ Language

Research shows that students remember incorrect examples as well as correct examples. In other words, students learn incorrect information; therefore, in this text, we avoid examples of what *not* to do as much as possible.

Fragments, Clauses, and Phrases

Now that you have mastered the major steps of the writing process, you are ready to focus on *how* you say something as well as what you say. You want to make sure you are constructing sentences in the manner typical of academic discourse.

As you work with this chapter, pay careful attention to *sentence fragments,* or incomplete sentences. Many students have trouble with sentence fragments. You may have experienced a teacher marking a sentence "frag" and you didn't always understand why. Some define a sentence fragment as a sentence missing a subject or a verb. However, a sentence with a missing subject or verb can still be a complete sentence if the subject or verb is implied. Likewise, sentences may be incomplete despite having both a subject and verb *part.* (The explanation of sentence fragments can get complicated!)

Fragments are hard to locate because often the missing meaning shows up in the next sentence and you may not realize that you have written one sentence as two.

What does work? Using some of the following editing techniques not only will make your writing more mature and interesting but can often help eliminate fragments.

One way to reduce the number of fragments in your writing and to expand and develop your supporting paragraphs is to add descriptive words, clauses, and phrases. The extra information you put into the sentence with these clauses or phrases can make your paragraph more interesting and informative, and the complex sentence structure makes your writing more effective. Furthermore, if you are incorporating additional *who, what, why, where,* and *how* information into a sentence, you are less likely to end up with a fragment. For example, instead of writing:

My boss made me rewrite the report.

Insert a clause to describe "who":

My boss, *who is a perfectionist,* made me rewrite the report.

You have told a little more about *who.* You can make the sentence even more informative and interesting by explaining *why.*

My boss, who is a perfectionist, made me rewrite the report *to make it sound more formal.*

Try adding a *what:*

My boss, who is a perfectionist, made me rewrite the report *on employee attendance policies* to make it sound more formal.

Sometimes you can add adjectives and adverbs to improve a sentence. Think *how, why, when, where.*

My *new young* boss, who is a perfectionist, made me *completely* rewrite the report on employee attendance policies to make it sound more formal.

Compare the last version to the first version:

My boss made me rewrite the report.

My *new young* boss, who is a perfectionist, made me *completely* rewrite the report on employee attendance policies to make it sound more formal.

Which sentence is more interesting? You can see it isn't difficult to write more interesting sentences.

How would these editing techniques help you with a fragment? Assume you were going through your draft sentence by sentence and you came to the fragment "While driving to work." This is a fragment because the word *while* makes the phrase dependent on further information: We don't know what happened "while" the first action (driving) happened. Applying the editing tool, you come up with "While driving to work *in my broken-down car.*" You still have a fragment, although a more interesting one. But you aren't through yet. You look for the *who:* "While driving to work in my broken-down car, *I.*" Continuing with expanding, you ask *what:*

While driving to work in my broken-down car, I *passed my boss.*

Now you have a complete sentence. Try another one:

While driving, I passed.

Here you have a complete thought, but you can continue to edit. Add a phrase: think *who, what, when, where,* and *how.*

While driving to work in my broken-down car, I passed my boss *in his Mercedes.*

Much better. (Is "Much better" a fragment? This is why fragments are so confusing. "It is," the subject and verb, are both implied. Thus the sentence is considered complete, but it isn't very interesting.) Now add some adjectives and adverbs to spice up your own sentence even more.

While *frantically* driving to work in my broken-down car, I passed my *frowning* boss in his *shiny new* Mercedes.

Notice that "frantically" tells *how.* We still don't have a *where.* You could add "in the parking lot" or "on the Interstate."

A second method that can reduce fragments is to be on the alert when you use a word ending in *-ing.* These words often signal a dependent clause, which means that it must be attached to an independent clause (a complete sentence). For example,

Signing my time sheet.

The reader doesn't know the *what, why,* or *how* pertaining to the signing. The *-ing* gives you the trouble. There are two ways to make this a complete sentence. The first is to remove the *-ing.*

I signed my time sheet.

The other way is to attach the phrase to the rest of the meaning:

Signing my time sheet made me realize how many times I had been late to work.

A third method of reducing fragments is combining your sentences into longer, more interesting ones. When you do this, you may combine those dependent clauses that you have written as fragments with the sentence they are dependent on. For example, fragments often begin with a *subordinator*—a word that makes the phrase dependent on further information. Combining the phrase with another sentence can solve that problem. You might write:

While driving to work. I passed my boss in his Mercedes.

Here you have a fragment and a complete sentence. The word *while* is a subordinator. This means the clause with the subordinator is meaningless by itself and must be attached to a complete sentence. Watch what happens when you combine the fragment and the sentence:

While driving to work, I passed my boss in his Mercedes.

The following words are subordinators and should warn you to check that you have a clause with a subordinator that should be attached to another sentence with a comma.

> *while, until, before, whenever, during, after, as, since, as soon as, when, as long as, where, wherever, though, although, even though, given that, so that, in order that, in order to, if, whether, unless, because*

In addition, if you combine your sentences using these words, you will improve your writing and reduce your chances of writing fragments.

Sometimes you will join two of your sentences by using a *relative pronoun*, a pronoun that "relates" to a word coming before it. Revision using relative pronouns makes a more interesting text and is helpful in avoiding fragments.

The most common relative pronouns are:

who, whom, whose, which, that

While driving to work in my broken-down car, I passed my boss in his Mercedes, *which was supposed to be much more powerful.*

Which refers to the Mercedes. (Be careful you don't misplace this relative pronoun. What would happen to the meaning if you put the phrase after the word boss?)

Sometimes, however, you will use *coordinators* to combine sentences. Coordinators are words that combine two complete sentences. An easy way to remember the list of coordinators is to think of the nonsense word SNOBFAY:

so, nor, or, but, for, and, yet

Be careful. When you use these words, you are joining two sentences that could stand alone. Joining them, however, can make your writing more interesting.

Take a short sentence from your draft, particularly one you suspect is a fragment. Complete this form, adding to the sentence as indicated by the prompt. Rewrite the new version of the sentence in every box.

You may wish to put examples on the board or have students do this activity in groups.

Prompt	Sentence
Original sentence	
Who (can be a name or adjective describing one if you already have a name.)	
What	
When	
Where	
Why	
How	

Read only the finished version to the class.

Go To ▶ 1. Go to an OWL that you have used and found helpful with earlier work in this book to read how the site presents sentence structure and punctuation.

2. Go to the *Writing Now* web site to read the article "Tuning In to the Keenest of Ears," from the *Journal of Science*. Pursue the research they propose to determine whether you have perfect pitch and to discover which musicians have it.

OPTIONS ▶ Customize

1. Pick one of your earlier essays from any chapter and write a conclusion.

2. In groups or individually, write a conclusion for an essay based on "The Joys of Journaling" from Chapter 1. Read the conclusions aloud to see how others handled them. You may discover new ways of handling conclusions.

3. Go back to pages 321–322, and reread "Raised on Rock-and-Roll." As you read the article again, pay particular attention to the sentence structure and examine it in the following ways:

   a. Circle all the subordinators. Examine the clause that the subordinator introduces. Could it stand alone? Mark any that you believe could stand alone with "SA."

   b. Highlight in yellow any examples of two independent clauses linked with a coordinator. (This means two sentences that could stand alone linked with one of the coordinating words.)

   c. Sometimes Quindlen uses punctuation to connect two complete sentences. Highlight any examples in blue.

   d. Find examples of her use of relative pronouns. Highlight them in yellow.

   e. Notice how descriptive Quindlan's language is. She *shows* instead of *tells.* Highlight your favorite descriptive sentence in blue.

   f. Rewrite paragraph 5 into shorter sentences. Read both versions out loud.

EDIT ▶ Revising for Sentence Structure

You may want to assign the rewriting of this draft as homework.

Read "Don't Confuse a Business with a Lifestyle." Examine the interesting sentences and details that McCormack includes. As you read, look for the sentence you find to be the best written.

Don't Confuse a Business with a Lifestyle

Mark H. McCormack

Success Secrets

1   I have always thought that successful musicians are the luckiest people in the world. Their careers meet all the criteria of what most people would call a perfect life:

- Job satisfaction? They love what they're doing.

- Recognition? They get instant approval from an adoring public.

- Working conditions? They perform in the toniest, most glamorous venues around the world.

- Job security? They can go on virtually until they die and are legendarily long-lived. In a sublime irony, their good fortune probably prolongs their lives.

- Remunerative rewards? Their earnings curve points steadily upward and increases regardless of age. In fact, it tends to increase because of age. Great musicians invariably earn more in old age—when they are revered as masters—than they do at any other point in their lives.

2   If I were categorizing careers that offered the most seamless marriage of business and lifestyle, classical music would be the ideal, the Holy Grail that the rest of us strive for.

3   I think golf runs a close second in the sense that golfers love what they're doing, have great working conditions, have long careers and get paid for doing what most of us would do for free. In my more smug moments, I also think the people in our company [International Management Group, a sports management firm] are lucky—because we've managed to create a business opportunity out of something we love, namely sports. We get paid to work at the sporting events the rest of the world is paying to attend. It's an attractive blend of business and lifestyle.

4   But it's an ideal that confuses a lot of people. They think they have a career or a business when in fact they're only creating excuses to pursue a lifestyle.

5   We see this all the time in the sports business.

Source: Mark McCormack, "Don't Confuse Business with a Lifestyle," *The Arizona Republic,* 10/8/98. Copyright © 1998 by Mark H. McCormack. Reprinted with the permission of McCormack Advisors International, Cleveland, OH.

6   People want to work for us because they love sports. They think it would be neat to have a business reason to spend the early weeks of autumn at the World Series. But they rarely consider whether they have the skills or personality to succeed at our type of business. All they know is they find the lifestyle appealing.

7   The brother-in-law of a promising athlete gives up his day job to manage the athlete's business affairs. He gives little thought to whether he's qualified for the job or that his lack of qualifications could jeopardize the athlete's affairs or that his business could be wiped out by a sudden injury. All he knows is that the sports business is more glamorous and interesting than his day job. He likes hanging around the fringes of sport. He's blinded by the lifestyle.

8   This error of people trying to create a business to justify a certain lifestyle certainly isn't exclusive to sports. Perhaps you've known people who enjoyed cooking and dining out and, therefore, decided to open a restaurant, ignoring the fact that few ventures have higher failure rates.

9   The problem with identifying an avocational interest and then matching it up with the right vocation is that the sequence should be reversed. If you can find a vocation at which you excel you stand a much better chance of melding it with your avocation.

10   It's certainly true in our company. For example, our golf division consists of many executives who have been passionate about the game of golf since they were youngsters. But they didn't succeed with us because of their golf skills or knowledge. It's also not the reason they were hired.

11   In at least two instances I can think of, we hired people for our accounting division who eventually gravitated to the golf side of our business. But they didn't start out that way. First, they had to establish their skills at accounting, which in each case took several years. Only then did they find their way into the golf side of our business.

12   Their passion for golf merely steered them in that direction. It didn't grant them automatic access. Their financial skills did that.

13   But that happens when you're clear about whether you're pursuing a business career or a lifestyle.

Analyze the Reading

1. Go back to the reading selection, locate the best-written sentence, and write it on the lines below. Try to include a similar style of sentence in your draft.

_____

_____

_____

You are now ready to write another draft of your central assignment. Revise your current draft, combining sentences using as many of the techniques listed above as you can.

Help Screen

Advanced Word Processing Tips

For a Works Cited page, you will want to use a hanging indent. In MS Word, you can create this format by selecting the information you want to use and then going to Format, Paragraph, Special, Hanging Indent. Set the spacing at .5".

When you are working on a paper with a classmate, or when you are going through several revisions, it is sometimes helpful to see the changes that you made. To do this in MS Word, go to Tools, Track Changes, Track Changes While Editing, then select whether to show changes on the screen, in the printed version, or both. To see the corrected version of the paper without the changes showing up, just take the checks out of the boxes in the Track Changes While Editing section.

To see how long your paper is, click on Tools, Word Count.

FILE ▶ Save As

00:45

After spending some time going over students' answers to the homework questions, you may want to allow class time to work on the drafts and/or allow for collaboration.

Research Essay with Conclusion

Take your final draft and perform all the revision and proofreading techniques you have learned so far.

Peer Revision Worksheet

Reviewed by: **Date:**

Focus of review: supporting details, conclusion, sentence structure

Reviewing paper written by:

Peer Revision Questionnaire

Ask yourself the following questions about your draft. Then, if possible, ask a friend or classmate to read your draft and answer the same questions about it. Also have your reader mark any nonconventional sentence constructions or punctuation. If your answers do not match, you haven't succeeded in communicating what you think you did. Where answers don't match well, discuss them together and try to think of ways to make your essay clearer.

- What is this essay about? (topic)

- What is the event or situation that prompted the essay? (prompt)

- What do you have to say about your topic? (thesis or main idea)

- Who is your intended audience?

- What is your purpose in writing about this?

- What personal experience (life, reading, TV, stories you've heard, and so forth) have you had with this topic?

- What purpose does each paragraph serve? How does each support the thesis?

- What methods of development did you use in each paragraph to support your thesis?

- Is there anything else I should know? Are there any questions in the reader's mind left unanswered by the essay?

Revision Checklist

❑ I have arranged my ideas in an order appropriate to the topic.

❑ I had someone read and annotate my essay.

❑ I have an appropriate title.

❑ I have a clearly stated topic.

❑ I have developed a topic that is appropriate, neither too broad nor too specific.

❑ All paragraphs support my overall topic.

❑ Each paragraph has a different focus relating to my topic.

❑ Each paragraph has well-developed supporting examples and/or facts.

❑ I revised my word choice to use descriptive and appropriate words.

❑ My tone is clear and consistent throughout the essay.

❑ I wrote an introduction or a summary that contained my assertion and an idea of what my essay is about.

❑ I used gender-neutral language.

❑ My pronoun references are clear.

❑ My pronoun use is appropriate.

❑ I used appropriate patterns of development for the topic, the purpose, the audience, and the introduction.

❑ I used a variety of sentence structures.

❑ I eliminated fragments and run-ons.

❑ I stated the name of the author and the title of the text in the first or second sentence of the summary.

❑ I clearly and accurately stated the author's thesis in the first or second sentence.

❑ I selected an appropriate technique to examine the text and include the major points the author made.

❑ I presented the author's points as presented in the text.

❑ The summary is accurate, complete, concise, and balanced.

❑ The summary is written in my own words.

❑ The summary is of appropriate length for the text and the assignment.

❑ My thesis is clearly stated and clearly responds to the author's thesis.

❑ My major points in response to the author's text are clearly stated.

❑ I keep my subjects and verbs consistent—either both singular or both plural.

❑ I keep any words or phrases in a series parallel.

❑ I checked for appropriate subject-verb agreement.

❑ I checked for appropriate and consistent verb tense.

❑ I checked for consistent pronoun usage.

❑ I included appropriate transitional words and phrases within paragraphs.

❏ I included appropriate transitional sentences between paragraphs.

❏ My examples are supported with enough detail.

❏ My facts are clearly explained.

❏ The entire essay is in my own words, unless it is a direct quotation in quotation marks.

❏ Word choice is clear, concise, and descriptive.

❏ All my sentences are complete sentences. The sentence structure is varied and interesting.

Proofreading Checklist

❏ I have read each sentence aloud, starting with the last one first and working backward to make sure each sentence is clear and uses appropriate language conventions.

❏ I used my proofreading frame to check for spelling.

❏ I asked a classmate to read my draft and complete the Peer Revision Worksheet.

C:\Prompts for Writing ▶

1. Write a paper responding to any of the articles in this chapter using examples and research to support your points.

2. Pick a topic in an area that interests you. Research it and write a three- to five-paragraph essay.

3. Select the central assignment from an earlier chapter. Evaluate the support of your main ideas, adding information where necessary. Can you add facts as well as examples? Then go through the revision step and compare the final essay with the original one you turned in.

4. In "Don't Confuse a Business with a Lifestyle," Mark H. McCormack argues that the life of a musician may not be as exciting or glamorous as people think. Read this article, making notations as usual. Then write a three- to four-paragraph response. You should defend your statements with *both* facts and examples. Therefore, you may have to read other material on the subject to gather examples of musicians' lifestyles (for example, the problems musicians have had with business managers, both those related to them and professional ones), and you will have to research the subject to get some facts to support your arguments, as well.

5. A student in another teacher's class submitted a research paper that someone else wrote. You do not know whether the paper was downloaded from the Web or purchased from a paper-writing service, but the teacher has clear evidence that the paper was written by someone other than the student. As a member of the Student Government Association, write an opinion on whether the student should fail the paper, fail the whole course, or be expelled from school for submitting a paper that someone else wrote as his or her own.

Go To ▶ Go to the *Writing Now* web site for additional readings on this subject. You will also find references on research and inferences.

Log Off ▶ Reflect and Review

Take some time to reflect on what you have learned about writing in this chapter.

How has your writing changed as a result of the discussions, readings, and activities in this chapter?

_____

_____

_____

_____

_____

_____

_____

Refer to the essay you wrote in Chapter 12. Examine your conclusions. How has your writing improved since that essay?

_____

_____

_____

_____

Is your sentence structure more varied and complex after you completed this chapter?

_____

How has your knowledge of the writing process changed as a result of the work you have done in this chapter?

_____

_____

_____

Shut Down

Now that you've finished your course, take some time to reflect on what you have learned and what you will bring forward to future writing classes and experiences.

What did you learn about **writing** that you want to remember?

_____

_____

_____

What did you learn about **revising** that you want to remember?

_____

_____

_____

What did you learn about **proofreading** that you want to remember?

_____

_____

_____

What did you learn about **being a writer** that you want to remember?

_____

_____

_____

What did you learn about **your own writing practices** that you want to remember?

_____

_____

_____

What did you learn about **college** that you want to remember?

_____

_____

_____

What did you learn about **yourself** in this course.

_____

_____

_____

What did you find especially helpful in this text? Why?

_____

_____

_____

What parts of the text did you especially enjoy using? Why?

_____

_____

_____

What parts of the text did you think weren't helpful? Why?

_____

_____

_____

Did you meet the goals you set for yourself when you began this course?

_____

_____

_____

INDEX

Note: Page numbers in *italics* indicate illustrations; page numbers followed by *n* indicate footnotes.